MONROE COUNTY TENNESSEE

CHANCERY COURT MINUTE BOOK

1832–1842

W.P.A. Records

Heritage Books

2024

HERITAGE BOOKS

AN IMPRINT OF HERITAGE BOOKS, INC.

Books, CDs, and more—Worldwide

For our listing of thousands of titles see our website
at
www.HeritageBooks.com

A Facsimile Reprint
Published 2024 by
HERITAGE BOOKS, INC.
Publishing Division
5810 Ruatan Street
Berwyn Heights, MD 20740

Nashville, Tennessee
The Tennessee Historical Records Survey
September 1940

International Standard Book Number
Paperbound: 978-0-7884-8809-2

TRANSCRIPTIONS OF THE COUNTY ARCHIVES

OF TENNESSEE

NO. 62. MONROE COUNTY (MADISONVILLE)

CHANCERY COURT MINUTE BOOK

1832-1842

Prepared by

The Tennessee Historical Records Survey
Division of Professional and Service Projects
Work Projects Administration

Sponsored

by

The Tennessee State Library

Nashville, Tennessee
The Tennessee Historical Records Survey
September 1940

The Historical Records Survey Program

Sargent B. Child, Director
Madison Bratton, State Supervisor

Research and Records Section

Harvey E. Becknell, Director
Milton W. Blanton, Regional Supervisor
T. Marshall Jones, State Supervisor

Division of Professional and Service Projects

Florence Kerr, Assistant Commissioner
Blanche M. Ralston, Chief Regional Supervisor
Betty Hunt Luck, State Director

WORK PROJECTS ADMINISTRATION

F. C. Harrington, Commissioner
Malcolm J. Miller, Regional Director
Harry S. Berry, State Administrator

W.P.A. RECORDS

The WPA Records are, for the most part, carbon copies of the original that was typed on onion skin paper during the Depression. Since these records were typed on poor machines by people who did not type in some cases and at the same time, they were read by persons not always sure of the older handwritten materials, the results are often less than perfect.

We have made every attempt to make as clear a copy as can be made from these older papers. Sometimes there are water stains and burned edges around the paper. This is the results of a fire at the home of one of the workers, Mrs. Penelope Allen, who was over most of the project. Sometimes, the index will be misleading in that they index by the middle name when a list of names are given in one family, i.e. "... the children of John Smith are, John, Jr., Mary Warren, and Oscar Sims. The indexer would list a Warren and a Sims in the index, when they should be Smith. Mountain Press has acquired a rather large number of finished and un-finished manuscripts. Many of these latter manuscripts are being typed and index now.

The WPA Records are now very scattered between the Tennessee State Library, various Public and Private Libraries and other collections. Some day, there is a hope that all of these can be collected and stored in one place. In spite of their many mistakes and problems, these are still the most complete collection of Tennessee records found anywhere.

MONROE COUNTY

CHANCERY COURT MINUTE BOOK
1832-1842

New Index

(NOTE: Page numbers in this index refer to
those of the original volume from which
this copy was made. These numbers are
carried throughout the copy within
parentheses.)

Campbell, Calloway, 166
Campbell, Charles, 157,166
Campbell, Robert, 304
Campbell, V.M., 197
Cannon, Guilford, 1,2,3,130,
    153,185,249,306,307,308.
Cannon, John O., 1,2,3,46,
    56,59,60,61,62,70,76,
    85,113,153,176,185,198,
    249
Cannon & Nelson, 183
Cannon, Newton, 59,60
Cannon, Robert, 234,319
Carey, Dempsey, 237,238,257,
    258
Carey, Nathaniel, 77, 142,
    213
Carey, Robert M., 77
Carey, Thomas, 21
Carey, Will H., 77
Caroline, (Negro),315,316
Carouth, Walter, 211
Carroll, Michael, 39,42,50,
    64,69,85
Carroll, William, 1, 3
Carson, Newton, 56
Carter, Asbury, 68,69
Carter, Charles, 38,47,48,
    68,69
Carter, Elizabeth, 37,40,50,
    57,68
Carter, Eliza P., 68,69
Carter, John P., 68,69
Carter, Julia F., 68,69
Carter, Lewis, 68,69
Carter, Micaijah, 50,57,68,
    69
Carter, Sally, 47
Caruthers, 324
Charles, (Negro) 128,129
Chesnut, George, 216
Chestnut, Henry, 217
Churchwell, George W., 39,
    55,63,75,78,79,87,94,
    95,96,102,107,113,137,
    139,152,156,157,167,
    185,189,197,248,331.
Citico Creek, 293,294,295,
    298,299,300
Clark, Thomas N. Jr., 253
Clark, Thomas N. Sr.,304
Cleveland, Eli, 40,42,170,
    175,193,201,216,313.
Cleveland, J.F., 211,223,224
    225

Cobb, David A.,150,151,255,
    321
Cobb, Prissa, 321
Coffin, Daniel L., 306,307,
    308
Coffin, James A., 1,2,3,45,
    48,59,60,61,62,78,93,
    96,110,138,159,196,197,
    306,307,308
Coker, Miria, 260,262
Coker, William, 234,246,260,
    262
Cole, John, 122,186
Coltharp, 279
Conassauga Creek, 72,90,255
Cook, Joseph, 4,6,14,16,35,
    144
Cook, R.F., 309,319
Cook, William A.,4,5,10,11,
    15,16,19,20,21,22,25,
    26,27,40,42,43,44,49
Cook, William H., 58,71,82,
    89,90,98
Cookson, Joseph, 263
Cookson & Wann, 141
Conner, H.W. & Co., 269,314
Cope, C., 75,139,152,156,
    167,185
Cope, M.C., 75,139,152,156,
    167,185
Copeland, John., 173,324
Counties:
    Blount, 1,2,3,49,128,
        270,271,273,291,299.
    Bradley, 59,60,61,121,
        168,246,262,263
    Hamilton, 221
    Roane, 24,277
Cowan, Andrew, 76,81,103
Cowan, Dickenson & Co. 215,
    229,275
Cowan, William W., 198,225
Craighead, J.P.N., 138
Crawford, Samuel, 21
Crawford, T. Hartley, 203
Creeks:
    Citico, 293,294,295,298,
        299,300
    Conassauga, 72,90,255
    Crooked, 271,289
    Estenaller, 53,66,110
    Fork Creek, 21
    Middle, 233
    Pistol, 287,288,297
    Sweetwater, 326

MONROE COUNTY

CHANCERY COURT MINUTE BOOK
1832-1842

ORIGINAL INDEX

M

McCarty vs Walker, 70,247,312
Meigs vs Turk, 120,137,171,188
Moore vs Cookson & Wann, 141,263
Mowry vs Lea, Entry Taker, 145,186,219,285
Mee, John vs L. Lea, 146,181
Mayfield, Thos. B. & Others vs Nancy Mayfield & Others,
           214,255,321
Mayfield, Nancy vs Mayfields - Cross Bill, 152,203,214,255,321
Maddy, James vs James Pelter, 175,209,225
Miller & Swan vs Harlan, 198,276
McEwen vs Matlock, 201,238,252
McGhee, Jno. vs Jno. Lyon, 213
McCarty, John L. vs N. Grubb, 222,250
Moore, Jesse C. vs L. Lea, 222,250
McClung & Wallace vs Blackstone, 313
Murrell & Humphreys vs Bush, 226
Morgan vs Henly & Others, 230,304
Morgan vs Jarnagin & Bacum, 230,274,304
McGhee, Barcklay & Others vs John McGhee et al, 249,270,
           283,286
Morgan, Gideon vs Jas. S. Bridges, 253,328
McAdams et als vs Sarah McAdams, 260
McBride vs McReynolds & Others, 282,314

N

Netherland vs Smiths, 203
Netherland vs Thompson Adm. 231

O

Oneal vs L. Lea, 156,186,220

P

Peck, Elliot - petition, 221
Prowell, S. vs L. Lea, 172
Parks vs Bryson & Taylor, 207,211
Parks vs Cleveland, 211,223,224

Q

Queener vs Queener, 196,222,269

R

Ross vs Turk, 120,137,171,188
Rothwell vs Reynolds et als, 144,158,170,195,242
Rogers, John vs F.A. Patton et al, 265,303
Rice O. vs Jameson & Fitzgerald, 283

Index to Minute Book, Chancery Court

(NOTE: These two whole indexes and the three names
on another are all given in original index)

(P-1)   Be it remembered that at a Court of Chancery began
and held at the Court house in the Town of Madisonville in and
for the Chancery District composed of the Counties of Blount,
Monroe & McMinn, in the state of Tennessee, on the Second day
of April A D. 1832, there was present:
        The Hon. William B.Reese Chancellar &c. By order
of the Court James A. Coffin is appointed Clerk and Master who
entered into bonds with approved security, which bonds are
directed to be spread upon the minute book and is in the words
and figures following viz.
        "Know all men by these present that we James A.Coffin,
John O. Cannon, Guilford Cannon and John Blair are held and
firmly bound unto William Carroll Governor in and over the
State of Tennessee and his successor in office in the sum of
Ten Thousand dollars, to which payment will and truly to be
made we bind ourselves and each of our executors, administrators
and assigns jointly and severally firmly by these presents.
Signed with our names and sealed with our seals this second
day of April 1832.
        The condition of the above obligation is such that
whereas the above bound James A. Coffin hath been appointed
Clerk and master of Chancery for the District composed of the
Counties of Blount, Monroe and McMinn in the state aforesaid;
now if the said James A. Coffin shall truly and honestly keep
the Record of said Court and discharge the duties of said office
according to law then the above bond to be void and of no
effect. Otherwise to remain in full force   (P-2)   and
virtue. Given the day and date above written

Signed, sealed &	James A. Coffin	(seal)
acknowledged	John O. Cannon	(seal)
in open court	Guilford Cannon	(seal)
Will B. Reese]	John Blair	(seal)
Chancellor &c)		

        Know all men by these presents that we James A.
Coffin, John O. Cannon and Guilford Cannon are held and firmly
bound unto William Carroll Governor in and over the state of
Tennessee and his successors in office in the sum of one
thousand Dollars, to which payment will and truly to be made
we bind ourselves and each of our executors, administrators
and assigns jointly and severally firmly by these presents.
Signed with our names and sealed with our seals this the second
day of April 1832.
        The condition of the Above obligation is such that
whereas the above bounded James A. Coffin hath been appointed
Clerk and master of Chancery for the District Composed of the
Counties of Blount, Monroe and McMinn in the state aforesaid,
Now if the said James A. Coffin shall will and faithfully

Collect & pay, in the manner required by law, or in the manner that shall hereafter be required by law, the firms and
forfeitures that may arise in said court, then the above
obligation to be void otherwise to remain in full force and
virtue.

Signed, Sealed   James A. Coffin   (seal)
& acknowledged   John O. Cannon   (seal)
in open Court   Guilford Cannon   (seal)
the day and
date above
written.
   Will B. Reese
   Chancellor &c.

(P-3)   Know all men by these present that we James A.Coffin
John O. Cannon and Guilford Cannon are held and firmly bound
unto William Carroll Governor in and over the state of Tennessee and his successors in office in the sum of five hundred
dollars to which payment will and truly to be made we bind
ourselves and each of our executors, administrators and assigns
jointly & severally firmly by these present. Signed with our
names and sealed with our seals this second day of April 1832.
        The Condition of the Above obligation is such that
whereas the said James A. Coffin hath been appointed Clerk and
Master of Chancery for the District Composed of the Counties
of Blount, Monroe and McMinn in the state aforesaid. Now if
the said James A. Coffin shall duly collect and pay into the
public treasury all such tax on causes as may arise in said
court of Chancery at such time and in such manner as is or
may be perscribed by law, then the above obligation to be
void, otherwise to remain in full force and virtue Given the
day and date above written.

Signed sealed and   James A. Coffin   (seal)
acknowledged in   John O. Cannon   (seal)
open Court   Guilford Cannon   (seal)
Will B.Reese   Chancellor &c.
        The said James A. Coffin then took the oath of
office, and also the several oaths prescribed by law.

(P-4)   William Lowry
                Vs.   In this cause the Council on
             Miller Francis   both sides being absent, by
               Treasurer &c. order of the court it is con-
tinued until next Term of this Court.
        Court adjourned until Court in Course.
                                    Will. B. Reese

        At a Court began and held at the Court house in
Madisonville on the 26th day of November 1832 there was present
the Hon William A. Cook Chancellor. -

Joseph Cook   )   In this cause four months are allowed John
    Vs   )   Denton to file his answer, and one month
Isaac Denton   )   allowed the other Defendants.
John Denton &)
James Denton   )

William Lowry & Al Com)
     Vs.   )
Miller Frances Treas.^r &c)
East Tennessee Dept -   Decree
        A Subponia ad Respondendum having been served upon
the Defendant having failed to appear and answer the same
according to exigency thereof; and the Plaintiff having
obtained an order that this cause should be taken pro confesso,

(P-5)   November Term 1832

Against the defendant and that it should be heard en parte
at this present term; and this Cause, now, this day, coming on
to be heard upon the said Bill and orders, & the said Defendant still persisting in his refusal to answer said Bill - It
is ordered adjudged and decreed by the Court, that the said
Miller Francis, treasurer of East Tennessee, and his successors
in office, be perpetually enjoined from selling the school
land mentioned in the Complainants Bill and it is further
ordered, that the said Miller Francis, treasurer of East Tennessee, pay the costs of this cause -

        Court adjourned until Court in Course -
                           Will A. Cook
(P-6)   MAY TERM 1833

        At a Court began and held in the town of Madison-
ville t̸h̸e̸r̸e̸ w̸a̸s̸ p̸r̸e̸s̸e̸n̸t̸, on the 27th day of May 1833, there
was present the Hon William B. Reese Chancellor &c -

Joseph Cook   )
     Vs   )   In this cause, John Denton, having
James, Isaac &)   failed to file his answer within the
John Denton   )   four months allowed him at last term,
presented an affidavit to procure leave to file his answer at
this term. Whereupon it is Considered by the Court, sufficient
Cause appearing in said Affidavit, that said Deft. John be permitted now to file his answer & that the judgment pro Confesso
be set aside. And it is further considered by the Court that
Deft. John be permitted to take the depositions of Defendants
James, and Isaac, when the cause may be at issue, subject how-
ever to all legal exceptions, on the hearing.

John Williams, Jacob Rogers   )
& son & Others   )
        Vs.   )   In this
I.B., James, Berry & Jacob F. Foute)   Cause

application being made in open Court for an injunction, the
appointment of a receiver &c - and an injunction being granted
in accordance with the prayer of the Bill, on the Complainants
giving security according to law; It is further ordered that
the Clerk and Master take upon himself the office of receiver,
and in pursuance of his said duty he is, so soon as subpoenas

and Copies of the Bill together with the Injunction are served
on the said Berry and Foute, to proceed forthwith to said
Defendants, and demand and receive from them, first all moneys
in their hands arising from the sale of the goods, wares, and
merchandise mentioned in Exhibit B and also all moneys collected on account of the notes & accounts contained in said Exhibit
B; - secondly all notes & accounts on hand and not collected,
set forth in said exhibit, and all notes given in liquidation
of the accounts in said Exhibit mentioned; - Also thirdly
any notes on accounts arising from the sale or exchange of any
of the   (P-7)   stock of goods in said Exhibit mentioned; -
Also, fourthly any receipts of attornies, Sheriffs, or other
officers for any of the above claims. These moneys when received he will safely keep until the further order of the
Court; and the notes and accounts which he may receive he will
forth with take the proper steps to have collected.

Thomas C. Henderson Adm &c   )
           Vs   )   The demurrer
Sarah Holt & J.W. Reagan   )   filed in this
Administrators &c   )   cause by

defendants coming on to be heard, it is considered by the Con
Court that said demurrer be sustained. -

                Court adjourned till tomorrow at 8 O'clock

                           W.B. Reese

                Tuesday, 28th May 1833 -
                Court met pursuant to adjournment.-

F̶r̶a̶n̶c̶i̶s̶/̶V̶.̶ B̶u̶l̶f̶i̶n̶c̶h̶   )
           V̶s̶   )   I̶n̶ t̶h̶i̶s̶ c̶a̶u̶s̶e̶
Thos. Hunt & A.P.H. Jordan)   t̶w̶o̶ m̶o̶n̶t̶h̶s̶ a̶r̶e̶
a̶l̶l̶o̶w̶e̶d̶ t̶o̶ t̶h̶e̶ D̶e̶f̶e̶n̶d̶a̶n̶t̶s̶ i̶n̶ w̶h̶i̶c̶h̶ t̶o̶ f̶i̶l̶e̶ t̶h̶e̶i̶r̶ a̶n̶s̶w̶e̶r̶ -

Thos C. Henderson adm   )
           Vs.   ) The plea filed
Sarah Holt & J.H. Reagan   ) by the Defendants is
Administrators etc.   ) disallowed reserving to the

sd
. defendants the right of insisting on the same matter in
their answer.

John McGhee   )   By consent, two
        Vs   ) .   months are
N.S. Peck & R.J. Meigs   )   allowed Defendants to file their
                                    answers -

(P-8)   Tuesday May 28, 1833
Francis V. Bulfinch   )   In this cause two months
        Vs.   )   are allowed Defendants
Th. Hunt & A.P.H. Jordan)   to file their answers.

Saml McConnell)
    Vs)
Commis^{er} OF Madisonville et al)

By Consent of parties this
Cause is left open for the
taking of testimony -

Jeremiah Jarnagin)
    Vs)
Lawsons & Routh)

By Consent, two months are
allowed Defts. to file their
answers.

John, Alexander & Matthew McGhee)
    Vs)
Hiram K. Turk & Jer.^h Frazier)

Decree

      Subpoenas ad respondendum having been served upon
the Defendants before the last term of this Court, and the Defendants having failed to answer; and the Bill having been
taken for Confessed at the March Rules 1833, and the cause
set for hearing upon the Bill and judgment pro. Confisso,
and the Defendants still persisting in their failure to answer;
and the cause now coming on to be heard upon the Bill and
judgment pro. Confisso, it is ordered, adjudged, and decreed
by the court that the Clerk and Master take and state an account ascertaining the sum due for principal and interest to
the Complainants severally upon the notes mentioned in the
bill, as well as on the sum paid to the state on forfiet use
of the land mentioned in the bill; and the Clerk having by
Computation ascertained and stated that there is due to the
Complainant John on the note first mentioned in the bill five
hundred and thirty three dollars and seventy two cents,
principal and interest down to this day, and upon the sum
paid to the state (P-9) Upon the forfeiture aforesaid the
further sum of six hundred and two dollars and fifty five
cents principal and interst; making together the sum of
Eleven hundred and thirty six dollars, twenty seven cents,
due to the said John Alexander, and Matthew W. upon the note,
secondly mentioned in the bill Three hundred and thirty four
dollars and ten cents, principal and interest down to this
day; making together the sum of one thousand four hundred
and seventy dollars and thirty seven cents; - It is therefore further ordered adjudged and decreed that unless the said
Defendants shall, within four months from this day deposite in
the office of the Clerk and Masters the said sum of $1470.37
cents, together with interest thereon, subject to the order
of complainants; then the said Clerk and Master, first giving
forty days notice of the time and place of sale, in some newspaper published in East Tennessee, shall, in the Town of
Madisonville in Monroe County, expose the South East Quarter
of the 12th Section, in the 1st Township and 3rd Range, East
of the meredian, and that half of the South West Quarter of
the same section which adjoins the said South East Quarter
mentioned in the said bill to sale, to the demand of the Complainants above mentioned, ~~and report to this Court, at the
next term, what he has done in the primises~~ and it appearing
to the Court that the lien of all the Complainants embraces
both tracts of land described in the bill, for the sum of

Eight hundred and sixty seven dollars, eighty cents, which
sum is composed of the principal and interest of the notes
mentioned in the bill; and that the tract first mentioned in
the bill is alone subject to the lien for the payment of the
purchase money due to the state - It is ordered that the said
tract of land mentioned (P-10) in the said bill be liable
only to the payment of the said sum of Eight hundred, sixty
seven dollars, eighty cents, and the tract first described in
the bill shall be liable to the whole sum of $1470.37 cents
and that the clerk and Masters shall only sell so much of each
tract as may be necessary to extinguish the heirs aforesaid,
according to the above principal; and report to this Court,
at the next term, what he has done in the premises.
            Court adjd till court in course -
                            W.B. Reese

November Term 1833

   At a Court began and held ~~at the Court House~~ in
the Town of Madisonville, on the 25th day of November 1833,
there was present the Hon. William A. Cook Chancellor &c.

Jeremiah Jarnagin) The parties in this cause having
   Vs.   ) compromised the same and paid the
Lawsons & Routh) costs which have accrued, it is

ordered by the court that the said suit be dismissed.

John, Alexander and) In this cause the Clerk & Master
Matthew W. McGhee) Reports that the several sums of
   Vs.   ) money due complainants not having
Hiram K. Turk and) been paid into his office within the
Jeremiah Frazer) time prescribed in the Decree, made

at last Term, he did, on the 16th Inst. After having given
forty days notice of the time & place of sale in the "Maryville Intelligences" offer for sale, at public auction, in
Madisonville, the two tracts of land mentioned in said Decree
and that the first mentioned tract, viz: the S.E. Quarter
of Sec. 12 was knocked off to John McGhee one of the compts.
at the price of $1200 he being the highest & best bidder and
that the last mentioned tract was also knocked off to said
(P-11) McGhee at the price of $300 making together the sum
of Fifteen hundred dollars all which is respectifully sub-
mitted.
   Which report of the Clerk & Master is, in all
things affirmed.
   Court adjourned till tomorrow 9 O'clock A.M.

          Will A. Cook

    Thursday November 26th, 1833
    Court met pursuant to adjournment

John McGhee   )
  Vs   )
Meshac Gentry   )   Decree
Allen D. Gentry &)
Jacob F. Foute   )

   The Chancellor declares that the slaves mentioned
in the bill namely Toney, Betsy, Mary, Jane, Folez, George
and Ritter ought to be made subject to the payment of the
sum of twelve hundred dollars with interest from the 19th of
September 1827 till paid, being the sum due from the Defendants Meshac and Allen D. to the complainant. Therefore unless the defendant deposit said sum and interest in the office of the Clerk and Master subject to the order of the Complainant within three months from this day, it is ordered,
adjudged, and decreed that the Clerk and Master of this Court,
after giving thirty days notice of the time & place of sale in

some newspaper published in East Tennessee, expose the said
slaves, or so many of them as may be sufficient to pay the
said debts and interest, the costs of this suit and the costs
of the suits brought by Samuel Edwards against the Defendants,
Meshac & Allen D. in the United States Circuit Court at Knoxville, to sale at public auctions; and out of the proceeds of
said sale, the clerk and Master is Directed to discharge the
Costs of this suit, pay the complainant the said sum of $1200.
and interest at six percent per annum from the 19th of September 1827 the Cost (P-12) of the above mentioned suit
of Samuel Edwards against the Defendants Meshac & Allen D.
the residue if any pay over to said last mentioned Defendants
and make report of his proceedings herein to this Court at
the next Term. It is further ordered that the Defendants, on
demand deliver said slaves to Complainant.

```
John, Alexander &    )
Matthew McGhee       )
     Vs              )          Decree
Hiram K. Turk &      )
Jeremiah Frazer      )
```

It is ordered that the Report made by the Clerk
and Masters of this Court, pursuance to the Decretal orders
made in this court at last Term, be in all things confirmed;
and it is adjudged & decreed that all the right and title of
the said Hiram K. Turk and Jeremiah Frazer of, in and to the
South East Quarter of the 12th section in the 1st Township
and 3rd Range East of the Meredian and that half of the South
West Quarter of the same section which adjoins the said South
East Quarter, be divested out of them and each of them, and
vested in the said John McGhee the purchaser thereof. At the
sale made by the Clerk and Master pursuant to said Decretal
Order. And it is further ordered that the Defendant deliver
possession of the premises to said John McGhee obtainaan injunction according to the course of the court - And that the
Complainants have execution against the said Hiram K. Turk
for the sum of thirteen dollars and forty eight cents, the
residue of their demand against him, and against said Defendants for the Costs of this suit.

It is considered by the Court that the Clerk &
Master be allowed fifteen dollars for his services (P-13)
in selling the land mentioned in the last Decree,
McGhee Vs. Turk & Frazer

```
John McGhee           )
    Vs                )
Nicholas S. Peck &  )         Decree
R.J. Meigs            )
```

The Chancellor declares that the several tracts of
land mentioned in the Bill: namely the North East and South
East Quarters of section 10th township 3rd Range 3rd East of
the Meridan; the North West Quarter of the same section except 65 acres out of the North East Corner of Said Quarter;

the South West quarter of the same section; the Northwest Quarter of section 15th in the same township and range all of which land is situated in the County of Monroe, ought to be subject to the payment of the aggregate sum of money due from the Defendant Peck to Complainant made up of the following sums viz $169.20 Cents and interest thereon from the 2nd of August 1824, of $914.72 cents and interest thereon from the 12th of September 1826, of 21 dollars and interest thereon from the 5th of September 1827; and 53 dollars and interest thereon from the 19th of December 1827.

It is therefore ordered adjudged and decreed that the Clerk and Master of this Court, should the said sum of money not be deposited in his office within three months from this day, subject to the order of complainant, after giving forty days notice of the time and place of sale in some newspaper published in East Tennessee, expose the above mentioned tracts of land to sale, or so much thereof as may be necessary; and out of the proceeds he is directed to pay complainant the aggregate aforesaid made up of the sums aforesaid and interest there   (P-14)   on at the rate of six percent per annum calculated down to the day of sale; to retain the costs of this suit and the probate and registration of the Deed of Trust; and the residue, if any, pay to the Defendant Nicholas S. Peck. The Clerk & Master is further directed to report hereof to this Court at the next term.

Joseph Cook   )
     Vs   )   Decree
James, John & Isaac Denton)

On this 26th day of November, 1833, came on this cause to be heard on Bill, answer, replication and proofs before the Hon. Will A. Cook Chancellor, and it is declared by the Chancellor that the land mentioned in Complainants Bill be regarded as a mortgage in the hands of John Denton to secure the payment of the several sums of money paid by John Denton and Isaac Denton on account of the complainant. And it is further ordered, adjudged & decreed by the Court that the Clerk and Master take an account of the several sums of money paid by the said John Denton and Isaac Denton, together with interest, on account of the complainant; and also of the rents and profits received by the respondents, or either of them, either by the rent of said land, or by the sale of timber off the same, and report to the next term of this Court, and all other matters and things in this cause are reserved until the coming in of said report.

(P-15)   John Williams   )   It is ordered that the
            Jacob Rogers et al)   Defendants James Berry and
                 Vs.   )   Jacob F. Foute deliver
            James Berry and   )   over to the Receiver all
            Jacob F. Foute   )   the papers specified in
Exhibit B. annexed to the Bill and the Receiver heretofore appointed proceed to demand and receive the same as directed by the order made in this cause at the last Term of this Court.

And on motion of Defendants in the above cause by
their Solicitor, one month is allowed them to file their answers,

Saml McConnell   )
)
Nathan Hendrix & others   )
commissioners of   )
Madisonville et al   )

        The plea filed by Defendants in this cause, is over-
ruled and they are allowed to plead de novo, or and are allowed to file two pleas, if they think proper or they may answer
at their election

        Court adjourned till Court in Course

                    Will A Cook

(P-16)   May Term 1834

At a court began and held in the town of Madisonville on the 26th day of Nov. 1834 there was present the Hon.
William A. Cook Chancellor &c.

Joseph Cook   )
     Vs.   )
Isaac Denton   )   Decree
James Denton &   )
John Denton   )

On this 26th day of May 1834 before the Hon. William
A. Cook Chancellor, came on this cause to be heard on the account
reported, with the matters of Equity reserved, and it appearing from the report, that a balance remained, on the 22nd of
this month against the complainant, and in favor of said John
Denton of 354 dollars; It is thereupon ordered by the Court,
no exceptions being taken that said report be confirmed - and
it is ordered, adjudged and decreed that unless complainant
pay said sum of Three hundred and fifty four dollars, with interest from the 22nd of this month to the Clerk and Master
within four months from this date, the Clerk and Master shall
sell the two quarter sections of land in the Bill mentioned,
after having given forty days notice, in some newspaper published in this Chancery District of the time and place of sale-
and that he report to the next term of this court. It is, also,
ordered, adjudged and decreed, that the Defendants pay the
costs of this cause and the clerk and Master shall retain the
same out of the moneys arising from the sale of said land and
deduct the same from the amount to be paid to said John Denton-
and it is further ordered, adjudged, and decreed that the said
John Denton be perpetually enjoined from all further proceedings in the action of ejectment complained of in the Bill.

(P-17)   Chancery Court at Madisonville, Te. May Term 1834

John McGhee   )
    Vs.   )   The Clerk and Master reports
Nicholas S. Peck &)   that in obedience to the
R.J. Meigs   )   order made in this cause at
                                last term, he should have
proceeded to advertise and sell the land referred to in the
decree ¢x¢¢¢ but that he was requested, both by complainant
and Defendant Peck to defer it till this term of the Court -
It is thereupon ordered that the Decree made in this cause
at last Term be revived; and that the Clerk and Master proceed accordingly.

John McGhee   )   The clerk and master reports that
    Vs   )   in obedience to the Decree made in
Meshac Gentry   )   this cause at last Term he advertised,
Allen D. Gentry &   )   and should have proceeded to sell the
Jacob F. Foute   )   negro slaves mentioned in said De-
                                cree; but that Compt. and Respondent

Allen D. entered into a written agreement, which is filed
with the papers in this cause, that the sale be postponed.-
It is thereupon ordered that the said Decree be
revived, and that, when the complainant shall so request,
the Clerk and Master proceed to advertise & sell as therein
directed.

Joseph Donohoo.)
 Vs.   ) This cause
Nathan Harris) having been
         compromised
         by the parties
and the costs having been paid; it is ordered by the court
that it be stricken from the docket.

(P-18)   May Term 1834

Isham Bradley)
 Vs.   ) Decree
Thomas Hunt)

   Be it remembered that at a chancery court began
and held at Madisonville, on the fourth Monday of May 1834,
On Monday the first day of said term and 26th day of said
Month before the Honorable Chancellor came on to be heard and
determined the above cause upon the Bill and answer, and it
appearing to the satisfaction of the Chancellor now here,
that the said Respondent was, on the 9th day of June 1832,
justly indebted to the said Complainant the sum of Sixty two
dollars thirty one cents, and that the said Respondent on the
said 9th day of June 1832 to secure the payment of said sum
of money to the said complainant with the interest accruing
thereon from the date aforesaid, made and executed his deed of
Mortgage in favor of said complainant conveying to said
Complainant and his heirs and assigns the tract of land therein described; Conditioned to be void provided said Respondent
should on or before the first day of June 1833 pay the said
Complainant the said sum of sixty two dollars and thirty one
cents with interest thereon accruing from the date of said
mortgage - and it further appearing to the satisfaction of
the said Chancellor that the whole of said debt amounting in
principal and interest up to this time to the sum of sixty
nine dollars and sixty three cents is justly due from said
Respondent to said Complainant - It is therefore ordered,
adjudged, and decreed by the said Chancellor, that the said
Respondent within three Calendar Months from this date deposit
in the office of the Clerk of this Court the said sum of sixty
nine dollars (P-19) and sixty three cents together with
the interest accruing thereon from the date of this Decree
until the date of said deposit: - It is further ordered,
adjudged and decreed, by the said Chancellor, that in default
of the said Respondent to make said deposit with the said
Clerk and Master of the court as aforesaid, the said Clerk
and Master after giving forty days notice in the nearest newspaper published in this Chancery District, and also twenty

days notice in writing to the Defendant in possession, shall
proceed to sell to the highest bidder on the public square in
said*tract of land described in said deed of mortgage or so
much thereof as shall be sufficient to pay and satisfy said
debt of sixty nine dollars and sixty three cents, with the
interest thereon up to the day of said sale, and shall also be
sufficient to pay the plaintiff costs in this behalf expended,
and that said Clerk and Master report all & singular his proceedings to the next term of this court.

Iridell D. Wright   )
     Vs.   )   Decree
John Dean   )

     This bill coming on to be heard and finally deter-
mined, before the Hon. William A. Cook, Chancellor on the Bill,
as confessed, from which it appears that on the 23rd day of
January 1832, respondent was indebted to complainant one
hundred and seventy five dollars and sixty five cents, to secure which the Respondent executed the mortgage mentioned in
complainant's Bill and it further appears that the debt now
due from Respondent to complainant secured by said Mortgage
is two hundred and one dollars and two cents- It is therefore
decreed by the court that the clerk and master - if the said
sum of two hundred and one dollars and two cents, be with interest, be not, within three months deposited in his office,
-sell the land mentioned in complainants Bill at public sale
in the town of Madisonville; (P-20) first having given
forty days notice of the time and place of said sale, in some
newspaper published in this Chancery District, and also twenty
days written notice to the Defendant in possession ~~and report~~
~~to next court what he has done in the premises~~. Out of the
proceeds of said sale the clerk and master will first pay the
costs of this suit, then the debt due complainant, and the
balance if any, pay over to Respondent- and report to next
court what he may have done in the premises.
     Court adjourned till tomorrow 8 O'clock A.M.

               Will A. Cook

         Tuesday May 27th 1834

Court met pursuant to adjournment

Matthew W. McGhee   )   In this cause
     Vs.   )   it being
Samuel Wear   )   represented that
                    it is necessary
                    that a survey
be made of the premises in dispute. Capt. Robert Wear is
appointed Surveyor for said purpose, and directed to survey
the ground mentioned in complainants Bill for which he claims
title according to the description in said Bill; and also the
land which Respt. alledges he was to make title for to complainant - that said wear make a plat of the same and have it
ready at next term of this court.

    * town of Madisonville, the said

James Humphreys)
    Vs   )   In this cause, on motion, Samuel Love is
John Knox   )   admitted as a Co- complainant with Compt.
               Humphrey's.

I.S. Porter   )   On motion, complainants are allowed to
John McGhee   )   amend their Bill by making Chas. H. Dorious
J.L. McCarter)   Trustee a Defendant.
   Vs.   )
George D. Edgar)

(P-21)   Thomas Carey   )
          Vs.   )
         Samuel Crawford)   Decree
         James Simpson and)
         David A. Deadrick)

     This cause coming on to be heard, on the Bill
answers, replication and proofs; before the Hon. William A.
Cook, Chancellor, and the matters and things therein being
fully considered by the court - It is ordered adjudged and
decreed that complainants Bill be dismissed, and the compt.
pay the costs of this suit.

John Lowry   )   Complainant came into court and by
   Vs   )   leave deposited with the Clerk and
John McGhee &   )   Master the sum of Four thousand two
W.P.H. McDermott)   hundred dollars, in paper on the
               United States Bank; and Defendant
McGhee by his counsil objected to the deposit being made,
especially in bank paper. Whereupon it is ordered by the
court that the Clerk and Master safely keep said sum of $4200
subject to the further order of this court.

James Humphreys &)
Samuel Love   )
   Vs   )   Decree
John Knox.   )

     Be it remembered that on this 27th day of May 1834
Came on this cause to be heard and finally determined before
the Hon William A. Cook Chancellor, upon the Bill, answers
replication, and proofs. After argument of counsel and consideration of the cause had, because it seems to the court
that complainant is entitled to relief; it is ordered, adjudged, and decreed that a moiety or an undivided half of all
water power, mill-seats, mills or other machinery propelled
by water, on Fork Creek in Monroe County, within the bounds
of the North West fractional quarter of section tenth, in the
third fractional (P-22) township and third range East of
the meridian, Hiwassee District, County of Monroe, Containing
one hundred and thirty six acres, be, and the same is hereby
divested out of Respondent, John Knox, and vested in complainant James Humphreys, and his heirs, forever, to have, hold
and enjoy one half of the profits of the water and mill seats

on the land aforesaid to him and his heirs it is further ordered and decreed that the clerk and master take an account in this cause, and ascertain what machinery has been erected by the Respondent on said fractional quarter, and the cost, thereof; and also what profits have been made thereupon up to the date of the report, and make his report to the next term of this court. It is further ordered that the respondent pay the costs of this cause for which an execution may issue.

Daniel Bain   )
   Vs.   )
Findley Orr &   )   Decree
James Meek   )

       This cause coming on for final hearing this 27th day of May 1834 before the Hon. William A. Cook Chancellor &c. on the Bill, answers, replication, and proofs, and it appearing to the satisfaction of the court that the complainant purchased from Findley Orr, one of the Respondents, the North East Quarter of section twenty five third township, second range, East of the Meredians, and also the North West quarter of the same section, township, and range, in Hiwassee District and Monroe County, for which said complainant executed his two promissary notes, for one hundred dollars each, the first payable on the 15th day of November 1831 and the other payable on the 15th day of November 1832 and assigned the certificate of the Treasurer of East Tennessee, to said Orr, for the South West quarter of section twenty five, township second, range second   (P-23)   East of the Meredian, Monroe County, Hiwassee District and took a bond on said Orr for the title to the two first named quarter sections of land, dated the 25th day of December 1830 - that said Orr bound himself in said bond to convey said quarter sections to complainant against the 25th day of December 1831, and to give said complainant possession of the premises against the 1st day of February 1831; - and it appearing to the court that said Orr has failed and refused to comply with his contract, as above set forth, and has kept said complainant out of the possession of the land mentioned in said bond, and that the contract between the complainant and Respondent is a bona fide contract; that the title or claim set up by Meek to the North East Quarter is merely colorable and without consideration: - and it also appearing to the court that the complainant is entitled to a specific performance of the contract set forth in said title bond and to have an account for the rents and profits of the two quarter sections aforesaid, from the 1st day of February 1831, until the possession be surrendered- It is, therefore, ordered, adjudged, and decreed by the court that all the right, title, interest, and claim that James Meek or Findley Orr the Respondents have in and to the aforesaid North East and North West quarters of section twenty five, township third, Range second, East of the Meredian, Monroe County, Hiwassee District, Ten, be vested out of the said Orr & Meek, and vested in the complainant, David Bain - and that all the right, title, interest and claim that the said David Bain may have in and to the south West Quarter of Section twenty five, township second, range second, East of the Meredian, Monroe County, Hiwassee District, be divested out of said Bain and vested in the said Findley Orr. It is further ordered and decreed that the clerk & master take an account of the value of the rents and profits of the two quarter sections said Orr was bound (P-24) to convey to complainant, from the 1st day of February 1831, and also ascertain the value of three acres which complainant had sold from and off of the quarter section, the certificate for which he has transferred to Respondent Orr; and also ascertain what may be due on the two notes mentioned, executed by complainant - what may be the difference between the value of said notes, together with the said three acres of land, and the amount of the amount of the rents and profits of the two quarter sections sold to compt. by Respondent Orr, and report to the next term of this court. It is further ordered that Defendant Compt pay all costs in this cause; and have execution for the same against Respondents.

John Williams, Jacob Rogers   )   In this cause the Clerk
and others   )   and Master reports that,
             Vs.   )   in obedience to the or-
James Berry & Jacob F. Foute   )   der made in this cause
                                    at the May Term 1833 of
this court, and also the additional order made at last Term, he did so soon as convenient after the last Term of this Court, demand of Respondents, as receiver, the moneys, notes, accounts, and receipts mentioned in said order; - that Respondent Berry replied that all the notes, accounts, and other papers connected with this suit were in the possession of Respondent Foute, who had the sole management of the concern, said Berry having removed to Roane County, that on application to Respondent Foute, he urged the superior advantages he possessed of closing the accounts as he was acquainted with the debtors &c and that said Foute as well as said Berry have, as yet wholly failed to comply with the order made at last Term, having placed in the hands of the said clerk and Master none of the moneys, notes, accounts & receipts referred to in the said orders of this court. It is thereupon ordered on motion of complainants, (P-25) Sol, that an Attachment issue against the Respondents James Berry and Jacob F. Foute according to the practice of this court.
          Court adjourned till tomorrow 8 O'clock A.M.

                              Will A. Cook

            Wednesday May 28th 1834
     Court met pursuant to adjournment.

John Lowry   )   By agreement of the parties, on
    Vs.   )   motion, leave is given Respondent
John McGhee &   )   McGhee to file a supplemental an-
W.P.H. McDermott   )   swer to complainants Bill.

Samuel McConnell)
   Vs)
Nathan Henderix & Others)
Commissioners of)
Madisonville et. al.)

The pleas filed by Respondents in this cause coming on to be argued and the same being fully considered by the court it is ordered that the said pleas be over ruled; and Respondents are

allowed till next term of this court to file their answers. It also appearing to this court that no security has been given for the prosecution of this suit, thirty days are allowed complainant to procure such security; and it is ordered that unless complainant give such security within said thirty days from this time, that his bill stand dismissed. It is further ordered that Defendants, who have pleaded, pay the costs of filing and over ruling the pleas.

On motion of the attorney General the Clerk and Master produced a receipt for the state tax by him collected for the year 1833, from the commissioners for building a court house in Madisonville, to whom he is required to pay the same. The amount collected being $7.90.

(P-26)   May Term 1834

Gideon Morgan)
   Vs.)   Decree
Joseph S. Millsaps)

Be it remembered that at a court of Chancery began & held at Madisonville on the 4th Monday of May 1834, before the Hon. William A. Cook, Chancellor, came on to be heard and finally determined, the cause of Gideon Morgan complainant Vs. Joseph S. Milligan Defendant, upon the Bill answers, replication and proofs, and the report of the clerk and master, with the exceptions thereto, of the complainant and Respondent, and the Chancellors being satisfied that the complainant is entitled to further relief, and having carefully inspected the report of the clerk and master and the exceptions thereto, it is ordered adjudged and decreed by the chancellor that the exception of Respondent to the Report of the clerk and master be overruled, and that the exception of the complainant to said report be sustained, and that the same be corrected so as to charge the Defendant with the sum of Three hundred and thirty six dollars - which said sum of $336. it is ordered, adjudged and decreed that the complainant recover against the Respondent, and that execution at law issue to collect the same. It is further ordered, adjudged and decreed, that, in the first instance, the complainant pay the costs of this suit, and have execution against Respondent for one half of the amount of the said costs

John Lowry)
   Vs)
John McGhee &)
W.P.H. McDermott)

The Rule intend to dissolve the injunction in this cause is discharged.

(P-27)　　　James Ainsworth　　　　　)
　　　　　　　　　　Vs　　　　　　　　)　On motion
　　　　　　William Ainsworth Sr.　　)　Two months
　　　　　　William Ainsworth Jr.　　)　are allowed
　　　　　　John McGhee and　　　　　)　Defendants
　　　　　　R.J. Meigs　　　　　　　　)　William
　　　　　　　　　　　　　　　　　　　　　　Ainsworth Sr.
& William Ainsworth Jr. to file their answers. -

Court adjourned till court in course

　　　　　　　　　　Willa A. Cook

November Term 1834

At a court began and held in the town of Madisonville on the 24th day of November 1834 there was present the
Hon. William B. Reese Chancellor.

John McGhee   )
    Vs   )
Nicholas S. Peck &   )   Decree
Return J. Meigs   )

It is ordered by the court that the report of the
clerk and Master made pursuant to the decretal orders heretofore made in this cause, be in all things confirmed; and it
is ordered, adjudged and decreed by the court that all the
right and title of the said Nicholas S. Peck and Return J.
Meigs of, in and to the North East and South East Quarters of
Section ten, township third, range third, East of the Meridian,
the North West quarter of the same section (except sixty five
acres out of the North east corner of said quarter) the south
West quarter of same section, the Northwest quarter of section
fifteen, in the same township and range, all of which land is
situated in the County of Monroe, be divested out of them,
and be vested in the said John McGhee and his heirs forever in
fee, the said McGhee being the purchaser thereof at the sale
made by the Clerk and Master pursuant to said decretal orders;
and it is further ordered that the defendant Nicholas S. Peck
deliver possession of the premises to said John McGhee upon
demand   (P-28)   thereof, and upon his refusal so to do, that
said McGhee obtain an injunction, according to the course of
this court. It is further ordered that the Clerk and Master
be allowed the sum of fifteen dollars compensation for his
services in selling the land mentioned in this Decree, and that
he apply the sum of thirty dollars, fifty one and a half cents,
reported to be in his hands, to the payment of said fifteen
dollars, and then to the costs of this cause, and pay over
the residue, if any to said Nicholas S. Peck; but if there be
not enough to pay the costs, let execution issue against said
Nicholas S. Peck for the balance. It is further ordered that
a copy of this decree be registered in the register's office
of said Monroe County.

John McGhee, John L. McCarty   )
    and Robt. L. Porter   )
        Vs.   )   Decree
George D. Edgar & Charles H. Dorious)

Be it remembered that this 24th day of November in
the year of our Lord 1834, came on the above cause to be finally heard, and the chancellor declares that the tract of land
mentioned in the bill, namely, lying and being in the County
of McMinn, bounded as follows, beginning at a Chestnut Oak,
Walker's south east corner, running West seventy six*beach on
the bank of the Hiwassee river, thence down the several meanders of said river, ninety four poles to a beech, and water
    * poles to a red oak and

birch, on the bank of said river, thence north forty poles, to a stake and pointers, thence east one hundred and sixty poles to a black oak and post oak, on the east line of Walker's reservation, thence south with the line to the beginning, containing seventy acres, it being part of the tract of land generally known as Major Walker's mill reservation ought to be subject to the payment of the several debts due complainants as stated in the bill, to wit, one hundred and twenty dollars and ten cents, due said John and John L. McCarty, due the 27th of December in the year 1832, and also the sum of one hundred and four dollars and (P-29) seventy cents due said Robert L. Porter, due the 27th of December 1832 - It is therefore ordered adjudged and decreed that the Clerk and Master of this court, should the said sums of money not be deposited in his office, within one month from this day, subject to the order of complainants, according to their respective debts or demands, after giving forty days notice of the time and place of sale, in some newspaper published in East Tennessee, expose the above mentioned tracts of land to sale, on so much thereof as may be necessary, and out of the proceeds pay complainants their demands with interest thereon from the 27th day of December 1832, up to the day of sale, and if there be not enough to pay each of said demands, then each shall be paid in proportion to the amount of his debt. Said clerk and Master shall return the costs of this suit, and also the costs of the deed of trust, and the residue, if any, pay over to the said George D. Edgar. The clerk and Master is further directed to report himself to the next term of this court.

John Lowry)	By consent of the parties two months
Vs.)	are allowed for taking additional
John McGhee &)	testimony, in this cause, at the end
W.P.H. McDermott)	of which time, it is to be set for
	hearing.

Frederick Bolinger)	
Vs.)	
Benjamin Griffith)	On motion of complainants Solicitor,
John Lotspeich)	this suit is dismissed as to Defend-
Matthew Small &)	ant Small on whom process has not
William Hogan)	been served.

James Humphreys &)	
Samuel Lane)	
Vs)	Decree
John Knox)	

It is ordered by the court that the report of the Clerk and Master, made pursuant to an interlocutory decree in this cause, be in all things Confirmed, there being no exceptions filed thereto. It is further ordered and decreed that Complainant (P-30) James Humphreys pay into the office of the Clerk and Master of this court within two months from this date, three hundred and seventeen dollars, eighty seven and a half cents, subject to the order of the defendant John Knox, it being the one half the costs of the machinery that has been

erected on the fractional quarter named in the pleadings in
this cause, which has been paid by said defendant after deducting the profits of said machinery. If said sum be not
paid within the time here stated, then it shall be the duty
of the Clerk of this court to issue an execution against said
James Humphreys in favor of Defendant Knox for the amount
thereof. It is further ordered that defendant Knox forthwith
admit said Humphreys into the joint possessions with himself
of the water power and machinery on the fractional quarter referred to in this cause, and that said John Knox, as heretofore ordered, pay the costs of this cause.

      Adjourned until tomorrow morning 9 O'Clock

                   W.B. Reese

          Tuesday November 25th, 1834
Court met pursuant to adjournment

John McGhee   )
    Vs.   )
Meshac Gentry   )   Decree
Allen D. Gentry &)
Jacob F. Foute   )

      It is ordered by the court that the report of the
Clerk and Master made in this cause be in all things confirmed;
from which it appears that the negroes named in the pleadings
were sold to the highest bidder on the 22nd day of this month
on the public square in the town of Madisonville, when and
where Allen D. Gentry became the purchaser for the sum of
seventeen hundred and ninety three dollars and eighty five
cents, paid into the Clerk's office, by the receipts of complainant. It is therefore ordered, adjudged and decreed that
all the right and title to said Negroes Tony, Betsy, Mary,
Jane, Toby, George and Ritter, which the said Allen D. Gentry,
Mishac Gentry and Jacob F. Foute have or either of them in
and to said negroes (P-31) be vested in said Allen D. Gentry
said purchaser and his heirs forever. It is further ordered
that the Clerk be allowed ten dollars, compensation for selling said negroes, and that he retain the same and the costs
of the cause out of the money in his hands.

Thomas C. Hindman   )
Administrator &c   )
    Vs   )   Decree
Sarah Holt and   )
James H. Reagan   )

      Be it remembered that on this 25th day of November
1834 Came on the above cause to be heard upon the Bill and
answers: because it seems to the Court that that portion of
complainants demand which is for moneys alledged to have been
received in the lifetime of Mildred Holt is barred by the
statute of limitations, yet that as to the balance of said
demand an account should be taken in this cause, it is ordered

and decreed by the court that the Clerk and Master take an
account in the above cause, and ascertain the amount of money
or effects belonging to the estate of Mildred Holt deceased
that came to the hands of said Irby Holt after the decease
of said Mildred Holt, or that may have come to the hands of
respondents since the death of said Irby Holt, and what dis-
position has been made of the same, and that said Clerk report
thereof to the next term of this court.

Indell D. Wright   )   On motion of complainants Sol.
        Vs   )   this cause is dismissed and the
John Dean   )   costs thereof assumed by the
                             complainant, for which let
                             execution issue.

William Duggan   )   The injunction granted in this cause
        Vs   )   is dissolved; and no motion of compts
James McKinney   )   sol: Respt is required to give bond
                         and security to refund in case the
$ḥ/X court so Decree.

(P-32)   Wednesday November Term 1834

Fredrick Balinger   )
        Vs   )
Benjamin Griffith   )   Decree
John Lotspeich &   )
William Hogan   )

        On this 25th day of November 1834 before the Hon.
William B. Reese, Chancellor, came on this cause for hearing,
on the Bill the answer of $ợḿṗ$ Defendant Lotspeich with the
replication thereto the answer of defendant Hogan, the pro
Confesso against defendant Griffith, the bill having been
discontinued as to the other defendant Small - and because it
appears to the court that the equity of the bill as to the
defendants Lotspeich and Hogan is satisfactorily answered, it
is ordered adjudged and decreed that as to them the bill be
dismissed, and that complainant pay the costs in this behalf-
And it is further ordered, adjudged & decreed that the Clerk
and Master take an account between Complainant and defendant
Griffith, as to all the matters of account suggested in the
Bill, and report to next court, preparatory to the final de-
cisions of the case.

Thomas Blackburn   )   On motion of complainants sol
        Vs.   )   this cause is taken as confessed
Robert Allen, Gilbert   )   against those Defendants upon
Blankenship & Others   )   whom process has been served;
                               and the Clerk and Master is
directed to issue an alias subponia for Defendant Robert Allen.

SAMUEL MCCONNELL   )   No copies of the Bill in this
        Vs   )   cause having issued, service of
The Commissioners of   )   the same having been waived,
Madisonville et-at-   )   and the Bill consequently having

became much mutilated by use. The clerk and master is directed to transcribe and certify a copy of said bill and file the same with the papers in same cause.

(P-33) Isham Bradley)
      Vs.   )   Decree
    Thomas Hunt)

    It is ordered by the court that the report of the Clerk and Master made pursuant to the decretal order made in this cause at last term of this court be in all things confirmed, and it is ordered, adjudged and decreed by the court that the right and title of the said Thomas Hunt in and to the lot of land mentioned in the pleadings in this case being a tract of land lying and being in Monroe County on Bat Creek containing twenty acres purchased by the said Thomas from Jessie Bright & upon which the said Thomas resided at the time the Bill in this cause was filed, be divested out of the said Thomas and his heirs and invested in John McGhee and his heirs in fee, the said McGhee being the purchaser thereof at the sale made by the Clerk and Master pursuant to said decretal order – and it is further ordered and decreed that the said Thomas Hunt deliver possession of the said premises to said John McGhee upon demand thereof made by him, and upon his refusal so to do, that said McGhee obtain injunction according to the rules of this court – It is further ordered that the Clerk and Master be allowed the sum of seven dollars and fifty cents compensation for his services in selling the land mentioned in this decree and that he apply the sum of seventy three dollars and forty two cents of the ninety five dollars and fifty cents reported to be in his hands to the payment of said complainants debt and that he retain the sum of $7.50 for his services and that the residue in his hands, if any, after the payment of costs, pay over to the said Thomas Hunt. It is further ordered and decreed that a copy of this decree be registered in Register's office of Monroe County.

Anderson P.H. Jordan) It is ordered by the court that
     Vs.   )   the injunction in this case is
William McConnell   )   dissolved.
John C. McConnell &)
Samuel D. Kelly   )
(P-34)

Matthew W. McGhee)
     Vs.   )   Decree
Samuel Wear   )

    Be it remembered that on this 25th day of November 1834 came on this cause to be heard and finally determined, upon the Bill, answer, replication and proofs, because it appears to the chancellor that complainant is entitled to a specific execution of the contract stated in the bill, it is therefore ordered, adjudged, and decreed by the court that

all the right and title that Matthew W. McGhee has in and to
the following described piece or parcel of land in Monroe County, to wit, beginning at a stake at the foot of the hill, in
a line of said Wears one hundred and forty four acre tract,
thence with the same due North, according to the true Meredian,
twenty nine and three tenth chains to a stake corner to said
Wears fifty acre fractions, thence with the same due east
twenty eight and five tenth chain to a stake at the foot of
the hill, thence along the same south thirty nine and three
fourth West, according to the Magrutical Meredian, forty and
nine tenth chain to the beginning containing ten acres, one
road and ten poles, being part of the south west quarter of
section twenty, four in range four East of the Meredian, and
second fractional township, in the Hiwassee District be and
the same is hereby divested out of said Matthew W. McGhee and
vested in said Samuel Wear and his heirs forever and it is
further ordered adjudged and decreed, that all the right and
title that Samuel Wear has in and to the following described
piece of land in Monroe County, to wit, beginning at a bunch
of hankberries on the bank of Tennessee river, Old Bark's
corner, running with his line due east, according to the
Magnetical Meredian, fifty five and four tenth chains to a
stake at the foot of the hill thence along the same south
twenty four West sixteen and three tenth chain to a stake,
North seventy two, West fifty one chain to the beginning containing ten acres, one road and ten poles,   (P#35)   being
part of said Wears twelve acres fraction in section twenty
four, North West quarter, be and the same is hereby divested
out of the said Samuel Wear and vested in said Matthew W.
McGhee and his heirs forever in fee. It is further ordered
that each forth with surrender said pieces or parcels of land
or possession thereof to the other; and that said McGhee and
Wear pay one half the costs of this cause for which execution
May issue.

Joseph Cook   )
      Vs   )
John Denton   )   Decree
Isaac Denton &   )
James Denton   )

        It is ordered by the court that the report of the
Clerk and Master made in pursuance of the decretal order here-
to fore made in this case be in all things confirmed; and it
is ordered, adjudged and decreed by the court that all the
right and title of the Complainant and of the said John Denton
of in and to the North East quarter of section fourteen, of
township three, range two; and of the south east quarter of
section eleven, township three, range two, both lying east of
the Meredian, Monroe County, Hiwassee District, be divested
out of them and vested in John McGhee in fee, he being the
purchaser thereof at the sale made by the Clerk and Master
pursuant to the said decretal order; and it is further ordered
that said Cook and Denton deliver possessions of the same to
said McGhee, upon demand made thereof, and upon their refusal
so to do that said McGhee obtain an injunction, according to

the course of this court. It is further ordained that the Clerk and Master be allowed the sum of ten dollars as compensation for his services in selling said land mentioned in this decree, and that he apply so much of the money in his hands, to the payment of the costs in this case, and of said ten dollars, and pay over the residue, if any, to the said John Denton. It is further ordered that a copy of this decree be registered, in said county of Monroe.   (P-36)

John Williams)
Jacob Rogers & son et al) Sufficient cause appearing
      Vs.) to the court from the affidavit
James Betty and) of Respondent James Berry the
Jacob F. Foute) said Berry is discharged
     from the attachment issued
in this case and it is ordered that said Berry pay the costs of said attachment.

Huldah Ball)
    Vs) On motion of Complainants Sol. the
Michael Girdner) bill in this Case is dismissed, and
     defendant assumes the costs, for which
lst execution issue.

Joseph R. Henderson &) In this case, on motion of Respon-
W.P.H. McDermott) dents Sol. one month is
    Vs) allowed
Nicholas S. Peck and) Defendants
his wife Nancy) to file their answers.

Joseph R. Henderson Ex^r &c)
W.P.H. McDermott) One month
    Vs) allowed
Nicholas S. Peck and wife) Defendants
Mary Wilson, John Henderson) to file their
et. al.) answers.

James M. Greenway) The Demurrer filed in this case,
    Vs.) to a part of complainants bill
Samuel Bicknell &) is by the court sustained so
Charles Riley) far as relates to lien of the
     vendor, and overruled as to the
judgment lien contended for by complainant, but receiving the latter point for consideration and decision on the final hearing.
Court adjourned until tomorrow 9 O'clock.

W.B. Reese

(P-37)   Wednesday November 26, 1834
      Court met pursuant to adjournment

Daniel Bain)
    Vs.)
Findley Orr and) Decree
James W. Meek)

This cause coming on for final hearing before the Hon. W.B. Reese Chancellor &c on this 26th day of November 1834 and it appearing to the court that the parties had compromised the matters in controversy in this cause and deposited with the clerk and master of this court their written agreement by them signed and sealed in which the kind of Decree to be made in this cause is specified- Therefore, in pursuance of said agreement, it is ordered adjudged, and decreed by the court that all the right and title of the said Findley Orr and James W. Meek to the North east quarter of section twenty five, township three, Range second, East of the Meredian; and also of the/ one hundred and fifteen acres of the east end of the North West quarter of section twenty five, township third, Range second, East of the Meredian, both tracts of said land lying in Monroe County, Hiwassee District, be divested out of the said Findley Orr and James W. Meek and vested in Complainant Daniel Bain. It is further ordered & decreed that said Orr and Meed deliver possession of said two tracts of land, to said Daniel Bain, on the 25th day of December next. And upon the refusal of them or either of them to do so, said Bain may obtain an Injunction according to the course of this court. It is further ordered that compt Bain and Respondent Orr, each, pay one half the costs of this cause, for which let execution issue; and that a copy of this decree be certified for registration in the said County of Monroe.

Francis V. Bulfinch Vs. Thomas Hunt & A.P.H. Jordon	The death Respondent Hunt is suggested by Compt Sol.
Thomas Hunt Vs. John Key & Elizabeth Carter	The death of Compt. Hunt is suggested.

(P-38)

| Anderson P.H. Jordon Vs. Wm. McConnell, John McConnell & Samuel D. Kelly | The Injunction in this case having been by order of the court dissolved, it is ordered |

adjudged and decreed, that the complainant and his securities Thomas Jordon and John Morrow are liable for the amount of the judgment rendered on the 18th day of June 1834, in the County Court of said County of Monroe, viz one hundred and seventy six dollars and forty six cents, with the interest on the same together with the further sum of seven dollars and eighteen cents the costs of said suit; and that execution issue for the same, in favor of Samuel D. Kelly, N.B. Upton, Wm. Upton, Sen. Wm. A. Upton and Joseph Upton, and it is ordered that said McConnells give bond & security to refund in case the two notes named in the pleadings as not due, be collected, and to   in case the said notes be transferred.

Joseph Smith and   )
Martha, his wife   )
        Vs.   )
Jesse Milton Adm. and   )   Decree
Jarrot Stow, Charles   )
Carter and wife,   )
and Edy Stow, Jr.   )

            Be it remembered that on this 26th day of November 1834 before the Hon. William B. Reese Chancellor came on this cause for hearing, on the bill, answers and proof; and after consideration had, it is ordered by the court that the Clerk and Master take an account in this cause, bottomed on the principals of the award mentioned in the pleadings - that he ascertain what has been received by the said Jesse Melton and Jarrot Stowe administrators; what has been paid out by them or either of them in the course of their administration; what land and how much descended to the heirs of Abel Stowe, deceased; what incumberance, if any was upon said land; what has been paid out by the said Jarrot or the said Jesse in discharge of the incumberance on said land; what, if anything, has been paid by said heirs on either of them or their assignes on said land; what land, if any, are yet due and owing from said estate, and to whom   (P-39)   Court adjourned until tomorrow at 9 O'clock.

                        W.B. Reese

            Thursday November 27th 1834
    Court met pursuant to adjournment

George S. Gilbert &   )
William L. Atlee   )   The decision of the clerk and
        Vs.   )   Master in sustaining exceptions
Samuel D. Kelly   )   to the answer of Defendant is
                                       affirmed: and the said defend-
                                       ant is allowed two months to
                                       amend his answer.

George W. Churchwell   )   The demurrer filed by
Peabody Riggs & Co.   )   defendants Turk and Coggburn
Poor & Kiser & Others   )   is overruled without cost and
Comps.   )   the said Turks allowed one
        Vs.   )   month to file their answers, so
Hiram K. Turk,   )   as not to delay trial. And on
Thos. J. Turk &   )   motion of complainants sol.
Others, Defendants.   )   the bill as to William Lowry,
                                       on whom process has not been
served, is discontinued; and also discontinued as to Defend-
ant Coggburn.

Michael Carroll   )   Ordered by
     Vs   )   the court
John Wear   )   that the
                       Clerk and Master,
                       examine the report

in this cause and report to next term the aggregate of said report.

         Court adjourned until Court in Course.

                   W.B. Reese.

(P-40)   May Term 1835

        At a court of Chancery began and held in the Town
of Madisonville, on the 25th day of May 1835, there was present the Honorable William A. Cook, Chancellor.

Thomas Hunt   )   The death
    Vs.   )   of Complainant
Elizabeth Carter &   )   having been
John Key, Adm.   )   suggested at
                              last term
                              of this
Court, and suit not having been revived it is considered by
the court that the same be abated.

Thomas Blackburn   )
      Vs.   )
Robert Allen, Gilbert   )   On motion
Blankenship, Spencer   )   of the sol-
Blankenship, Betsy   )   icitor of
Watson, John Watson,   )   Respondents
Polly Farmer, John   )   three months
Blankenship, Sally   )   are allowed
Adams, William   )   Respondents
Adams, Saml. Johnston Jr.)   to file their
& Wm. Upton   )   answers; -
                                 So as not to delay trial.

John McGhee, Arthur H. Henly   )   In this
John Calloway, & Thos. Calloway)   cause the
          Vs.   )   subpoena
Henry Stephens & R.J. Meigs   )   ad ress
                                       pondendum
and copy of the bill, not having been served on Respt. Stephens;
on motion of Compts. Sol an alias is ordered to issue.

Benjamin C. Jameson   )   In this
        Vs.   )   case the
Eli Cleaveland &   )   Compt.
George Yoakum   )   dismisses
                          his bill
and assumes the costs; for which let execution issue.

          Court adjourned until tomorrow morning 9 O'clock.
                              Will A. Cook

(P-41)   Tuesday May 26th 1835
               Court met pursuant to adjournment

John McGhee,   )
John L. McCarty   )
and Robert S. Porter   )
        Vs.   )   Decree:
George D. Edgar &   )
Charles H. Dorious   )

It is ordered by the court that the report of the
Clerk and Master, made pursuant to the decretal order here-
to fore made in this cause, be in all things confirmed; and
it is ordered, adjudged and decreed by the court that all
the right and title of the said George D. Edgar and Charles H.
Dorious of in and to a certain tract of land lying and being
in the County of McMinn, bounded as follows: - Beginning at
a Chestnut Oak, Walkers south East corner, running West seventy six poles to a red oak and beach on the bank of Hiwassee
River, thence down the several meanders of said river, ninety
four poles to a beach and water birch, on the bank of said
river, thence north forty poles to a stake, and pointers,
thence east one hundred and sixty poles to a black oak, and
post oak, on the east line of Walker's Reservation, thence
south with said line to the beginning, Containing seventy
acres, it being part of the tract of land generally known as
Major Walker's Mill Reservation, be divested out of them, and
each of them, and be vested in Lewis Ross, the purchaser of
the sale made by the Clerk and Master pursuant to said decretal order, and in his heirs forever in fee; and it is
further ordered that the defendants George D. Edgar and Charles
H. Dorious deliver possession of the premises to said Lewis
Ross, upon demand thereof, and upon their refusal so to do
that said Lewis Ross obtain an injunction according to the
course of this court. It is further ordered that the Clerk and
Master be allowed the sum of ten dollars Compensation for his
services in selling the land named in this decree, and that
he apply the sum of twenty eight dollars and thirty cents, reported to be in his hands to the payment of said ten dollars,
and then to the costs of this cause, and pay over the residue,
if any to the said George D. Edgar; but if there be not
enough to pay the costs, let execution issue against said
Edgar for the balance. It is further ordered that a copy of
this decree be registered in McMinn County.

(P-42)   Tuesday, May Term 1835

Matthew W. McGhee   )   In this cause an injunction is
       Vs.   )   ordered to issue, to enforce
Samuel Wear   )   the execution of the Decree
                            rendered at last Term, according
to the course of this court.

Samuel Ainsworth   )   On affidavit of Compt.,
       Vs.   )   it is ordered that the
William Ainsworth Sen. &   )   Rule sitting this cause
William Ainsworth, Jr.   )   for hearing on Bill and
                                 answers, be set aside;
and that the cause be open for testimony.

Michael Carroll   )   Be it remembered that on the 26th
       Vs.   )   day of May 1835, came on to be heard
John Ware   )   and determined before the Hon: Will-
                        iam A. Cook, Chancellor, this cause
upon the bill, answer, replication, proofs and the report of

the commissioners heretofore appointed to take an account between complainant and Respondent, when it was ordered, adjudged, and decreed by the court that the Clerk & Master of
this court take an account between the parties for the term
of one year from the date of the articles of partnership,
referred to in said bill -, charging Defendant with the proceeds
of the mill and forge during the time he had possession thereof and that he strike a balance between them; and that he
take an account of the profits which the ^Defendants might
have made by the forge & mill by diligence and skill in the
management thereof for and during the time he retained the
possession thereof after the lapse of one year from the com-
mencement of the partnership, and also of the other matters
referred to in the former decretal order, and that he report
to the next term of this court. It is also ordered, adjudged
and decreed by the court that the Complainant and Respondent,
each pay his own costs, for which executions may respectively
issue.

~~B.C.-Jameson~~)
    Vs.)
~~Eli Cleveland &~~)
~~George Yoakum~~)

(P-43)   James M. Greenway)   This cause coming on to
               Vs.   )   be heard on the bill,
        Samuel Becknell &)   answers replications and
        Charles Riley   )   proofs, and argreement of
                                Council having been had;
It is considered by the court that complainant is not entitled
to relief, that his bill be dismissed, and complainant pay
the costs in this cause.
              Court adjourned until tomorrow morning 9 O'clock.

                            Will A. Cook

              Wednesday May 27th 1835
           Court met pursuant to adjournment

Frederick Boliger   )   On affidavit of A.D. Keys
      Vs   )   Sol. of Respondent
Benjamin Griffith   )   Griffith, said Griffith
Matthew Small   )   is allowed to file his
W. Hogan &   )   answers and by consent, it
J. Lotspeich   )   is ordered that the order
                            heretofore made in this
cause directing an account to be taken, be continued, and by
consent, compt. file his replication to said answers.

John Locke, Politiah   )   In this
Shelton, R.N. Gillespie,   )   cause the
Hannah Gillespie,   )   subpoena ad
Wm. N. Gillespie, Sidney   )   respondendum
Ann Gillespie, Mary   )   having been
Leuty, Stanton Leuty, Thomas)   executed; and
Leuty, & Burton Leuty.   )   defendant having

Vs.   )   failed to
Gideon Morgan, Jr.)   file his
                                   answer; the
Bill is taken as confessed and set for hearing en - parte.

William Duggan   )   This cause coming on to be heard
    Vs.   )   before the Hon. W.A. Cook Chancellor
James M. Kinney   )   upon the Bill, answers, replications,
                            and proofs; and it appearing that
complainant is not entitled to relief, it is considered by
the court that his Bill be dismissed, and that complainant
pay the costs in this cause.
  (P-44)

John Morris   )
    Vs.   )   In this cause, the same having come
John Hawkins   )   on for final hearing on the Bill,
                            answer replication and proofs after
agreement of counsel, it is considered by the court that
complainants bill be dismissed without prejudice, and that
complainant pay the costs.

John Lowry   )
    Vs.   )   This cause having come on to be
John McGhee and   )   heard, on this the 27th day of
W.P.H. McDermott   )   May 1835 before the Honorable
                            William A. Cook Chancellor, upon
the Bill, answers, replication and testimony; and agreement
of counsel having been had; because it appears to the court
that complainant is not entilted to relief; it is ordered
adjudged, and decreed by the court that complainants Bill
be dismissed and that he pay the costs. From which Decree
of the Chancellor, complainant prays an appeal to the Supreme
Court to be holden in Knoxville on the second Monday of
July next, which appeal is granted to him, he having entered
into bond and security to prosecute said appeal, according
to law.

John Williams, Jacob Rogers & Others   )   Sufficient
                Vs.   )   cause ap-
James Berry & Jacob Foute   )   pearing to
                                             the court, from
the affidavit of Respondent Foute, and from his deposited
with the clerk and master a portion of the notes mentioned
in Exhibit B, the said Foute is discharged from the attachment issued in this cause and permitted to file his answer.

Anderson P.H. Jordon   )
        Vs.   )   This cause coming on by
Wm. M.McConnell &   )   consent to be determined
Jno. McConnell and   )   upon Bill and answers, it
Samuel D. Kelly   )   is considered by the court
                             that complainants Bill be
dismissed and that complainant pay the costs.

(P-45)

Thomas Henderson)   In this case the subpoena ad
   Vs.)   respondendum having been served
John Lowry and)   on Respt. John Lowry, and he
William Lowry)   having failed to answer; on
                 motion of Compts. sol the bill
as to him is set for hearing pro confesso.

Richard Stephens)   Be it remembered that on this 27th
   Vs.)   day of May 1835 came on this cause
Isaac Baker)   to be heard and determined on the
William Upton)   bill, answers, (of Respondents
Henry Orman &)   Baker & Upton, and the Pro Confesso
Spencer Blankenship)   as to the other defendants) and
                 replication and proofs; and the
matters and things therein contained being fully considered
and understood; and it appearing that the complainants is
entitled to have a specific performance of the contract
mentioned in the pleadings, and that respondents Orman and
Baker had agreed to divide the land therein named, being a
certain tract purchased by Respondent Baker of Spencer Blankenship containing eighty acres and that Orman by said agreement was to have the North end of said tract of land to be
divided according to quantity, without respect to improvements
but it not appearing that said land had been specifically
measured and marked; it is ordered, adjudged and decreed by
the court, that the title to the North end of said Eighty acres,
(to be divided according to quantity and quality without respect to improvements) be divested out of the said Defendants
and each of them and vested in complainant in fee simple.
And it is ordered that Robert Wear and James A. Coffin be
appointed commissioners to divide and mark said land according to quantity and quality and report to the next term of
this court and it is further ordered that Respondents Baker
and Upton Complainant Complainant pay the note of twenty
five dollars mentioned in Respondent (P-46) Bakers answer, and that said Baker have execution for the same upon
said note being surrendered up to Complainant, or filed in
the office of the Clerk and Master for the benefit of Complainant. And it is ordered that Respondents Baker and
Upton pay the costs in this cause, and that execution may
issue for the same.

John Sharp)
   Vs.)
Thomas L. Triomery)

The Chancellor is pleased to order an account in
this cause, and directs that the Clerk and Master in taking
said account ascertain the amount of receipts against the
gin named in the pleadings at the date of the compromise
between complainant and respondent and the amount of set off
or deduction to which respondent was then entitled; and that
he also take testimony as to the value of cotton at that time,
and report hereof to next Term.

Samuel McConnell   )
    Vs   )
Charles Kelso Commiss-   )
ioner of Madisonville et al)

It is agreed by the parties, that the answer of
Charles Kelso shall stand as an answer for all the defendants
not answering separately - and that notice for taking depositions may be served on Charles Kelso and John O. Cannon
for all, except defendants Peck and Hendricks.

Charles Kelso Commiss-   )
ioner of Madisonville et al.)
    Vs) C. Bill   )
Samuel McConnel   )

It is agreed by the parties that the notice for
taking depositions may be served on Charles Kelso and John
O. Cannon for all of the complainants - and Defendant has one
month to file his answer.

(P-47)   Wednesday May 27, 1835

Joseph Smith and   )
Martha Smith   )
    Vs   )
Jesse Melton, Jarrot   )
Stowe, Edy Stowe,   )
Charles Carter and   )
Sally Carter   )

Be it remembered that on this 27th day of May 1835
came on this cause to be finally heard and determined on the
bill, answers, replication, proof and the report of the Clerk
and Master: and it appearing to the satisfaction of the court
that the complainant Joseph is entitled to relief; that there
remained in the hands of the administration Jesse Melton on
the 24th day of April 1830 which he ought to have paid out in
discharge of the incumberance on the land and distributed to
the heirs $581.03 - that Joseph Smith paid out on the 29th
day of December 1832, Three hundred and thirty eight dollars
and seven cents, and that Respondent Charles Carter on the same
day paid fifty four dollars and twenty five cents - the
amount of the incumberance on his part of the land mentioned
in the pleadings and it further appears that Joseph H. Smith
is entitled to the distributive share of John Stowe deceased,
of said estate; and it also appears that Jarrot Stowe administrator had in his hands on the 21st day of September 1831. Two
hundred and seventy two dollars and sixty two cents of said
estate, which still remains unaccounted for. That said estate
in the hands of said Melton, adm. consisted in part of two
notes - one on Complainant Joseph for one hundred and eleven
dollars, twelve and a half cents; the other one Respondent
Charles Carter for the sum of Two hundred and thirty two
dollars and seventy three cents; - that respondent Charles
Carter was entitled to a credit of one hundred and sixty dollars

and five cents - being his distributive share of said estate
and one third of Jarrot Stow's, due from Jesse Melton, administrator, after discharging the incumberance on the land
and that Joseph H. Smith is entitled after the extinguishment
of his note, to the sum of sixty two dollars and ninety two
cents, being the share of Complainants and of John Stow, including what was due Jarrot Stow. It is therefore (P-48)
ordered, adjudged, and decreed by the court that Respondent
Melton pay the Complainant Joseph H. Smith and wife the sum
of four hundred dollars and forty eight cents and thirty four
cents being the balance due complainant for his share, and
the share of John Stow decd of said estate, including the advances and interest thereon made by said Smith for the land
and two thirds of Jarrot Stow's part due from Jesse Melton
adm. It is further ordered and decreed by the court that Respondent Charles Carter have a credit on his note upon which
judgment has been obtained in the Circuit Court for Monroe
County by Jesse Melton administrator, of forty six dollars and
seventeen cents, - the credit to bear date when said note fell
due; and also a credit for the further sum of one hundred and
thirteen dollars and eighty eight cents, to bear date the 29th
of December 1832. And it is further ordered and decreed that
Respondent Jarrot Stow pay to complainants Smith the sum of
one hundred and thirty dollars and fifty six cents, being the
amount Complainant and John Stow is entitled to of said
estate in the hands of Jarrot Stow, administrator, and that
said Jarrot pay to the said Charles Carter and wife the sum
of sixty seven dollars and twenty three cents being their share
of said estate in the hands of said Jarrot, administrator.
And it is further ordered and decreed by the court that each
distributer pay one fourth of the costs in this cause, and it
being suggested to the court that Respondent Jarrot is probably
insolvent; it is ordered that, in the first instance, Complainants pay two thirds, and Respondent Carter one third of said
Jarrot Stow's part of the costs, and that they have execution
over against said Jarrot.

   James a Coffin Clerk and Master of the Chancery
Court produced in court, the receipt of William M. Stokely
Treasurer of the Court House Commissioners, (P-49) for the
state Tax by him collected for the fiscal year ending October
1st 1834, amounting to $15.38.

   Court adjourned until Court in course.

        Will A. Cook

November Term 1835

        Be it remembered that at a court began and held on
this November 23, 1835 at the court house in the Town of Madisonville, for the Chancery District composed of Blount,
Monroe and McMinn Counties, there was present the Honorable
William B. Reese, Chancellor.

Samuel McConnel   )
        Vs.   )
The Commissioners of   )
Madisonville et al   )

        Complainant, with the leave of Court dismissed his
Bill as to Respondents Nicholas S. Peck and Nathan Hendrix.
        Court adjourned until tomorrow.
                                        W.B. Reese

                Tuesday November 23, 1835

        Court met pursuant to adjournment

Thomas Blackburn   )
        Vs.   )
Robert Allen   )
Gilbert Blankenship   )
and others   )

        Complainant by his attorney suggests the death of
Respondent Robert Allen.

Thomas C. Henderson Adm   )
        Vs.   )
Sarah Holt & James H.   )
Reagan, Adm. and Admx.   )

        The order made in this cause at November Term 1834,
directing an account is continued.
        Court adjourned until tomorrow morning 9 O'Clock.
                                        W.B. Reese
(P-50)   Wednesday November 25th 1835
        Court met pursuant to adjournment.

Richard Stephens   )
        Vs.   )
Isaac Baker   )
William Upton   )
Spencer Blankenship   )
and Henry Orman   )

        In this cause, by leave of court, complainant is
allowed to file his amended Bill, and it is filed accordingly.

Fredrick Bolinger)
    Vs.)
Benjamin Griffith)
John Lotspeich &)
Wm. Hogan)

   The order heretofore made directing an account to
be taken in this cause is continued until next Term.

Michael Carroll)
    Vs.)
John Ware)

   The order made at last Term directing an account to
be taken in this cause is continued; and the parties directed
to produce before the Clerk and Master the original books and
papers relating to the partnership between the parties, and
to appear and be examined as required, touching said partnership.

George S. Gilbert and)
William L. Atlee)
    Vs.)
Samuel D. Kelly)

   This cause is continued for taking testimony; and
is, by agreement of the parties, to stand for hearing at
next term.

John Key, administrator)
of Micaijah Carter)
    Vs.)
Elizabeth Carter Guardian)
the Minor heirs of)
said Micaijah Carter)
Deceased)

   This cause coming on for hearing on the bill and
Answer, and the matters and (P-51) things therein duly
considered, the Chancellor is pleased to order an account,
and to direct the Clerk and Master that in taking the account
he ascertain the amount of the estate of said Micaijah Carter
deceased, which came to the hands of complainant as administrator; the amount of bona fide debts, duly authenticated yet
due from said estate, and to whom due and owing – and also
whether the land named and described in the bill can be sold
with less disadvantage to the heirs than any other part of
the real estate of said Micaijah Carter deceased.
   Court adjourned till tomorrow 9 O'Clock.

         W.B. Reese

Court met Thursday Nov. 26, 1835 pursuant to adjournment

Joseph R. Henderson)
William P.H. McDermott)
John Jackson and)   Decree
Amos Biram)
    Vs.)

Nicholas S. Peck and)
Nancy Peck)

   This cause coming on for final hearing upon Bill,
Answers, replication and proofs, the Chancellor was of opinion
that complainants were entitled to relief. It is therefore
ordered adjudged and decreed that defendants be perpetually
enjoined from prosecuting the action of ejectment named in
the pleadings; that the same be dismissed, and that Nicholas
S. Peck pay the costs thereof. It is further ordered and decreed that all right and title acquired by Nicholas S. Peck
and Nancy Peck to the North West fractional quarter of section
twenty two, township three, range three, east of the Meredian,
Monroe County, Hiwassee District, by virtue of the entry No.
4139 for one hundred and fifty acres, in the name of Nancy
Peck, and also by the grant No. 2495, founded upon said entry,
and dated the 29th day of January in Year 1833, each of (Г-52)
which are made exhibits to the Bill, also all right they have
to said land as heirs at law of Andrews Henderson, deceased,
be divested out of said Nicholas S. Peck and Nancy Peck, his
wife. It is further ordered that Nicholas S. Peck pay the
costs of this cause, for which execution may issue, from which
decree Nicholas S. Peck and wife the Defts. pray an appeal to
the Supreme Court at Knoxville which is granted, they having
entered into bond according to law.

Joseph R. Henderson &)
William P.H. McDermott)
   Vs)
Mary Wilson, Nicholas S.)
Peck, & his wife Nancy Peck,)
Jacob J.M. Peck, John Hen-)
derson, Robert N. Henderson,)   Decree
David Wear, and his wife)
Betsy Wear, Charles W. Norwood)
and his wife Melinda Norwood)
Shadrach Inman and his)
wife Sally K. Inman)

   This cause was heard upon the Bill, answers of
Jacob J.M. Peck, Nicholas S. Peck and wife replication and
proofs Because it seems complainants are entitled to relief,
it is ordered adjudged and decreed by the court that all the
interest, right and title defendants have of, in and to the
south East quarter of the section of land granted to Joseph
Phillips; as named in the pleadings, lying and being in the
County of Monroe, in the Hiwassee Destrict situated on Tellico
River, lying in the third range, east of the Meredian third
township as heirs at law of Andrews Henderson, deceased be and
the same is hereby divested out of them and vested in Complainant William P.H. McDermott the purchaser from Joseph R.
Henderson, the executor of Andrew Henderson deceased, as an
estate in fee simple. It is further ordered that Joseph R.
Henderson, the executor, executed to said McDermott a deed
for said land as executor of Andrew Henderson, deceased- It

is further ordered that Nicholas S. Peck pay the costs of this
cause so far as he and wife are parties, that the Bill be dismissed as to Jacob J.M. Peck; that complainants pay   (P-53)
the costs of making him defendant, and that the complainant
Joseph R. Henderson pay the residue of the costs as Executor
of Andrew Henderson, deceased, from which decree Nicholas S.
Peck and wife Nancy Peck, and Jacob J.M. Peck pray an appeal
to the Supreme Court of Knoxville which is granted they having
entered into bond with security.

James Ainsworth   )
        Vs   )
William Ainsworth Sen &   )
William Ainsworth Jun.   )

        By consent of complainants solicitor it is ordered
by the court, that notice for taking depositions may be served
by Respondents on Isaac Burrilson:

John Locke and Palatiah   )
Shelton, Executor of William   )
S. Leuty, dec., and Robert   )
N. Gillespie, and Hannah his   )
wife, late Hannah Leuty,   )
William N. Gillespie and   )
Sidney Ann his wife, late   )
Sidney Ann Leuty, Stanton   )   Decree:
Leuty, Thomas Leuty,   )
Burton Leuty, and Mary   )
Leuty, widow, children   )
and legatus of William   )
S. Leuty, deceased,   )
Complainants   )
        Vs.   )
Gideon Morgan Junior   )
Respondent   )

        Be it remembered that on this 26th day of November
in the year of our Lord 1835, came on this cause to be finally heard: - and it appearing to the court that Complainants
Bill had been taken as confessed against the defendant at the
last Term of the Court: - and the Clerk and Master having
made the following report - that is to say - "In this cause
the Clerk and Master reports that the interest of $1202.24
cents, the amount stated in the bill and deed of Mortgage, as
due from defendant, from February 27th 1828, until the 26th
day of November 1835, amounts to $559.00 cents - principal
$1202.24 cents - interest $559.00 Cents - total $1761.24 cents."
Thereupon the Chancellor declares that the tract of land mentioned in the bill, namely, all that tract or parcel of land
called Major Walkers upper reservation, or mill place, situated on Estenallee Creek in McMinn County, Tennessee, containing six hundred and forty acres excepting   (P-54)   one
tract of seventy acres, sold by said Walker to Henry McCorkle,
one tract of fifty acres sold by said Walker to William Dennis

Hampton, leaving a tract of 495 acres, being the same sold to said defendant by Spencer Beavers, Esquire, Sheriff of said County of McMinn, as the property of said Walkers and conveyed by said sheriff's deed to said defendant hearing date the 18th of October 1825, bounded as follows, to wit, Beginning on a large black oak and post oak McCorkle's Corner on said reservation line one hundred and ten poles to Hampton Corner, a small White oak and hickory, thence West, with said Hampton's line 89½ poles to Hampton's Corner, thence North 135 poles with Hampton's and Camps line to the East and West line of said reservation - thence West with said reservation line 230 poles to a small pine, the North West Corner of said reservation, thence south with said reservation line 334 poles to a small elm and spanish oak, on Hiwassee river, the south west corner of said reservation, thence up the several meanders of the river to a birch and water birch McCorkles corner thence North with McCorkle's line 40 poles to a stake and pointers thence east with said line 160 poles to the beginning, ought to be subjected to the payment of the said sum of $1761.24 cents the amount reported as aforesaid by the Clerk and Master, as due from the Defendant to the Complainant up to this day, together with legal interest until paid. It is therefore ordered adjudged and decreed that the said Defendant Gideon Morgan, junior be allowed (P-55) the term of three months from this date, to deposit the said sum of $1761.24 cents, in the office of the clerk and master of this court, subject to the order of Complainants John Locke and Palatiah Shelton, and if said money should not be deposited in said term, then the Clerk and Master shall, after giving thirty days notice of the time and place of sale, in the Tennessee Journal, a newspaper published in Athens, in McMinn County, proceed to sell said tract of land at public auction, at the court house in the town of Athens, and out of the proceeds of said sale, pay the Complainants their said demand, with interest thereon from this day, the costs of this suit, and also the costs of the mortgage deed, and the residue, if any, pay over to said defendant. And the clerk and master shall report at the next term of this court how he shall have executed this order.

John Sharp   )
  Vs.   ) Decree:
Thomas G. Triomery)

   This cause coming on for final hearing on the report of the Clerk and Master; It is considered by the court, that complainants bill be dismissed, and that complainant pay his own costs, including the costs incurred by the report of the Clerk and Master; - and that Respondent pay the balance of the Costs.

George W. Churchwill)
and Others   )
   Vs.   )
Hiram K. Turk &   )
Thomas J. Turk   )

By consent of parties, it is ordered that the Clerk and Master take an account and ascertain the balance due complainants without prejudice to either party.
(P-56)

Findley Orr)
    Vs.)
Arthur Orr)

In this cause complainant comes into court and dismisses his bill and assumes the cost, for which let execution issue.

Samuel McConnell)
    Vs.)
Jesse Melton, Jones Griffen,)
Samuel Bicknell, Iredell)
D. Wright, Charles Kelso,) Bill
John O. Cannon, Charles) and
Riley, Anderson P.H.) Cross
Jordan, Thomas) Bill
Hunt, Arthur H.)
Henly, Creed Fulton,)
Newton Carson)
David V. Waugh,)
Isaac Anderson) Decree:
George W. Foute)
and James M. Greenway)

The Bill in the above named cause and also the cross Bill of the above Respondants against said McConnell coming on to be finally heard upon the Bills, answers, replication and proofs and agreement of counsel having been had it is ordered, adjudged and decreed by the court that the Bill of the complainant Samuel McConnell against said defendants be dismissed and that Complainant pay the costs, for which let execution issue.

It is further ordered that the Cross Bill of the above named Respondents, be dismissed and that they pay the costs of the same, for which let execution issue.-

From which Decree of the Court as requests the Bill of Complainant McConnell, the said McConnell prays an appeal to the Supreme Court to be holden in Knoxville on the second Monday of July next, which is granted, he having entered into bond with security according to law.
(P-57)

John Key, administrator)
of Micaijah Carter)
Deceased.)
    Vs.)
Elizabeth Carter, Guardian)
of the Minor heirs)
of said Micaijah Carter)

This cause coming on for final hearing on this November 26,
1835 on the Bill, answer and report of the Clerk and Master,
and the matters and things therein contained being only considered - It is ordered and decreed by the court that the
report of the Clerk and Master sell at the Court house door
in the Town of Madisonville, the land mentioned in the pleadings
first giving thirty days notice in the Tennessee Journal printed
at Athens - if the time and place of sale, and the proceeds of
said land first apply to the payment of the costs in this cause,
and the remainder pay over to the said John Key to be applied
to the payment of the debts mentioned in the report of the
Clerk and Master, and the remainder, if any, pay over to the
said lines as directed by law.

Return J. Meigs and   )
Elihu S. Barclay   )
        Vs.   )
John B. Hood, and   )
the Commissioners   )
of the Town of Athens   )

It appearing to the Court that Defendant John B.
Hood is a nonresident, that publication had been made as required by law, requiring said John B. Hood to appear and answer, and the said Hood failing to appear and put in his answer, It is ordered that said bill be taken for confessed
against said John B. Hood; and the commissioners of Athens
having filed their answer; on motion of complainants the
cause is set for hearing.
(P-58)

William H. Cooke   )
        Vs.   )
The Heirs of Samuel   )
Thompson deceased,   )
and the heirs of   )
Alfred Thompson   )
deceased.   )

In this case subpoena, having been served on Jeremiah
Lillard, Mary Riggs, Michael C. Derrick and Emily Derrick,
Elizabeth Masters, & Miranda Thompson and they having failed
to answer. It is ordered that complainants bill be taken for
confessed against said defendants.

Anderson Hodges   )
        Vs.   )
Joseph A. Mabry   )

This cause coming on to be heard on the Bill and
answer on a motion to dissolve the Injunction it is ordered
that the Injunction be dissolved; and that Respondent have
execution against Complainant Anderson Hodges and his securities in the Injunction bond, Thomas Hodges and Reuben Faukner
for the sum of seventeen hundred and eighty dollars and sixty
cents, with interest thereon until paid; and the further sum

of six dollars two and a half cents costs at law upon Defendant giving bond with security to refund in case the final determination of this suit be against him.

James P. Haynes   )
        Vs.   )
William G. White   )
Samuel White and   )
Irby Boyd   )

        This cause coming on to be heard on a motion to dis-
solve the Injunction, on the bill, and answer of William G.
White one of the respondents. It is ordered that the Injunction
in this case be dissolved; and a procendo awarded Respondent
William G. White that he may proceed on his judgment at law.
(P-59)   Court adjourned until Court in course.
                                W.B. Reese

June Term 1836

Be it remembered that at a court of Chancery began
and held at the Court house in Madisonville on the 20th day of
June 1836, for the Chancery District composed of the Counties
Monroe, McMinn, and Bradley, in the Eastern Division of the
State of Tennessee, there was present the Honorable Thomas L.
Williams Chancellor.

By order of the court James A. Coffin is appointed
Clerk and Master of this court for the term of six years, who
entered into bond, with approved security, which bonds having
been ordered to be spread upon the minute book, are in the
words and figures following, to wit.

"Know all men by these present that we James A.
Coffin, John O. Cannon, E.H. Wear, Thomas H. Calloway, and
Martin Henderson are held and firmly bound unto Newton Cannon
governor in and for the State of Tennessee, and his successors
in office, in the sum of Ten Thousand dollars, to which payment will and truly to be made, we bind ourselves and each
of our executors, administrators & assigns jointly and severally, firmly by them presents, signed with our names and
sealed with our seals, this 20th day of June 1836.

The condition of the above obligation is such that
whereas the above bound James A. Coffin hath been appointed
Clerk and Master of the Chancery Court at Madisonville for
the ninth Chancery District composed of the counties of Monroe
McMinn & Bradley in the state of Tennessee (P-60) and in
the Eastern Division of said State, for the term of six years,
now if the said James A. Coffin shall truly and honestly keep
the record of said court and discharge the duties of said office, for the said term of six years, according to law then
the above bound be void, and of no evvect otherwise to remain
in full force and virtue. Given the day and date above written.

Signed, sealed)	James A. Coffin	(Seal)
and acknowled-)	E.H. Wear	(Seal)
ged in open)	Thomas H. Calloway	(Seal)
Court June 20)	John O. Cannon	(Seal)
1836)	Martin Henderson	(Seal)
Test)		

Thomas L. Williams Chan.

Know all men by these presents that we James A.
Coffin, John O. Cannon, E.H. Wear, Thos. H. Calloway, and A.
Hood are held and firmly bound unto Newton Cannon, governor
in and over the state of Tennessee, and his successors in
office in the sum of one thousand dollars, to which payment
will and truly to be made, we bind ourselves and each of our
executors administrators and assignes jointly and severally
firmly by these presents. Signed with our names and sealed
with our seals the 20th day of June 1836.

The Condition of the above obligation is such that
whereas the above bounden James A. Coffin hath been appointed
Clerk and Master of the Chancery Court at Madisonville for the

ninth Chancery District in the state of Tennessee composed of
the Counties of Monroe, McMinn and Bradley, in the eastern
division of said state, for the term of six years; now if
the said James A. Coffin shall faithfully collect and pay in
the manner required by law, the fines and forfeitures   (P-61)
that may arise in said Court, then the above obligation to be
void, otherwise to remain in full force and virtue.

Given the date and day above written.

Signed, sealed	)	James A. Coffin	(Seal)
and acknow-	)	E. H. Wear	(Seal)
ledged in open	)	Thos. H. Calloway	(Seal)
Court June 20th	)	John O. Cannon	(Seal)
1836.	)	Alex. Hood	(Seal)
Test. Thomas L.	)		
Williams Chan.	)		

Know all men by these present that we James A.
Coffin, John O. Cannon, E.H. Wear, Thos. H. Calloway, & A.
Hood are held and firmly bound unto Newton Cannon governor in
and over the state of Tennessee and his successors in office,
the sum of five hundred dollars, to which payment will and
truly to be made we bind ourselves and each of our executors,
administrators and assignes jointly and severally firmly by
these presents. Signed with our names and sealed with our
seals the 20th day of June A.D. 1836.

The condition of the above obligation is such that;
whereas the said James A.Coffin hath been appointed Clerk and
Master of Chancery for the term of six years, for the Chancery
Court held at Madisonville in the Eastern Division of Tennessee
for the ninth Chancery District composed of Monroe, McMinn
and Bradley counties; Now if the said James A. Coffin shall
duly collect and pay into the public treasury all such tax or
causes as shall arise in said court of Chancery, at such time,
and in such manner, as is or may be prescribed by law, then
the above obligation to be void; otherwise to be and remain
in full (P-62) force and virtue. Given the date and day

above written.	)		
Signed, sealed	)	James A. Coffin	(Seal)
and acknow-	)	E.H.WEAR	(Seal)
ledged in open	)	Thos H. Calloway	(Seal)
Court June	)	John O. Cannon	(Seal)
20, 1836	)	Alex. Hood	(Seal)

Test
Thomas L. Williams, Chan.

The oath of office and the several oaths prescribed by law were then administered to said Clerk and Master
James A. Coffin by the Chancellor -

Fredrick Bolinger	)
Vs	)
Benjamin Griffith	)

In this cause the time is enlarged for taking the
account heretofore ordered, until next term of this court; and

if the account ordered should not be taken by next term; the
cause is to stand for hearing and it is ordered that compt pay
the costs of this term.

James Ainsworth   )
        Vs.   )
William Ainsworth Sen.   )
William Ainsworth Jun.   )
John McGhee and   )
Return J. Meigs   )

        The parties in this cause by their solicitors waive
all objection that might be taken to the competency of the
Chancellor now presiding and, by order of court, this cause
is remanded to the rules, and the deposition of William
Ainsworth Sen, one of the Respondents, may be taken, subject
to all just exceptions; and complainant may take the Deposition of W.W. Erwin, again -

Noble Tunnell   )
     Vs.   )
Michael Ghormley   )

        By consent of the parties this cause is continued
till next term, for the taking of testimony.

(P-63)   Monday June Term 1836

George S. Gilbert and   )
William L. Atlee   )
        Vs.   )
Samuel D. Kelly   )

        On this affidavit of Complainant Atlee, this cause
is remanded to the rules, for taking further testimony.

Anderson Hodges   )
     Vs.   )
Joseph A. Mabry   )

        It appearing from the endorsement on the Sceri
Facias issued in this cause against compt. and also from the
admissions of Compts sol that this cause is settled between
the parties, and that complainant is to pay the costs; it
is ordered that complainants bill be dismissed, and that he
pay the costs in this cause for which execution may issue.

George W. Churchwell   ) .
and others   )
        Vs   )
Hiram K. Turk and   )
Thomas J. Turk   )

        By consent this cause is continued until next term
of this court.
                Court adjourned until tomorrow morning 8 O'clock-
                                Thomas L. Williams

Court met pursuant to adjournment on Tuesday morning June 21st 1836.

John McGhee)
Jno. Calloway)
Arthur H. Henley &)
Thomas H. Calloway)
   Vs.)
Henry Stephens)

  At the suggestion of Complainants Sol. three months are allowed Respt Henry Stephens to file his answer in this cause.

   (P-64) Tuesday June 21, 1836

Thomas Henderson)
  Vs.)
William Lowry)

  On the affidavit of complainant this cause is remanded to the rules, and four months allowed the parties for taking testimony; at the expiration of which the cause may be set for hearing, and shall stand for trial at next Term.

Hiram K. Turk)
  Vs.)
George C. Harris)

  The Demurrer filed in this case is over-ruled and defendant allowed to insist on the same matter in his answer.

John Ramsey and)
Thomas Sliger)
  Vs.)
John Sliger)

  This case having been settled by the parties and the costs paid, it is ordered to be stricken from the docket.

John Steel, Samuel)
Blackburn & Mira)
T. Blackburn by)
her next friend, the)
said Samuel -)
  Vs)
David Bell and)
Samuel Bell)

  The Demurrer in this case is over-ruled and two months allowed defendants to file their answers so as not to delay trial.

Jarrot Stow)
  Vs)
Joseph Smith)
and Martha)
Smith)

Complainant by his solicitor dismisses the bill in this cause, and assumes the costs, for which execution may issue.

Michael Carroll)
    Vs)
John Wear)

In this case a dimuation of the record from the Circuit Court being suggested a Certiorari is awarded.
(P-65)

Return J. Meigs,)
and Elihu S. Barclay)
Compts.)
    Vs.)
John B. Hood and)
Archibald R. Turk,)   Decree
Onslow G. Murrell,)
James F. Bradford,)
Solomon Bogart)
Joel K. Brown,)
William W. Anderson,)
Urial Johnston,)
James H. Fyffe)
and Elijah Hurst,)
Respondents)

Be it remembered that on the 20th day of June, 1836, this cause came on to be heard upon the bill, the pro Confesso taken against said John B. Hood, and the answer of the Commissioners of the town of Athens- Whereupon it is ordered, adjudged, and decreed that said defendant John B. Hood be allowed the term of two months from the date of this decree, to deposit in the office of the Clerk and Master of this court the sum of five hundred and fifty dollars and fifty two cents, being the amount of complainants said judgment against him, including legal interest up to this date as appears by the Report of the Clerk and Master subject to the order of Complainant Return J. Meigs; and should said John B. Hood, fail to deposit said sum as herein required, the Clerk and Master of this court shall proceed to sell said lot number 46, in the Town of Athens at public auction, at the court house in said town, after first giving forty days notice of the time and place of said sale by publication in some newspaper published in said town of Athens; and upon application of Complainants by their solicitor it is ordered that said town lot be sold on a credit, one third of the purchase money to be paid in six months, one third in twelve months, and the other third in eighteen months, said several payments to be secured by note with sureties to be approved of by the Clerk and Master; and out of the proceeds of said sale must be paid the costs of this suit, and then Complainants demand, and if (P-66) there be anything over it is to be paid to Defendant Hood; and the Clerk shall report to next term of this court, how he shall have executed this order.

John Locke and))
Palatiah Shelton,)
Executors of)
William S. Leuty dec.)
and Robert N. Gillespie,)
and Hannah his wife,)
William N. Gillespie)
and Sidney Ann his)
wife, Stanton Leuty,)
Thomas Leuty,)
Burton Leuty and)
Mary Leuty, widow)
children and legatus)
of William L. Leuty,)
deceased, Complainants)
     Vs.)
Gideon Morgan, Junior)
Defendant)

         Final Decree

     Upon reading the report of the Clerk and Master
of this Court, made in pursuance of the decretal order rendered
at the last term, in which report it is shown that the Clerk
did in obedience to said decretal order, and in the manner
therein required, sell the land mentioned and specified in
complainants bill, to John Camp, he being the highest and
best bidder for the sum of fifteen hundred and fifty dollars,
which amount is paid into the office of said Clerk and Master.
It is ordered by the Chancellor that said report be in all
things confirmed; and it is ordered, adjudged and decreed by
the court that all the right and title of the said Gideon
Morgan, Junior, of in and to the tract of land mentioned in the
bill and decretal order, namely, all that tract or parcel of
land, called Major Walker's upper reservation, or mill place,
situate on Estenallie Creek, in McMinn County, Tennessee,
containing six hundred and forty acres, excepting one tract of
seventy acres, sold by said Walker to Henry McCorkle, one
tract of fifty acres, sold by said Walker to Sterling Camp,
and one other tract of twenty five acres, sold by said Walker
to William Dennis Hampton, leaving a tract of four hundred and
ninety five acres, being   (P-67)   the same sold to said defendant by Spencer Beavers Esquire, sheriff of said County of
McMinn, as the property of said Walker, and conveyed by said
Sheriff's deed to said defendant, bearing date 18th of October
1825, bounded as follows; to wit, Beginning on a large black
Oak and post oak McCorkle's corner on said reservation line,
thence running North with said reservation line, one hundred
and ten poles to Hampton Corner, a small white oak and hickory,
thence West with said Hampton's line eighty nine and a half
poles to Hampton's Corner, thence North one hundred and thirty
five poles with Hampton's and Camp's line to the East and
West line of said reservation thence West with said reservation
line two hundred and thirty poles to a small pine, the North
West corner of said reservation thence south with said reservation line three hundred and thirty four poles to a small elm
and spanish oak, on Hiwassee River, the south West corner of
said reservation, Thence up the several meanders of the river

to a bark and water birch, McCorkles Corner, thence North
with McCorkles line forty poles to a stake and pointers,
thence east with said line one hundred and sixty poles to
the beginning, be divested out of the defendant Gideon Morgan,
Junior, and out of the heirs, devises and legatus, of William
L. Leuty, deceased, and each of them, and be vested in said
John Camp, the purchaser of the sale made by the Clerk and
Master as aforesaid, and in his heirs, in fee; and it is further ordered that the defendant Gideon Morgan, junior, declare
possession of said premises & upon his refusal so to do that
said John Camp obtain and injunction according to the cause
of this court.

It is further ordered that the Clerk and Master be
allowed as compensation for his services in selling the land
named in this decree three per-cent on the purchase money received by him, amounting to the sum   (P-68)   of forty six
dollars and fifty cents, after the payment of which sum, and
the costs of this suit, out of the said sum of fifteen hundred
and fifty dollars, the balance of said sum shall be paid over
by the Clerk and Master to complainants John Locke & Palatiah
Shelton: and it is ordered that a certified copy of the Interlocutory decree in this case & this decree be registered
in the office of the Register of McMinn County.

John Key, administrator   )
of Micaijah Carter decd.   )
          Vs.   )
Elizabeth Carter, guardian   )
pendente lite of Charles P.   )
Julia F, John P. Eliza P.   )   Final Decree.
Asbury, and Lewis   )
Carter, Minor heirs of   )
said Micaijah Carter   )
decd.   )

Chancery Court, 9th District. June term 1836. This
cause coming on to be finally heard and determined on this 21
st day of June 1836 before the Hon. Thomas L. Williams Chancellor for the Eastern division of Tennessee on the bill, answers, replication, proof and the report of the Clerk and
Master of the present term of this court, from which it appears
that the Clerk and Master did in pursuance of the interlocutory
decree in this cause, proceed at the Court house door in the
town of Madisonville to sell at public outcry the thirty six
acres of land mentioned in the pleadings lying and being in
Monroe County in the south west quarter of the 28th section,
Township second, Range second, East of the Meredian, bounded
as follows: Beginning at the Northeast Corner of said quarter
thence West sixty eight poles, nine links; thence south ninety
three and a half poles, thence East 52 poles 9 links; thence
North forty poles, thence East sixteen poles, thence North
fifty three and a half poles to the beginning, after having
given   (P-69)   the notice required, when Robert Russell of-
fered and bid for said land, one hundred dollars, which was
the last and highest bid, and the same was knocked off to him

the said Russell. It is therefore ordered adjudged and decreed by the Court that said report be in all things confirmed; that the title to said thirty six acres of land be divested out of the said Charles P. Julia F. John P., Eliza P., Asbery and Lewis Carter heirs at law of Micaijah Carter, deceased, and vested in the said Robert Russell and his heirs; that the Money arriving from said sale be first applied to the payment of the costs in this cause, and then to the complainant, to satisfy the different claims mentioned in the report of the Clerk and Master, at a former term, of this court, and the residue, if any, pay over to the said Elizabeth, guardian of said heirs; and that a copy of this decree, and the decree made in this case at last Term, be registered in the register's office of Monroe County, It is further ordered that the Clerk and Master be allowed, for his services in selling said land, the sum of five dollars.

Michael Carroll, Compt.)
                Vs.   )   Decree
John Ware, Respt.   )

Be it remembered that at a term of the Chancery Court began and held for the Eastern Division of Tennessee at the court house in Madisonville, on the third Monday of June 1836. And on Tuesday the 21st day of said month came on to be finally heard and determined before the Honorable Chancellor Thomas L. Williams, the above cause, upon the decretal order heretofore made in this Court, and the Report of the Clerk and Master made to the present term of this court: It/is/ordered (P-70) Appearing to the satisfaction of the Court, from the report of the Clerk and Master, that, upon a balance struck between complainant and Respondent in said report in favor of Complainant for the sum of fourteen hundred and forty five dollars and forty six and a half cents that favor of Complainant Complainant is entitled to relief for the agreement therein stated; It is ordered adjudged and decreed by the court that the report of the Clerk and Master made to the present term of this court be in all things confirmed that Complainant recover against Respondent the sum of fourteen hundred and forty five dollars forty six and one half cents. It is further ordered that John O. Cannon heretofore, appointed commissioner, to take an account in this cause be allowed the same fee that Clerks and Masters were allowed at the time his services were rendered, for similar services; that each party pay one half said commissioner's fees, and that said commissioner be entitled to an execution against both complainant and defendant for his said fees.

It is further ordered, adjudged, and decreed that the partnership heretofore subsisting between the parties be dissolved; and that execution issue against the parties for their respective costs in accordance with the order heretofore made in this cause, and that execution issue against the Respondent for the amount of this decree.

John L. McCarty, Executor)
of John Walker, Jr. Decd.)
         Vs)
Betsy Walker)
(P-71))
William H. Cook, Compt.)
         Vs)
Jeremiah Lillard and his)
Wife, Jemima, Samuel)
Thompson, Miranda)
Thompson, Francis Thompson,)
Catharine Thompson, and)
Alfred Thompson, Children)
and heirs of Alfred Thompson,))
deceased, and Mary Thompson,)
widow and relicit of Samuel)
Thompson Sr. decd-; And)
Daniel Thompson, Samuel)
Thompson, Robert Thompson,)
Miranda Thompson, John)
Thompson, William)
Thompson, Amy Thompson,)
Sarah Thompson, Samuel)
Riggs and Mary his)
wife, Michael C. Derrick and)
Emily his wife, and Elizabeth)
Masters, Children and heirs)
at law of Samuel Thompson Sen.)
deceased, Respondents.)

A certiorari is awarded in this case to compts to be directed to the Clerk of the Circuit Court for McMinn County for a complete record.

Decretal order

Be it remembered that on the 21st day of June 1836, the above stated cause came on to be heard upon the Complainants bill, the answers of Mary Thompson, Samuel Thompson, for himself and as guardian of the minor heirs of Alfred Thompson deceased, and as guardian of the minor heirs of Samuel Thompson Sr. deceased Daniel Thompson, Jemima Lillard and Samuel Riggs, and the pro confesso, as to defendants, Jemima Lillard, Mary Riggs, Michael C. Derrick, Emily Derrick, Elizabeth Masters and Miranda Thompson - Whereupon it is ordered adjudged and decreed by the court,

that complainants judgments are liens upon the interest of the heirs of Alfred Thompson, deceased, in the iron works and lands mentioned in Complainants bill, and to make the same available for complainants demand. It is ordered that the Clerk and Master of this court proceed to make sale of said land mentioned in complainants bill, at public auction to the highest and best bidder, at the court house door in the town of Athens, s̶a̶i̶d̶ ̶l̶a̶n̶d̶s̶ ̶b̶e̶i̶n̶g̶ (P-72) in McMinn County first having given forty days notice of the time and place of said sale by publication in the "Tennessee Journal" or some other newspaper published in said town of Athens; said lands being the north west quarter of Section 36 in Township 5, and range first East, being the quarter section of land on which the iron works are erected, the South West quarter of section 25, in Township 5, and Range 1st East, the south west quarter of section 36, in township 5th and Range 1st East, the North East quarter of section 15 i̶n̶ ̶t̶o̶w̶n̶s̶h̶i̶p̶ in township 5, and Range 1st East, the North East quarter of section 35 in township 5 and Range 1st. East, the North East quarter of section 36 in township 5 and range 1st East, the North East quarter of Section 31st in township 4, and range 2nd, East, and one hundred and twenty acres of the North side of the North West

quarter of section 31st in township 4th and range 2nd East,
all said several tracts of land situated on the waters of
Conassauga Creek and East of the Meredian line in Hiwassee
District and that the proceeds of said sale be partitioned
amongst the several claimants and heirs as they are respectively entitled as appears from the pleadings in this cause,
that is to say, the interest of the heirs of Alfred Thompson
decd in said partnership, being one third part thereof and
one sixth part being two childrens parts to which said Alfred
was entitled out of his father's interest in said partnership
being the one half thereof be paid to complainant in discharge
of his said judgments, then the balance to be paid to the
heirs of the said   (P-73)   Alfred Thompson deceased, that
one sixth   part of the whole proceeds of the sale, and one
twelfth part (or a Child's part of the interest of Samuel
Thompson Jun.: And that the balance of the proceeds of the
sale be paid of the interest to which Samuel Thompson, the
father, was entitled, be equally divided between his other
heirs mentioned in the pleadings: to wit, Robert Thompson,
Miranda Thompson, John Thompson, William Thompson, Amy, & Sarah
Thompson, Samuel Riggs and Mary his wife, Michael C. Derrick
and Emily his wife, and Elizabeth Masters and the Clerk shall
report at next term how he executes this decree.

Joseph Smith and   ) By consent of
Martha Smith   ) Complainant,
        Vs.   ) Sol, two months
Jarrot Stow   ) are allowed
Jesse Melton &   ) defendants to file
Saml. Blackburn   ) their answers.
Joshua Parsons and   )
Hugh Ghormley   )
        Vs   Q
John Calloway
A.H. Henley and   )
Thomas H. Calloway   )

By consent of parties by their Solicitor the answer
of Thomas H. Calloway is allowed to stand for the other defendants.

Court adjourned until Court in Course.

Thomas L. Williams.

(P-74)   December Term 1836

Be it remembered that at a Court of Chancery for
the 9th Chancery District in the state of Tennessee began and
held at the Court house in Madisonville on the 19th day of
December 1836, there was present the Hon. Thomas L. Williams,
Chancellor.

Frederick Bolinger)
        Vs.   )
Benjamin Griffith   )

On affidavit of Complainant this case is continued
until next term, and the time enlarged for taking the account
heretofore ordered; and it is ordered that complainant pay
the costs of this term.

Noble J. Tunnell   )
        Vs.   )
Michael Ghormly   )

This cause coming on for hearing; Complainants
bill (his solicitor assenting thereto) is dismissed; and it
is ordered that complainant pay the costs of this cause for
which let execution issue.

Hardy C. Tatum   )
        Vs.   )
Jesse Kerr & Richard   )
White   )

The order made at rules setting this cause for
hearing it set aside as to Respondent Kerr is set aside, and
the Case remanded to the Rules.

Gideon Morgan)
        Vs   )
David Vann   )

This Case coming on for Hearing on a motion to
dissolve the Injunction in this case; it is ordered that the
Injunction be dissolved; on Respondents entering into bond
with security to refund in case of a final dicision against him.

Samuel McConnell   )
        Vs   )
Abraham Utter   )

This cause coming on for hearing on a motion to
(P-75)   dissolve the injunction, and argument of council
having been had. It is ordered that the Injunction in this
case be dissolved, on Respondents entering into bond with
approved security approved by the Clerk and Master to refund
in case of a final decision against him; and that Respondent
Abraham Utter recover of Samuel McConnell the Complainant and
Hamilton Bradford and Levi Bailey his security in the Injunction Bond the sum of Three hundred and seventy nine dollars
and thirty one cents, the amount of the judgement rendered in

the circuit Court of McMinn County, besides costs with interest thereon from the 28th day of October 1830, until paid.

Thomas Meredith, & Edward Spencer, surviving partners of the firm of Manning, Meredith & Co. Joshua Medtant and Peter Mason - Complainants.

against

Phillip E. Thomas, Evan P. Thomas, William G. Thomas, and William E. George, C. & M.C. Cape, R.B. Allen, Enoch Blackburn, Samuel Blackburn and George W. Churchwell, Respondents.

This Case coming on for final hearing upon the bill, the answers of Thomas and George, George W. Churchwell, Samuel Blackburn, and the replication to said answers, and the pro-Confesso as to the other Respondents, publication having been made and they having failed to answer; and agreement of Counsel having been heard and it appearing to the Court that Complainants are not entitled to the relief prayed - It is ordered, adjudged and decreed by the court that complainants Bill be dismissed and that complainants pay the costs in this cause. The Bill in this Case is dismissed without prejudice as to Respt. S. Blackburn

(P-76)   Monday Dec. 19, 1836

Patrick S. Peck, Complainant
            Vs
Joseph R. Henderson - Ex of Andrew
Henderson, decd - Polly Wilson, John Henderson, Nicholas S. Peck and his wife Nancy, Charles W. and Malinda Norwood, David and Betsy Wear, Robert N. Henderson & Shadrach & Sally K. Inman. Respondents.

Complainant, by his Solicitor John O. Cannon dismisses his Bill: It is therefore ordered by the Court that the said suit above named be stricken from the Docket, and that Complainant pay the costs in said cause.

Andrew Cowan, Compt.   )
        Vs.   )
Oswell Phillips, Respt.   )

In this case a rule is entered that compt. may show cause if any he can for the dissolution of the Injunction.

Gideon Morgan   )
        Vs.   )
David Vann   )

This cause coming on for hearing on the Bill and answer, on a motion to dissolve the Injunction. It is ordered that the Injunction be dissolved and that Respondent have execution against Complainant Gideon Morgan and his security in the Injunction Bond. John G. Glass for the sum of Two hundred and thirty dollars, the amount of the judgment in the Circuit Court of McMinn County, together with interest on the same from the 2nd day of August 1836 until paid, on Respts entering into bond with security to refund in case of a final decision

against him.
(P-77)   Court adjourned till tomorrow morning 9 O'clock.
                                        Thomas L. Williams

                    Tuesday Morning - Dec. 20, 1836.
                Court met pursuant to adjournment-

James Ainsworth   )
      Vs   )
William Ainsworth Sen.   )
William Ainsworth Jr.   )
R.J. Meigs & J. McGhee.)

        On affidavit of Respondent William Ainsworth Jun.
this case is continued until next Term of this Court, and remanded to the rules for taking testimony on both sides.

Mary Smith & Others   )
          Vs   )
John Smith et al   )

        On affidavit of John Smith one of Respondents this
case is continued till next term & remanded to the rules.

John K. Farmer   )
      Vs   )
Nathaniel Carey   )
Will H. Carey   )
Robert M. Carey   )

        In this case five months are allowed defendants
to file their answers.

H.K. Turk   )
    Vs   )
George C. Harris)

        On affidavit of compt. this case is continued till
next Term and remanded to the rules for taking testimony -and
on motion of Respt. sol. a rule is entered that he show cause
if any he can why the Injunction in this case shall be dissolved.

Kelso & Pursley   )
      Vs   )
James Hall   )

        Respt. allowed till next Wednesday to file his
answer to demurrer.

(P-78)   Tuesday Dec. 20, 1836

Thomas Blackburn, Compt.   )
        Vs   )
Robert Allen, and others   )
Respondents   )

        The Demurrer filed in this case is overruled.

James A. Coffin Clerk and Master of this court presented the Treasurer receipt for the state Tax by him collected - which is as follows -

"10$\frac{66}{100}$ Knoxville Dec. 10, 1836 - No. 194.

Received of James A. Coffin Ten Dollars 66 cents, audited to him by No. 194 and due on account of Revenue by him collected, as Clerk of Chancery Court held at Madisonville from 1st Oct. 1835 to 1st Sept. 1836.

And McMillan Cashr.
for Treasurer of Tennessee.

George W. Churchwell et al)
    Vs   )
Hiram K. Turk et al   )

  On this 20th day of December 1836, came on this cause for hearing before the Hon. Thomas L. Williams Chancellor, upon the bill of Complainants, the answer of the Respondents, the replication the report of the Clerk and Master and proofs and it appearing to the satisfaction of the court that the complainants are entitled to relief. It is ordered, adjudged and decreed by the court, that the report of the Clerk and Master be in all things affirmed, and that unless the Respondent Hiram K. Turk deposit in the office of the Clerk & Master the sum of fourteen hundred and fifty dollars and sixty five cents with interest thereon from the 18th day of August 1835, within three months from this day, that the said Respondent and George Henderson (P-79) the security declares to the Clerk and Master the negro Rhoda, and all other property and notes mentioned in the deed of trust, that have not heretofore been sold or desposed of by the said George W. Churchwell, under the deed of Trust, and that the Clerk and Master proceed to expose the same to public sale after giving thirty days notice of the time and place of sale, the said property for the satisfaction of the debts of Complainant - and if the Respondent H.K. Turk or the said George Henderson should fail and refuse to deliver over said property to the Clerk and Master for the purpose aforesaid, then the Clerk and Master shall proceed to ascertain the value of said property and report all his proceedings to the next term of this court.

Return J. Meigs and   )
Elihu S. Barcklay Compts.)
    Vs.   )
John B. Hood & Archibald)
R. Turk, Onslow G. Murrell) Final Decree
and Others Commissioners)
of Athens Respondents)

  Upon reading the report of the Clerk and Master made in this cause, on this 19th day of December 1836, in which it appears "that, in obedience to the decree rendered in this cause at last Term, the said Clerk and Master did after having advertised sale therein required, the time and place of sale, proceed to sell, at the court house door in

Athens, the Lot of ground named in the said decree, namely
Lot No. 46, in the Town of Athens, on the 10th day of December,
1836, when Return J. Meigs Complainant, by his agent Alexander
D. Kizer, was the highest and last bidder; whereupon the said
Lot No. 46 was sold to the said Return J. Meigs at the price
of one hundred and fifty five dollars, which was the amount of
his bid. It is ordered, adjudged and decreed by the court
that   (P-80)   said report be in all things confirmed, and
that the title to the said Lot No. 46 in the Town of Athens be
divested out of the said John B. Hood, and out of Archibald R.
Turk, Onslow G. Murrell, James F. Bradford, Solomon Bogart,
Joel K. Brown, William W. Anderson, Urial Johnston, James F.
Fyffee, and Elijah Hurst, Commissioners of the town of Athens,
and vested in Return J. Meigs shall have possession of said
lot, to obtain which, if necessary, process may issue according to the cause of this court.

And it is ordered, that out of the amount of said
sale, said Return J. Meigs pay the costs of this suit: that
after deducting the costs, the balance of said sale be credited
on the demand of the complainant Meigs, mentioned in the decretal order; and that the Clerk and Master be allowed the sum
of $12/50 cents, for selling the said Lot. It is further or-
dered that a copy of the decretal order and of this decree be
registered in the office of the Register of McMinn County.

George S. Gilbert and   )
William L. Atlee   )
        Vs.   )
Samuel D. Kelly   )

On the 19th day of December 1836 came on this cause
for hearing before the Honorable Thomas L. Williams, Chancellor,
upon the Bill of Complainants, the answer of Respondent, the
replication and proofs, when it is ordered, adjudged and decreed
by the court, that the Clerk and Master proceed to take an account in this case of all the advances made by Respondent to
Complainants either in money or property and on what account,
and also of the value of the work done by complainants for Respondent, and the value of the work agreed to be done by Complainants for Respondent, embraced, within the bond executed
by   (P-81)   Complainants to Respondent, and what amount of
money and property and notes he has received of Complainants,
or any account whatever, and report to next Term of this Court,
and the equity of the case is reserved until the final hearing.

Isaac Denton Adm.   )
inistrator of   )
Robert Rollins   )
        Vs   )
Betsy Rollins and   )
others, Respts.   )

This case is remanded to the rules, and let the
Clerk appoint some discreet person as guardian pendente Lete
of the minor heirs of said Robert Rollins decd. the guardian
heretofore appointed having failed to answer the bill.

James P. Haynes   )
Arson Haynes adms.   )
of John Haynes decd   )
       Vs.   )
Elizabeth Haynes &   )
Others   )

      On affidavit of Compts. Sol. it is directed process in this case issue to Carter County T. for Respondents.

Andrew Cowan, Compt   )
      Vs.   )   Bill of Review
Oswell Phillips, Respt.)

      This case coming on to be heard on a motion to dissolve the Injunction. It is ordered & adjudged ~~and decreed~~ that the Injunction be dissolved, and that Respondent have execution against Complainant Andrew Cowan and Carter Melton and William Burk his security in the Injunction bond for the sum of Two hundred and seventy one dollars and seventy one cents with interest thereon from the 5th day of May 1836, the date of the decree in the Circuit Court for McMinn County and also the costs in the Circuit Court on Respondents (P-82) entering into bond with security approved by the Clerk and Master to refund in case of a decision against him on the final hearing.

Miram K. Turk   )
    Vs.   )
George C. Harris   )

      This case coming on to be heard on a motion to dissolve the Injunction, It is ordered that the Injunction be dissolved, and that Respondent have execution against Complainant for the sum of fifty one dollars, with interest on the same from the 21st day of September 1833, the date of the Jurtius Judgment On Respondents executing bond with security to refund in case of a final decision against him.

William H. Cook, Complainant
          Vs
Jeremiah Lillard and Jemima his wife, Samuel Thompson, Miranda Thompson, Francis Thompson, Catherine Thompson, and Alfred Thompson, Children of Alfred Thompson decd. Mary Thompson widow of Samuel Thompson Sen. decd. and Daniel Thompson, Samuel Thompson, Robert Thompson, Miranda Thompson, John Thompson, William Thompson, Amy Thompson, Sarah Thompson, Samuel Riggs, Mary Riggs, Michael C. Derrick, and Emily Derrick, and Elizabeth Masters, Children and heirs of Saml. Thompson Sen. decd. Respondents.

      The Clerk and Master presented his report of the sale made by him in this case; when on affidavit of Defendant Miranda Thompson; It is ordered that the Clerk and Master proceed to sell again in accordance with the decree rendered at last term the land described in (P-83) said Interlocutory decree, and refund to Complainant the money by him paid into office, on his bid.

James P. Haynes)
   Vs   )
William G. White) Final Decree:
Samuel White &   )
Erby Boyd   )

   Be it remembered that on this 20th day of December
1836 by consent of the Consel of the parties this cause came
on to be finally heard and determined upon the Bill, and answers of the Respondents William G. White and Samuel White,
and the pro Confesso of the defendant Erby Boyd, and by the
consent of the counsel for the complainant and Defendant, It
is ordered, adjudged and decreed by the Court that the Complainant's bill as to the said William G. White and Samuel
White be dismissed; and that the said William G. White and
Samuel White recover of the Complainant all their costs in
this behalf expended for which an execution may issue according to the course of this Court and by the consent of the
Counsel aforesaid, It is further, ordered, adjudged and decreed by the court, that the defendant Erby Boyd pay to the
complainant James P. Haynes the sum of Two hundred and five
dollars together with the interest thereon from the 31st day
of December 1828 till paid, it being the balance of the
purchase money with the interest thereon in the hands of the
said Erby Boyd, for the negro boy Phillip mentioned in Complainants Bill together with all the costs by the complainant
in this behalf expended and that the Clerk retain out of said
sum the costs in their cause - for which let execution issue
for which an execution may issue according to the Course of
this court.

Anderson P.H. Jordan)
   Vs   )
William Bayless and)
Martin Hunt Adms.)
of Thomas Hunt   )

   Two months are allowed Defendants to file their
answers so as not to delay the hearing of the cause at next
term.
(P-84)

John Steele, Samuel   )
Blackburn and Mira   )
T. Blackburn by her   )
next friend Compts.   ) Decree
   Vs.   )
David Bell and   )
Samuel Bell assignes   )
of F.S. Heiskell   )
Respondents.   )

   Be it remembered that on the 20th day of December
1836, this cause came on to be heard by consent of parties
upon the Bill, answers, replication and proofs, the bill of
sale mentioned in the bill from N.B. Upton to Mira T. Blackburn
dated August 25th 1836, being produced to the court, and the

parties admitting the bill of sale from Samuel Blackburn to
John Steel, was executed as stated in the bill, and the is-
suance of the execution in favor of Respondents under which
the boy was made or the negro girl Ann: And the levy on said
girl were also admitted- where upon it is ordered, adjudged
and decreed by the Court that the Injunction granted in this
case be made perpetual and that Respondents and all others
under them be restrained and prohibited from selling said
negro girl Ann. And it is further ordered and adjudged that
Respondents David and Samuel Bell pay the Costs in this cause
for which let execution issue, From which decree of the
Chancellor Respondents pray an appeal to the Supreme Court
to be held in Knoxville on the Monday of June 1837, which is
granted on their entering into bond with security as required
by law.

(P-85) Michael Carroll   )
              Vs   )   Bill of Review:
        John Ware   )

On affidavit of John O. Cannon Respts Sol. It is
ordered that before Michael Carroll Compt. in the original
Bill be permitted to take out execution on the Decree rendered
in said cause, he be required to give security to refund in
case the Bill of Review be decided against him.

Court adjourned till Court in Course.

Thos. L. Williams.

Thursday March 18th 1841

Court met pursuant to adjournment

Robert M. McEwin En &   )   Complainants sol
Elizabeth McEwin En &   )   suggested the
) Vs.   )   death(of
Henry Matlock   )   Complainant
John McPherson et al   )   Elizabeth McEwin

John Austin   )   This cause coming on to be heard
        Vs   )   before the Hon. Thomas L. Williams
Jacob Lingerfelt   )   Chancellor, upon the Bill, answers
                              Replication, & proof, and it
appearing to the Court that complainant is not entitled to
relief; It is ordered, adjudged and decreed by that complainant pay the costs, for which let execution issue. From which
decision of the Chancellor Complainant prays an appeal.

(P-86)   June Term 1837

        At a court of Chancery began and held at the Court-
house in Madisonville on the 19th day of June 1837, there was
present presiding, the Hon. Thomas L. Williams Chancellor.

Frederick Bolinger .)
        Vs   )
Benjamin Griffith   )

        On affidavit of complainant this case is remanded
to the Rules and four months allowed for the Clerk and Master
to complete his report.

James Ainsworth   )
        Vs   )
William Ainsworth Sen.   )
William Ainsworth Jun.   )
John McGhee & R.J. Meigs   )

        Sufficient cause being shown on affidavit of Respon-
dent William Ainsworth Sen. this case is continued, and remanded to the rules, for taking further testimony.

Hardy C. Tatum   )
        Vs.   )
R. White and Jessee Kerr   )

        On affidavit of complainant this cause is continued;
and remanded to the Rules for the purpose of taking Deposition of.

Gideon Morgan   )
        Vs.   )
David Vann.   )

        This case coming on to be heard on the Bill,
answers and Replication; and it appearing that complainant is
not entitled to relief - It is ordered and decreed that complainants Bill be dismissed and that complainant pay the costs
of this suit, for which execution may issue.

(P-87)   June Term 1837

Joseph R. Henderson Ex.   )
and W.P.H. McDermott   )
        Vs   )
Nicholas S. Peck & wife   )
Nancy, Jacob Peck & others·)

        The Demurrer filed in this case by Nicholas S.
Peck & wife is overruled - and said Respondents allowed
until the first Rule day to file their answers.

Samuel Blackburn   )
        Vs   )
George W. Churchwell   )
Thomas & George et al   )

On affidavit of Respondent Churchwell, it is ordered that complainant give other good security, or that his present prosecution security justify on or before the first day
of next Term.

Court adjourned till tomorrow morning half past
7 O'Clock -

Thos. L. Williams.

Tuesday June 20, 1837
Court met pursuant to adjournment.

Thomas Henderson	)	On affidavit of Respondent Will
Vs.	)	Lowry this case is continued and
John Lowry & Will Lowry	)	remanded to the Rules - and Re-
		spts may serve notice to take

Deposition on Wm. Gillespie, Compts Sol.

Samuel McConnell	)	On affidavit of complainant this
Vs	)	case is Continued until next term
Abraham Utter et als	)	for taking testimony.

Charles Kelsoe &	)	
Jas Pursley	)	The Demurrer
Vs	)	filed by Respondents in this
John & M. Hall	)	case is overruled; and
		Respts required to answer -

and required to do so on or before 2nd Rule day-

(P-88)   Tuesday June 20, 1837

William Hale	)	
Vs	)	Decree:
Jacob Smezbough	)	

Be it remembered that at a Chancery Court began
and held at Madisonville in the County of Monroe in the 9th
District in the Eastern Division of the State of Tennessee
this cause came on to be heard and determined, upon complainants Bill: - Which had been taken for confessed and regularly
set for hearing - It appears to the court that Complainant is
entitled to the relief prayed; it is therefore ordered and
decreed that the Injunction issued in this cause be made perpetual, that Respondent take nothing by the judgment stated
in the pleadings. It is further ordered and decreed that
complainant pay the costs in the first instance, but recover
the same from defendant for which he may have execution for
the costs at law and in equity.

John McGhee and	)	
John Calloway,	)	By the consent of the parties
Arthur H. Henly &	)	This case is to be transfered
Thos. H. Calloway	)	to the Chancery Court held at
Executors of	)	Knoxville soon as the testimony
Joseph Calloway	)	shall have been taken.
Vs	)	
Henry Stephens &	)	
R.J. Meigs	)	

William J.J. Morrow   )
George D. Edgar &   )
John Mize   )
    Vs   )
Indell D. Wright &   )
Samuel Bayless   )

    By consent of parties, it is ordered that this case be transfered to the Chancery Court at Knoxville.

Indell D. Wright   )
    Vs   )
Will J.J. Morrow   )
George D. Edgar   )
Thomas Henderson, I.W. Meek)
and Samuel Bayless   )

    By consent of parties this case is transfered to the Chancery Court at Knoxville.

(P-89)   William H. Cook, Complainant)
                     Vs.)
    Jeremiah Lillard, and his)
    wife, Jemima, Samuel)
    Thompson, Miranda)
    Thompson, Francis)   Final Decree
    Thompson, Catharine Thompson)
    and Alfred Thompson,)
    children & heirs of)
    Alfred Thompson, deceased, -)
    and Mary Thompson,)
    widow of Samuel)
    Thompson, Senr. deceased.)
    and Daniel, Samuel,)
    Robert, Miranda, John,)
    William, Amy, and Sarah)
    Thompson, Samuel Riggs and)
    his wife Mary, Michael C.)
    Derrick and his wife, Emely;)
    and Elizabeth Masters, and)
    Children & heirs at law of)
    Samuel Thompson Sr.)
    decd, Respondents)

    Upon reading the report of the Clerk and Master made in obedience to the order made in this cause at last Term and in pursuance of the Decree rendered at the term previous of this court, in which report it is stated that the Clerk and Master did make the advertisement required as to the time and place of sale, in the Tennessee Journal, and did accordingly on the 8th day of April 1837, proceed to sell at the Court house door in the town of Athens, all the several tracts of land specified in said decree viz: the North West quarter of Section 36, in Township 5, Range 1st East: the South West quarter of Section 36, in Township 5, Range 1st East; the North West quarter of Section 15, in Township 5, and

Range 1st East; the North East quarter of Section 35, in
Township 5 and Range 1st East; the North East quarter of
section 36, in township 5, and Range 1st East; the North
East quarter of section 31 in Township 4, and Range 2nd East;
and 120 acres of the North Side of the North West quarter of
section 31, in Township 4 and Range 2nd East, all said tracts
situate in McMinn County, Tennessee: - When and where the
said several tracts of land were sold and knocked off to
Complainant William H. Cook, he being the highest and best
bidder, at the time of Twelve hundred and fifty two dollars
of which sum said complainant has paid into office &c. (P-90)
Wherefore it is ordered adjudged, and decreed by the court
that said Report be confirmed; that the title to said several
tracts of land viz - The North West quarter of Section 36, in
township 5 and Range first East; the North East quarter of
Section 15, in Township 5 and Range first East, The North East
quarter of section 35 in township 5, and Range first East the
North East quarter of section 36, in Township 5, and range
first East; the North East quarter of Section 31, in township
4, and range 2nd East; and 120 acres of the North Side of the
North West quarter of Section 31 in Township 4 and Range
second East; all said several tracts of land situate on the
waters of Conassauga Creek, and East of the Meredian line in
the Hiwassee District in McMinn County, Tennessee; be divested
out of the said Jeremiah Lillard and his wife Jemima; and Samuel, Miranda, Francis, Catharine, and Alfred Thompson, children and heirs at law of Alfred Thompson decd; and Mary Thompson
widow of Samuel Thompson, senior, deceased; and Daniel,Samuel,
Robert, Miranda, John, William, Amy, and Sarah Thompson,
Samuel Riggs and his wife Mary, Michael C. Derrick and his
wife Emily, and Elizabeth Masters; children and heirs at law
of Samuel Thompson Sen. deceased; and out of each and every
one of them, and vested in William H. Cook, the purchaser as
aforesaid, and his heirs forever.

And it is further ordered that the Clerk and Master
pay the proceeds of Said sale to the respective claimants,
according to the Shares and proportions to which they are respectively entitled, as ascertained, declared and Stated in
the Interlocutory Decree rendered in this cause; the Shares
of John William, Amy and Sarah Thompson Minors and children
of Samuel Thompson Sen. deceased to be paid to their legally
constituted guardian or guardians.

It is further ordered that the Clerk and Master retain out of the proceeds of said sale to be in the first
place deducted, the costs of this cause, including (P-91)
the sum of fifty Dollars which it is ordered by the Court that
said Clerk and Master James A. Coffin be allowed for his
services in executing the Interlocutory Decree and order in
this cause, and also the costs of the suits at law mentioned
in the pleadings.

And it is further ordered that a certified copy of
this Decree and of the Interlocutory Decree be Registered in
the office of the Register of McMinn County; and it is further
ordered, if it be necessary, that process issue, according to

the cause of this court, directed to the Sheriff of McMinn
County, commanding him to put the purchaser aforesaid in
possession of the aforesaid purchased premises.

Hiram K. Turk   )
        Vs   )
George C. Harris   )

        On affidavit of complainant this case is continued
till next Term - for taking the deposition of Calvin M. Hickey.

Joseph H. Smith and   )
Martha Smith   )
        Vs   )
Jarrot Stow, Jesse   )
Melton & L. Blackburn   )

        On affidavit of Respondent Jarrot Stow this case is
continued till next term for taking testimony.

Will Upton, Will A.   )
Upton, Joseph Upton   )
and David Lowry   )
        Vs   )
Jacob Baker, Isaac   )
Denton, C.S. Calloway,   )
& Joe Donohoo   )

        The Demurrer filed in this case is overruled, and
Defts allowed two months to answer so as not to delay.-

Mary Smith, guardian &   )
Will Smith   )
        Vs   )
John Smith, Joseph   )
Smith, Jur. Smith   )

        Respondents have leave to amend their answer by
pleading the Statute of limitations.

(P-92)   June 20, 1837 - Tuesday

George S. Gilbert and   )
William L. Atlee   )
        Vs.   )   Decree:
Samuel D. Kelly   )

        On this 20th day of June 1837 Came on this cause
for final hearing before the Hon. Thomas L. Williams Chancellor
&c upon the bill of Complainant, the answer, as amended, of
respondent, the replication, the proofs and report of the
Clerk and Master, and it appearing to the satisfaction of the
Court that the Complainants are entitled to relief. And it
further appearing to the satisfaction of the Court that respondent has advanced to Complainants the sum of Four hundred
and twenty seven dollars and fifty cents, and that respondent

had received of Complainants two hundred and seventy one dollars and Eighty four cents in work, and one hundred and seventy dollars on account of a note on A.P.H. Jordon, which has been paid Respondent; and also one hundred and eleven dollars and six cents on the sale made by the Trustee F.A. Kanty, under the Deed of Trust, making in all the sum of Five hundred and twenty two dollars and ninety cents, leaving one hundred and twenty five dollars and forty cents in favor of Complainants - It is therefore, ordered, adjudged, and decreed by the Court that Complainants recover of the Respondent said sum of one hundred and twenty five dollars and forty cents, and that Respondant be enjoined from proceeding to collect his judgments at law upon the note of three hundred dollars for the Barouche, and that he be perpetually enjoined from suing on the bond of Complainants for the work therein stipulated to be done upon the house of Respondant - and it is further ordered adjudged and decreed by the Court that the Respondants pay the costs, for which execution may issue.

(P-93)   Joshua Parsons and   )
         Hugh Ghormley   )
                Vs   )
         John Calloway, Thomas   )   June Term 1837:
         H. Calloway & A.H.   )
         Henly, Ex. of Joseph   )
         Calloway, deceased   )

This cause coming on to be heard before the Chancellor Thomas L. Williams on the Bill, answers, replication, and proof - It appearing to the Satisfaction of the court that Complainants are entitled to the relief prayed; It is ordered, and adjudged that the Clerk and Master of this court take an account between the parties to this bill; that he ascertain the value of the partnership property mentioned in the Bill received by each of the Complainants and Defts. testator; and that he report to the next Term of this court.

Richard Stephens   )
        Vs   )
Isaac Baker   )
William Upton   )   Decree:
Henry Orman &   )
Spencer Blankenship)

This cause coming on for final hearing before the Hon. Thos. L. Williams Chancellor on the Report of Robert Wear and James A. Coffin made to the present term of this court: from which it appears that the equal division as to quantity of the 80 acres of land made by Orman and Baker was agreed by Complainant might be reported as the true line, between Complainant & Baker. It is therefore ordered by the Court that the title to the North side of the said 80 acres named in the pleadings viz 40 acres, be divested out of the said Baker, William Upton, Henry Orman and Spencer Blankenship and vested in the said Richard Stephens and his heirs in fee. It is further ordered that Robert Wear, Surveyor, and James A.

Coffin be allowed the sum of seven dollars and fifty cents each for their services in the division of said land - and that this Decree together   (P-94)   with the Interlocutory decree be registered in the Registers office of Monroe County.

Anderson P.H. Jordan   )
         Vs.   )
William Bayless and   )
Martina Hunt admrs   )
of Thomas Hunt, Decd.   )

Be it remembered that on this 20th day of June 1827 before, the Hon Thomas L. Williams Chancellor came on this cause to be heard and determined on the bill answers and proof which being read and understood - It is ordered adjudged and decreed by the Court that the Clerk and Master take an account in this cause; that he ascertain the amount of the Judgments recovered against complainant by Respondents; the advances made to Thomas Hunt by complainant since the date of the notes mentioned in Complainants bill; the debts of the said Hunt which have been paid by Complainant; the grain and other articles furnished Thomas Hunt and his family by complainant, the amount of books taken to Alabama belonging to Complainant, as well as any other dealings that may have taken place between them since the giving of the notes afore-said, and the dates of said payments or advances &c. and that he have power to bring before him the parties and examine them on interrogatories in writing, and that he strike a balance and report to next term of this court.

Samuel Blackburn   )
         Vs   )
George W. Churchwell   )
Thomas & George et als   )

The decision of the Clerk & Master in overruling the first exception filed to the answer of Thomas & George is overruled by the Chancellor.

(P-95)   George W. Churchwell   )
         and others   )
              Vs   )
         H.K. Turk and   )
         Thomas Turk   )

On motion of Compt it is ordered by the Court that Hiram K. Turk deliver to the Clerk & Master of this court, in the town of Madisonville within three months from this day all the property covered by the deed of Trust to Compt. G.W. Churchwell in this case, and upon failure to do so, that he appear at the next term of this court and show cause why an attachment should not issue against him; and that a copy of this order be served upon him.

Court adjourned till Court in Course.

Thomas L. Williams

(P-96)   December Term 1837

        At a court of Chancery began and held at the court
house in Madisonville on the 18th day of December 1837 there
was present the Hon. Thomas L. Williams, Chancellor.

George W. Churchwell, William
Woodward, & Andrew Jones,
Samuel A. Keyser & Issac
Schaefer, John F. Poor &
Michael F. Keyser, George
Peabody, Samuel Riggs and
Jeremiah D. Peabody, Philip
E. Thomas & William George,
Charles Fisher, & B. Meyers, &
I. W. Curl and James Curl,
Complainants.
                Vs.
Hiram K. Turk and Thomas Turk,
Respondents.

        It is ordered that the order made in this case
at last term be revived.

        James a Coffin Clerk and Master of this court
presented the Treasurer's receipt for the state tax by him
collected for the fiscal year ending the 1st of September
1837 which is as follows and ordered to be entered on the
minutes -
        $14 $\frac{50}{100}$ Knoxville, Dec. 14th No. 485

        Received of James A. Coffin Fourteen Dollars and
fifty cents audited to him by No. 485 and due on account of
Revenue by him collected as Clerk of the Chancery Court at
Madisonville from 1st September 1836 to 1st September 1837.

                            And McMillan Co.
Signers   for Treasurer of
duplicates   Tennessee

(P-97)   December Term 1837, Monday

Frederick Bolinger   )
        Vs   )
Benjamin Griffith   )

        Compts by his Solicitor R.H. Hynds Dismisses his
Bill. It is therefore ordered that this case be stricken
from the Docket, and that complainant pay the costs which have
accrued, for which let execution issue.

Thomas Henderson   )
        Vs.   )
William Lowry   )
and John Lowry   )

This case coming on for final hearing upon the Bill. answer of William Lowry, Replication, the pro confesso as to John Lowry, and proofs, and it appearing to the Court that complainant is not entitled to relief, it is ordered that his Bill be dismissed and that he pay the costs, for which let execution issue.

Hardy C. Tatum)
    Vs)
Jesse Kerr and)
Richard White)

On affidavit of Respondent Kerr this case is continued till next term of this court.

Arson Haynes and)
James P. Haynes)
Adms. of John Haynes)
decd.)
    Vs)
Elizabeth Haynes)
and others)

A copy of the bill and a summons to answer having been executed on Respt. Elizabeth Haynes Guardian pendante lite, & she having failed to answer, It is ordered that an alias Summons be issued, requiring her to answer the bill as guardian pendante lite of James P., Martha Jane, William and John Haynes minor heirs of John Haynes, deceased.

(P-98)   Monday December Term 1837.

Singleton McKeel and)
James Shelton Compts.)
    Vs)
Absolom Hooper &)
Sharritt Foster)

Compts by their Solicitor John F. Gillespie dismiss their Bill filed in this case and assume the costs for which let execution issue.

Ann Turk Compt.)
    Vs)
William Turk and)
Archibald Turk Respts)

It appearing to the court that this case has been adjusted by the parties, Compt. by his Sol. Dismisses the Bill of Complainant; Whereupon Respt. William Turk by his Solicitor assumes the costs, for which let execution issue.

William H. Cook Compt.
    Vs
Jeremiah Lillard & his wife
Jemima et als Respt.

It appearing to the satisfaction of the court from an inspection of the papers on file in this case, that, in transcribing the final decree rendered in this case at last Term, there was an error as to the discription of said land two quarter sections having been omitted, It is ordered that said Decree be corrected So as to conform to the Report of the Clerk & Master of the Sale of said land, the description of which is as follows - Viz. "The North West quarter of Section 36, in Township 5 and Range first, East, the South West quarter of section 25, in Township 5 and range first East; the South West quarter   (P-99)   of section 36 in Township 5 and Range first East; The North East quarter of section 15, in Township 5, and Range first, East; The North East quarter of Section 35, in Township 5 and range first east; the North East quarter of section 36, in Township 5, and Range first East, The North East quarter of Section 31, in Township 4 and Range second East; and 120 acres of the North side of the North West quarter of section 31 in Township 4 and Range second East.

```
Mary Smith et als      )
        Vs             )
Joseph, John and       )
Irene Smith            )
```

On motion of Compts. Sol. It is ordered that Compts. be permitted to retake the deposition of John B. Jackson.

Court adjourned till tomorrow morning 9 O'clock.

Thomas L. Williams

Tuesday Dec. 19th 1837
Court met pursuant to adjournment.

```
Joshua Parsons and          )
Hugh Ghormley               )
        Vs                  )
Executors of Jos. Calloway  )
```

This case is again referred to the Clerk and Master who is directed to report at next Term, the advances made by each Respondent, and the amount due each on acct of the partnership note to M.W. McGhee.

```
Charles Kelso and      )
James Pursley          )
        Vs             )
John Hall and          )
Margaret Hall          )
```

The decision of the Clerk and Master as to the 3rd and 4th Exceptions filed to Respt. Jno. Hall's answer is sustained, and his decision as to the 1st. & 2nd exceptions is overruled.

(P-100)   Tuesday December Term 1837

Frances V. Bulfinch Compt.)
     Vs.)
Anderson P.H. Jordan &)
Admrs. & heirs of Thomas)
Hunt, decd. Respts.)

     It appearing that no steps have been taken in this case for more than one year past, it is ordered that it be stricken from the Docket, and that Compt pay the costs for which let execution issue.

James Gettys)
     Vs)
Margaret E. Walker)
James H. Walker &)
William T. Walker)
Minor Children of)
W.L. Walker, decd)

     Samuel A. Coffin Clerk and Master is, by the court appointed Guardian, pendante lite of the Respts.

Samuel McConnell, Compt.)
     Vs)   Decree
Abraham Utter, Respt.)

     This 19th day of December 1837, before the Honorable Thomas L. Williams, Chancellor, came on this case to be finally heard and determined upon the original, amended and Supplemental bills, answers of Respondent, replication and proofs. It appears, to the Court that Complainant is entitled to the relief prayed by him, that the injunction granted in this cause had been dissolved, that on the 14th of January 1837 respondent with Thomas J. Caldwell and William Upton, his sureties, duly executed a bond to refund to Complainant whatever sum or sums of money that might be collected from him on the judgment rendered upon the dissolution of Said Injunction. That a fieri facias had been issued upon said judgment, upon which it (P-101) appeared by the return of the Sheriff of McMinn County there had been collected and paid over to Respondent Utter, on the 27th day of March 1837, the sum of five hundred and twenty five dollars. It is therefore ordered and decreed by the court that the said Abraham Utter, Thomas J. Caldwell and William Upton refund and pay to the Complainant Samuel McConnell the said sum of five hundred and twenty five dollars with the further sum of twenty three dollars twelve and one half cents, interest thereon up to this time amounting in all to five hundred and forty eight dollars, twelve and one half cents; for all of which an execution may issue. It is further ordered and decreed by the court that Respondent Utter pay the costs of this cause, and also the costs of that at law named in the pleadings. But that Complainant McConnell pay the same in the first instance, and have execution against Abraham Utter, Respt.

Anderson P.H. Jordan)
Compt)
     Vs)
William Bayless Adm.)   Decree:
and Martina Hunt)
Admx. of Thomas)
Hunt, decd. Respondents)

       This 19th day of December 1837 came on this cause
to be heard and determined before the Honorable Thomas L.
Williams, Chancellor, upon the Bill, answers, replication,
proof, and the Report of the clerk and master ordered at last
term. Said report shows that on the 18th of May, 1836, Respondents recovered judgments, as administrator & administrix
of Thomas Hunt, deceased, against complainant for the sum of
three thousand one hundred and thirty seven dollars binder
costs of suits. That complainant is entitled to credits upon
said judgments, to the amount of two thousand eight hundred,
fifty four dollars, and twenty three cents leaving a balance
due Respondents on the 19th December 1837 of Two hundred and
eighty (P-102) two dollars and seventy seven cents. Said
Report is not excepted to. It is therefore ordered and decreed that said Report be in all things confirmed, that Respondents be perpetually enjoined from proceeding at law
upon Said judgments, but that they recover from Complainant
the said sum of Two hundred and eighty two dollars and seventy
seven cents, the amount reported due as aforesaid for which
let an execution issue from this court. It is further ordered
that respondents pay the costs of this cause, out of any assets
in their hands of the estate of Thomas Hunt deceased, for
which an execution may issue.

      Court adjourned till tomorrow morning nine O'Clock.

                    Thomas L. Williams

          Wednesday Dec. 20, 1837
       Court met pursuant to adjournment

Samuel Blackburn Compt.)
     Vs)
George W. Churchwell)
and others, Respondents)

       The decision of the Clerk and Master is sustaining
the five first exceptions to Respondent G.W. Churchwells amended answer is sustained; as also is his judgment in overruling
the Smith exception and said Churchwell is allowed until the
second rule day to file his amended answer, at which time, if
he fail to answer, the Bill, as to him, is to be taken as confessed, and said Churchwell is ordered to pay the costs of
said insufficient answers.

(P-103)   December Term 1837. Wednesday

Andrew Cowan, Complt.   )
      Vs   )
Oswell Phillips, Respts.)

      It appearing that no steps have been taken in this case since December 1836, It is ordered that it be stricken from the Docket, that complainant pay the costs for which let execution issue.

Joseph R. Henderson, Exr.)
and Will P.H. McDermott   )
      Vs   )
N.S. Peck, Nancy Peck,   )
Jacob J.M. Peck et als.   )

      On affidavit of N.S. Peck this case is Continued till next term; and Respondents are permitted to cross examine John Jackson before the Clerk and Master. The deposition of Caleb Star is also permitted to be taken.

James Ainsworth Complt.   )
      Vs   )
William Ainsworth, Sen.   )
William Ainsworth Jr.   )   Decree:
John McGhee and   )
Return J. Meigs, Respts.)

      On this 20th day of December, 1837, Came on this case for hearing before the Honorable Thomas L. Williams Chancellor, upon the bill of complainant, the answers of Respondents William Ainsworth Sen. & William Ainsworth, Jun. the replications thereto, the judgments pro confesso against Respondents McGhee and Meigs, and the proofs, and because it appears to the court that it is necessary to take an account in this cause, the Chancellor is pleased to order adjudge and decree that the Clerk (P-104) and Master proceed to take and state an account between the parties in which he shall ascertain what amount of money is due to respondents John McGhee for principal and interest upon the note for which the Deed of Trust was executed; and that he also take and state an account of the debts due the bank of North Carolina in which Respondent William Ainsworth, Sen. was principal, and Complainant and William Ainsworth Jun. were sureties deducting therefrom the debt of $141. due from complainant in his own right and the debt of $181. due from him as administrator, stating the balance after those deductions, and that he ascertain how much of those Bank debts were paid by William Ainsworth Sen. and how much by complainant, and that he state the half of the amount paid by complainant, and calculate interest upon that sum from the time of the payment to the taking of the account; and that he further ascertain how much, if any, of said money was borrowed and paid on account of the Hugh's debt to Scruggs for whom complainant and Respondent William Ainsworth, Jun. were bail and that he report to the next term of this court when a final decree will be made, and until which time, as it appears to the court that William Ainsworth

Jun. was the surety to said notes, the point, whether the last
surety or endorser can be called upon for contribution is reserved - and further that William Ainsworth Sen. and William
Ainsworth Jun.   (P-105)   pay the costs of this cause.

William A Upton and Mahala Upton, his wife, Margaret Blair;
Martha Blair, and Mary M. Blair, Minors and heirs at law of
William S. Blair, decd by their Guardian James Hall, Complt.
                              Vs
John McGhee, Respondent.

        This 20th day of December 1837, came the Complain-
ants by Spencer Jarnagin their Solicitor, and the Respondent
by Robert H. Hynds his attorney, and agree, and do set this
cause for hearing upon the Bill and answer, and waive all
objections to the Hon. Thomas L. Williams Chancellor presiding
in this cause, on account of his being a relation of Respondent, John McGhee, and request that he hear and determine the
same, Upon the Bill and answers. It is further agreed, and
ordered by the court that the Clerk and Master proceed to
sell at auction, at the Court house in Madisonville, Monroe
County, Tennessee, the land named in the Bill, to the highest
bidder, after thirty days previous notice in the Tennessee
Journal, printed in Athens, Tennessee, for cash; that he also
ascertain and report the amount due by William S. Blair, deceased or by the firm of McGhee & Blair, to the Respondent
John McGhee, for principal and interest, and that he report
hereof at next term for further order of this court.

(106-P)   December Term 1837, Wednesday

Isaac Denton Complt.;)
            Vs   )
Betsy Rollins et als)

        It is ordered that the Clerk and Master take an
account in this case, and report at next Term.

Hiram K. Turk   )
        Vs   )
George C. Harris   )

        This case is continued till next Term.

Thomas C. Hindman Adm.   )
of Mildred Holt, decd.   )
            Vs   ) .
Sarah Holt & James H.   )
Reagan, adms of Irby   )
Holt, decd.   )

        This 20 of Dec. 1837 before the Honorable Thomas
L. Williams, Chancellor, came the exceptions to the Report of
the Clerk and Master to be argued, and because it appears to
the court that said report is not warranted by the interlocutory
decree, or justified by the evidence in the cause, it is ordered

by the court that said exceptions, be sustained, that the report be set aside, and that the Clerk and Master take an account pursuant to the interlocutory decree heretofore entered in this cause.

Court adjourned till court in course.

Thomas L. Williams.

(P-107)   March Term 1838

        At a court of Chancery began and held at the
Court house in Madisonville on the 18th day of March 1838,
there was present the Hon Thos. L. Williams, Chancellor.

Charles Kelso and   )
James Pursley   )
        Vs   )
John Hall and   )
Margaret Hall   )

        Respondent Margaret Hall is required to answer the
Bill filed by Complts within four months from this time.

George W. Churchwell & Others)
            Vs   )
Hiram H. Turk & Thos. Turk   )

        It is ordered that the order heretofore made in
this cause and revived at last Term, be revived -

Hardy C. Tatum   )
        Vs   )
Jesse Kerr & Rich White)

        On affidavit of Respt Kerr this Case is continued
till next Term and the deposition of William Kerr is allowed
to be retaken, as well as the deposition of Nath. Magill and
Complt. being a non resident of this state, notice may be
served on his counsel of record.

H.K. Turk   )
    Vs   )
George C. Harris   )

        This case coming on for trial on the Bill, answer,
Replication and proofs, and the same being duly considered,
It is ordered by the court that the Bill of complt. be dismissed; and that complt pay the costs for which let execution
issue.   (P-108)

Joseph Smith and   )
Martha Smith   )
        Vs   )
Jarrot Stowe,   )
Jesse Melton and   )
Samuel Blackburn   )

        In this case the Clerk and Master is ordered to
take an account and all matters are reserved for the final
hearing.
        Court adjourned till tomorrow morning 8 O'Clock -

                            Thomas L. Williams

                Tuesday March 19, 1838
        Court met pursuant to adjournment.

John Williams and others)
        Vs)
James Berry and Jacob F.)
Foute)

      The death of complainant John Williams is suggested.

Charles Kelso and)
James Pursley)
      Vs)
John Hall and)
Margaret Hall)

      It is ordered that if, in this case, Respondent
Margaret do not file her answer within the time allowed on
yesterday, an attachment nisi issue.

William A. Upton)
Mahala Upton et als)
      vs)
John McGhee)

      By consent of parties, by their solicitors, this
Bill filed in this case is amended as to the description of
the land. (109)

Hiram K. Turk)
      Vs)   Injunction Bill
George C. Harris)

      This cause having been on yesterday heard and the
bill dismissed, now on motion of Respondents Solicitor,
judgment is hereby entered against the said Complainant in
favor of Respondent for the sum of fifty one dollars the
judgment enjoined together with the further sum of thirteen
dollars and seventy seven cents interest on the same till
this time - for which let execution issue - & also for all costs.

Isaac Denton Adm.)
      Vs)
Betsy Rollins et als)

      The order made at last Term directing an account
in this case is revived.

Joseph R. Henderson &)
Will P.H. McDermott)
      Vs)
N.S. Peck and wife)
Jacob J.M. Peck)
David Wear and)
Wife et als.)

      On affidavit of Jacob Peck who appeared as Sol-
icitor for David Wear and his wife Betsy, this case is remanded to the Rules.

```
A.H. Henly          )
Th. H. Calloway     )
and Others -        )
School Trustees     )
        Vs          )
Heirs of            )
And.Miller          )
```

   The Demurrer filed in this case is set for
argument at next Term.

P-110)   Tuesday March Term 1838

```
James Gettys            )
        Vs              )
Margaret E. Welcker     )
James Henry Welcker &   )     Decree:
William Thomas Welcker  )
heirs at law of         )
William L. Welcker      )
```

   On this 19th day of March 1838 this cause came on
to be finally heard before the Honorable Thomas L. Williams,
Chancellor, Upon the Bill and answers of defendants, by their
guardian, James A. Coffin. It appeared to the court that
William L. Welcker in his life time, was the owner of a tract
of land in McMinn County in the state of Tennessee, Containing fifteen acres more or less, situate lying and being in the
County and state aforesaid, on the South side of Estanalla,
beginning in the dividing line between Nathaniel Smith and
Stephen Kelly, at a stake on the South Side of William Lowrys
Mill pond, thence down the meanders of said pond eighty eight
poles to a stake in Lowry's line, thence south four and a
half east, with the old line 22 1/3 poles to a Stake, thence
South 37° east along the main road 39 poles to a stake, thence
east to said dividing line between Smith and Kelly, thence
North with said dividing line thirty one poles to the beginning. That complainant had purchased and paid for said land
and was put into possession and that said William L. Welcker
had departed this life and the legal title (P-111)   to
said tract of land had descended to defendants as his heirs
at law. It is therefore, ordered adjudged and decreed by
the court that all the right interest and title in and to
Said tract of land that has descended to, or is now vested
in said Margaret Elizabeth Welcker, James Henry Welcker, and
William Thomas Welcker as heirs at law of said William L.
Welcker be divested out of them and vested in said James
Gettys and his heirs forever, and for him to have and hold
said tract of land in fee. It is further ordered that a
copy of this decree be registered in the Register's office of
McMinn County, Tennessee, and that James Gettys pay the cost
of this cause for which an execution may issue. Said heirs
have six months after full age to impeach this decree.

Thomas C. Hindman)
Administrator of)
Mildred Holt, deceased)
     Vs)   Decree:
Sarah Holt and)
James H. Reagan,)
Administrators of)
Irby Holt, deceased)

     This 19 day of March before the Honorable Thomas L. Williams Chancellor came on this cause for final decree upon the report of the clerk and master from which it appears that Respondent James H. Reagan has received of the estate of Mildred Holt deceased, since the death of his intestate Irby Holt the sum of Two hundred and sixty dollars, to which Complainant is entitled as administrator (P-112) of said Mildred Holt. Said report is unexcepted to and is in all things confirmed. It is therefore ordered adjudged and decreed by the court that said James H. Reagan pay the said sum of Two hundred and sixty dollars to Complainant, and that execution issue therefor. It is further ordered and decreed that defendants Sarah Holt and James H. Reagan pay the costs of this cause, for which execution may issue.

Carey S. Calloway &)   William Upton
Isaac Denton)   William A. Upton
     Vs) No. 76)   Joseph Upton
Joseph Donohoo)   & David Lowry
                        Vs) No. 78
                    Carey S. Calloway,
                    Jacob Baker
                    Isaac Denton and
                    Joseph Donohoo.

It is ordered that the necessary steps be taken in the two above stated causes, that they may come on for trial together.

     Court adjourned till Court in Course.

                Thos. L. Williams

(P-113)   Monday Sept. Term 1838

     Be it remembered that at a court of Chancery began and held at the Court house in Madisonville on the 3rd Monday, being the 17th day of September 1838, there was present the Hon. Thomas L. Williams, Chancellor.

Samuel Samples)
     Vs)
Joel Kelly)

     On motion of Respts. Sol. A Rule is granted to show cause why the Injunction in this case should be dissolved.

     On motion - Levi Truit Esq. was duly qualified as a Solicitor in this Court.

William Ainsworth)
    Vs)
John Davis)

On motion a Rule is granted to show cause why the Injunction in this case should be dissolved.

Joseph Smith & his wife)
Martha Smith Complts)
     Vs)
Jarrot Stowe, Saml. Black-)
burn & Jesse Melton, Respts.)

The death of complainant Martha Smith is suggested by Complts. Sol. J.O. Cannon.

George W. Churchwell, William)
Woodward, and Andrew Jones,)
Samuel A. Keyser, and Isaac)
Schaffer, John F. Poor, and)
Michael F. Keyser, George Peabody,)
Samuel Riggs and Jeremiah)
Peabody, Philip E. Thomas &)
William George, Charles Fisher)
and B. Meyers, & J.W. Curl and)
James Curl.)
     Vs)
Hiram K. Turk and Thomas Turk)

It appearing to the satisfaction of the court that Respondent Hiram K. Turk has deliberately disobeyed (P-114) the orders heretofore made in this cause it is ordered by the Chancellor that an attachment issue directed to the Sheriff of McMinn County (or to the sheriff of any other County should it be necessary) Commanding him to take the body of the said Hiram K. Turk and have him personally present before the Hon. Chancellor at our court of Chancery to be held at the Courthouse in Madisonville on the 3rd Monday of March next unless the said Hiram K. Turk shall, with good and sufficient sureties in the sum of Two hundred Dollars enter into bond to make his personal appearance at the next Term of our said court on said 3rd Monday of March next, and Clear himself of the contempt of court with which he stands charged, or be dealt with as the case may demand.

John Hartly)
  Vs)
George Winton)

On motion of Respts Sol. a Rule is granted to show cause why the Injunction in this case may be dissolved.

Sam'l Patterson)
    Vs)
Garland Smith &)
David Kelsoe)

The Plaintiff in this case dismisses his Bill -

having paid the costs of the same.

Court adjourned till 8 O'Clock tomorrow.

Thos. L. Williams

(P-115)   Tuesday Sept. 18th 1838
              Court met pursuant to adjournment.

John Parsons and   )
Hugh Ghormley Complts.   )
            Vs   )   Final Decree:
John Calloway   )
A.H. Henly &   )
Thomas Calloway   )
Exrs. of Joseph   )
Calloway, decd.   )
Respondents   )

        This cause coming on to be finally heard and de-
termined at a Chancery Court at Madisonville on the 3rd
Monday of September 1838, and 17th day of the month before
the Honorable, Thomas L. Williams Chancellor &c. Upon the
Bill answers, Replication and proofs and the Report of the
Clerk and Master, and it appearing to the satisfaction of
the Chancellor, that said Testator in his lifetime, had
entered into partnership with Complainants in the purchase
of the property as charged in said bill for which said note
was executed to Matthew W. McGhee, and upon which judgment
was recovered by said McGhee in the court of Pleas and Quarter
Sessions of Monroe County against Respondents on the 19th day
of March 1835 for $124.64½ cents debt and $7.06¼ costs of
suit. It also satisfactorily appearing that said testator
received of said property purchased as aforesaid the value
of $76.50 and that Complainant Ghormley receive the balance
of said property so purchased, and that complainant Parsons
received no part of said property, and it also satisfactorily
appearing that said Defendants are equitably & justly liable,
on account of the interest enjoyed by their said testator in
said partnership property to pay and satisfy of the principal
and interest of said judgment at law the sum of $117.64; and
it further appearing that said complainant Ghormly ought to
pay the balance of said judgment. It is therefore adjudged
(P-116)   and decreed by the court that said Defendants pay
and satisfy said sum of $117.64 of said judgment, and two
thirds of the costs of said suit at law, and also two thirds
of the costs of this cause, for which execution may issue.
and that Complainant Ghormley pay the balance of said Judgment at law and of this cause. That said judgment at law
against Complainant be perpetually enjoined as to Complainant
Parsons, and be also perpetually enjoined as to Complainant
Ghormley for the amount herein decreed against said defendants.

Mary Smith Guardian &c   )
and William Smith   )
        Vs   )
Joseph Smith, Israel C   )
Smith & John Smith,   )
Executors of   )
William Smith, decd   )

       Be it remembered that on this 18th day of September 1838, this cause came on to be heard and determined on the bill, answers, Pleas, Replication and proofs and it appearing to the satisfaction of the court that an account should be taken in this cause; It is ordered adjudged and decreed that the Clerk and Master take an account, in which he shall state.
    1St.   The amount of money belonging to the estate of James Smith, deceased, which came to the hands of William Smith the Respondents testator, or to the Respondents, together with what would be the legal interest thereon from two years after the time it came to his or their hands until it was paid out.
    2nd   The amount of money paid out by the Respondents (117) or their testator for and on account of debts against the estate of said James Smith,deceased.
    3rd   The amount of money paid out by Respondents or their testator to the complainants or either of them for and on account of the distributive shares of the heirs at law of James Smith, deceased, out of the estate of said deceased.
       The Clerk and Master is further ordered to report said account at the next Term of this court. All matters of Equity together with the decision upon the plea of the Statute of limitations are reserved until the coming in of the report.

William A. Upton, Marshall Upton,
Margaret Blair, Elizabeth Blair,
James Blair, William Blair,
Martha Blair, and Mary M.
Blair, Complainants
      Versus
John McGhee, Respondent

       This 17th day of September 1838 came on this cause for final hearing decree upon the interlocutory decree and report of the Clerk and Master. Said Report is in all things confirmed. It appears that the Clerk and Master of this Court, in obedience to the interlocutory decree did, on the 16th day of June 1838, proceed to sell at public outcry, at the court house door in Madisonville the North East quarter of Section thirty-six, third fractional township, and third Range east, containing forty seven and a half acres, also ninety-eight acres of the South West quarter of same section; same fractional township, and same range, lying between the reservations of Calvin Smith and John Ross on Little Tennessee River: - At which said sale John McGhee became the purchaser of said two tracts of land at the sum of seven hundred and

P-118)   twenty seven dollars and fifty cents, he being the
highest and best bidder.   It is therefore ordered and decreed
by the court that all the right and title the said William A.
Upton, Mahala Upton, Margaret Blair, Elizabeth Blair, James
Blair, William Blair, Martha Blair and Mary M. Blair as widow,
heirs and distributies of William S. Blair, deceased, had or
have, of, in and to the said tracts of land be divested out
of them and vested in the said John McGhee and his heirs forever in fee.   It is further ordered that the costs of this
cause be first paid out of the proceeds of said sale, and the
residue applied toward the payment of the debts due said John
McGhee named in the bill, by William S. Blair, deceased, and
that a copy of this decree be registered in the Register's
office of Monroe County, where said lands lie: - And that the
Clerk be allowed Twenty dollars for his trouble in setting
said lands, to be taxed in the bill of costs.

Isaac Denton Adm of   )
the Estate of Robert   )
Rollins decd.   )   Decree:
          Vs   )
Betsy Rollins, the   )
Widow, and Nancy   )   ~~This Cause~~
Jane, William, John   )   ~~coming~~
& Fanny, minor   )   ~~on for~~
Children, and heirs   )   ~~final~~
of Robt. Rollins, decd.)   ~~decree~~

        This cause coming on to be finally heard and de-
termined before the Hon. Thomas L. Williams, Chancellor &c.
On the 17th day of September 1838, upon the Bill, the pro
confesso as to the Respondents, and the   (P-119)   Report
of the Clerk and Master.   It appearing to the satisfaction
of the Chancellor that said complainant has advanced in the
payment of debts against the estate of said, Intestate over
and above the amount of the assets, that came to his hands
to be administered the sum of $81.83½ cents including prin-
cipal and interest and that said complainant is entitled to
satisfaction for the amount so advanced by him as aforesaid ,
out of the real estate mentioned in said Bill.   It is therefore ordered, adjudged and decreed, by the Chancellor, that
the Clerk and Master of this court, proceed to sell at the
court house in Madisonville, after giving thirty days notice
of said sale, by advertisement at three public places in
Monroe County, the East half of the south west quarter of
section 11 of Township 3rd of Range 2nd East of the Meredian
in Monroe County, and that said Clerk & Master report to the
next term of this court.

E.B. Loyless   )
     Vs   )
Luna Payne &   )
John M. Gibbs   )

        Be it remembered that on this the 18th day of September 1838, this cause came on to be heard on Complainants Bill, and Respondents pro Confesso, and it appearing to the satisfaction of the court that an account should be taken in this cause: - It is ordered, adjudged and decreed that the Clerk and Master take an account in this cause, in which he shall state -

1st   The amount of the balance of the purchase money due to the defendant John M. Gibbs from the Defendant Luna Payne with the legal interest thereon.

(P-120) 2nd   The amount of money due from the defendant Lune Payne to the complainant, with the legal interest thereon. And report said account to the next Term of the Court.

Lewis Ross, Complt)
  Vs   )
Hiram K. Turk)

  It appearing satisfactorily to the Chancellor that the defendant Hiram K. Turk has wilfully disobeyed the Injunction here-tofore issued in this cause. It is ordered that an attachment issue directed to the Sheriff of McMinn County, commanding him to take the body of said Hiram K. Turk and have him personally present at a court of Chancery to be held at the court house in Madisonville on the 3rd Monday of March next; unless he, the said Turk shall enter into bond with good and sufficient sureties, in the sum of Two hundred dollars, to make his personal appearance, before the Hon. Chancellor at the next Term of said Court, on the 3rd Monday of March next, at the court house in Madisonville, and clear himself of the contempt of court with which he stands charged, or be dealt with as the case may require.

Return J. Meigs, Complt)
  Vs   )
Hiram K. Turk, Respt.)

  It appearing satisfactorily to the Chancellor that Defendant Hiram K. Turk has wilfully disobeyed the Injunction-heretofore issued in this cause. It is ordered that an attachment issue directed to the (P-121) Sheriff of Bradley County, commanding him to take the body of said Hiram K. Turk and bring him personally before the Chancellor at a court of Chancery to be held at Madisonville on the 3rd Monday of March next; unless he the said Turk shall enter into bond with good and sufficient sureties in the sum of Two hundred dollars, to make his personal appearance, at the next term of said Chancery Court, at the court house in Madisonville on the 3rd Monday of March next and clear himself of the contempt of Court with which he stands charged, or be dealt with as the case may required.

Hardy C. Tatum)
  Vs   )
Jesse Kerr and)
Richard White)

This case coming on for final hearing upon the bill, answer of Respondent Kerr, Replication and proofs, and the pro confesso as to Richard White and it appearing to the Chancellor that Complainant is not entitled to the relief prayed - It is ordered that his bill be dismissed and that he pay the costs incurred, for which let execution issue.

John Hartly)
    Vs)
George Winton)

      This case coming on, on a motion to dissolve the Injunction - It is ordered that the Injunction be dissolved, on Respondents entering into bond, with security to refund, in case of a final decree against him.

(P-122)   Samuel Sample)
          Vs)
      Joseph Kilby)

      This case being heard on a motion to dissolve the Injunction, It is ordered that the Injunction be dissolved, on Respondents entering into bond with good security to refund in case of a final decree against him.

Silas Perry)
   Vs)
Abil Pearson &)
Thomas A. Anderson (-)

      This case coming on to be heard on the Bill and answers, on a motion to dissolve the Injunction, it is ordered by the chancellor that the Injunction in this case be dissolved, on Respondents executing bond with good security to refund in case of a final decision in favor of Complt.

Matthew W. Smith)
and others, Complts.)
      Vs)
Richard Stephens,)
Daniel Prince & others)

      This case coming on to be heard on the Bill and the Plea of Richard Stephens, Daniel Prince, Abel Richeson, John Cole and Philip Trotter, It is ordered by the Chancellor that the Plea of said Respondents be sustained, and that the Bill, as to them be dismissed.

Charles Kelso and)
James Pursley)
     Vs)
John Hall and)
Margaret Hall.)

      In this case it is ordered that an Injunction issue in accordance with the Petition of Complts, this day presented.

(P-123)   William Ainsworth)
                    Vs   )
            John Davis   )

       An alias Injunction is awarded in this case

Amos Brimer & Wife   )
        Vs   )
Jesse Leming and others   )

       The Bill in this case is by permission of the
Chancellor, amended, so as to insert the name of Thomas Isbill
of North Carolina, as a Respondent.

James Ainsworth   )
        Vs   )
William Ainsworth, Sr.   )
William Ainsworth, Jr.   )
John McGhee and   )
R.J. Meigs   )

       In this case J.F. Gillispie Respondents Sol Pre-
sented a cross-bill and made a motion to file the same,
which was by the Chancellor disallowed; and also presented
a petition for a rehearing of the Interlocutory Decree;
which was also disallowed.

David Sellers, Complt   )
        Vs   )
William Ainsworth &   )
James Adair   )

       Be it remembered that on this 18th day of September
1838, this cause came on to be heard and determined on the
Bill of complainant, answer of Respondent William Ainsworth,
Pro Confesso of Defendant James Adair, replication and proofs
and it appearing to the satisfaction of the court that an
account in this cause should be taken, It is ordered, adjudged and decreed that the Clerk and Master take an account
showing the amount due from Defendant James Adair (P-124)
to the complainant, together with the legal interest thereon,
and report said account to the next term of the court.

       It is further ordered that the question on the
lapse of time and the Statute of limitations be reserved till
the coming in of the Report.

Joseph Smith and   )
Martha Smith   )
        Vs   )
Jarrot Stowe,   )
Jesse Melton &   )
Sam'l Blackburn   )

       In this case it is ordered that the Clerk and
Master ascertain the amount of the Decree upon which suit
was instituted that is coming to complt Joseph Smith in right
of his wife; and the amt coming to him on account of advances
made for the administrators and purchasers from other heirs
of Abel Stowe, decd. the amt. carried by the Mortgage mention-

ed in the pleadings, and the amount of the decree against Respt Stowe.

```
Joseph R. Henderson      )
Executor and William     )
P.H. McDermott           )
        Vs               )
Nicholas S. Peck, and    )
his wife, Nancy Peck,    )
formerly Nancy Henderson,)
Jacob J.M. Peck, and     )           Decree
others who are           )
heirs at law of          )
Andrew Henderson         )
deceased.                )
```

        This 18th day of September 1838, this cause came on to be heard before the Honorable Thomas L. Williams Chancellor & upon the Bill (P-125)   answers, Replication, bill taken as confessed as to the defendants who have not answered, also the proofs in the cause. It appears to the Honorable court that complainants are entitled to the relief prayed in their bill; It is therefore ordered, adjudged and decreed that the legal title be vested in defendants to the South East quarter of the tract of land called Phillip's reservation, situate on Tellico river in the County of Monroe in the third Range east of the Meredian being the tract owned by Andrew Henderson deceased, by purchase from Joseph Phillips, and named and described in the bill be divested out of them, and that the same be vested in the Complainant William P.H. McDermott, the purchaser under the other complainant Joseph R. Henderson, the executor of Andrew Henderson deceased, in him and his heirs forever. It is further ordered that if either of said defendants have possession of any part of said quarter section of land, or any one under them, that they forthwith surrender the same to said William P.H. McDermott, after notice of this decree, and that if not surrendered that a writ of possession issue. It is further ordered and decreed that Defendants Nicholas S. Peck and his wife Nancy Peck, and Jacob J.M. Peck pray an appeal to the next term of the Supreme Court, to be held at Knoxville, on the first Monday of July next, which appeal is granted, on bond with security being given according to law.   (P-126)

```
John Key, admr      )
of Alfred Pogue     )
        Vs          )
George C. Harris    )
and others          )
```

        Ordered that an Injunction issue to all creditors of complts, Intestate making them parties to the bill.

```
James Ainsworth
        Vs
William Ainsworth, Sr.
```

William Ainsworth, Jr.   )
John McGhee and   )   Final Decree
Return J. Meigs   )

      This 18th day of September 1838, before the Honorable Thomas L. Williams Chancellor &c. Came on this cause to be finally heard and determined upon the Bill, answers, Replication and proofs and the report of the Clerk and Master Said Report is in all things Confirmed, the exceptions thereto being overruled by the Court. It seems to the Court that Complainant is entitled to relief, and it appears from the Report of the Clerk and Master, that the complainant had paid as Surity for Respondent William Ainsworth, Sr. the sum of Three thousand seven hundred and ninety nine dollars and forty seven cents, for which William Ainsworth Jr. was jointly bound with him as cosurety for said William Ainsworth Sr. and that William Ainsworth, Jr. was liable on the 6th day of August 1838 to refund to Complainant for principal and interest, the sum of one thousand eight hundred and ninety nine dollars, seventy three and a half (P-127) cents, as co-Surity for said William Ainsworth Sen. It further appears that William Ainsworth Jun was indebted to John McGhee, on the 6th day of August 1838 for principal & interest in the sum of one thousand and sixty two dollars and fifty three cents, to secure which the deed of Trust named in the bill was given. Thereupon the court was pleased to order, and does order, adjudge and decree, that said William Ainsworth, Jr. pay to Complainant the said sum of one thousand eight hundred and ninety nine dollars, seventy three and a half cents, with interest thereon from the 6th day of August 1838 till paid. It is further ordered and decreed that the tract of land named in the Bill be sold by the Clerk of this Court after forty days notice in some news paper printed in Athens, if said William Ainsworth Jun. shall not within three months pay the said sum, and out of the proceeds of said land first pay the amount due said John McGhee and then the amount decreed to Complainant and if not sufficient to pay the same that an execution issue for the residue; From which decree the Respondents William Ainsworth Sen. and William Ainsworth Jr. pray an appeal to the next Supreme Court to be held at Knoxville on the first Monday of July 1839, they having by direction of the Chancellor given bond and security. On failure to prosecute said appeal with effect to pay and satisfy the costs of said appeal and also the cost of said suit in this court, and said appeal to them is granted and it is ordered by the Chancellor that the cross Bill (P-128) presented by said appellants and moved to be filed, and the petition presented by them for a rehearing of the interlocutory decree, be copied by the Clerk, and be made a part of the transcript in this cause.

Hannah and her children
Elias, Charles, Mary, Martha and
Rhoda by their next friend
John Lowry

Vs
Patrick McClung and James Houston
Executors of William McClung,
decd.

Be it remembered that on Tuesday the 18th day of
September, 1838 came on the above cause to be heard and determined before the Honorable Thomas L. Williams Chancellor
&c upon the Bill and answer & proof - and after argument of
Counsel and mature deliberation of the court - It is ordered and decreed by the court that Hannah and her children
Elias, Charles, Mary, Martha, and Rhoda Slaves belonging to
the estate of William McClung, deceased, late of the County
of Blount in the state of Tennessee, be emancipated according to the terms of the last will and testament of the said
William McClung decd. And it further appearing to the satisfaction of the court, for the admission of the parties that
one of the said slaves has offspring one child, born since
the institution of this suit, and being entitled to all the
rights and (P-129) privileges of its mother, be also
emancipated by whatever name, and it is further adjudged and
decreed by the court, as part of the decree herein made that
the said Hannah, Elias, Charles, Mary, Martha, Rhoda and the
child since born as aforesaid by whatever name forthwith
leave and forever quit the state of Tennessee - bond with
John Lowry, John Waugh and David Caldwell as security approved
by the court, executed to the Governor for the time being
undertaking that the said Hannah, Elias, Charles, Mary,
Martha, Rhoda and the child since born as aforesaid by whatever name shall and will forthwith leave and forever quit
the said state of Tennessee and it further is ordered and
adjudged by the court that John Lowry, the next friend of the
said Hannah, Elias, Charles, Mary, Martha, Rhoda and the
child pay the costs in this behalf expended for which execution may issue.

Court adjourned till Court in Course.

Thomas L. Williams

(P-130)   Monday March Term 1839

        Be it remembered that, at a court of Chancery be-
gan and held at the Court House in Madisonville for the 9th
Chancery District in the Eastern Division of Tennessee, there
was present The Hon Thomas L. Williams, Chancellor.

A. & J.P. Haynes   )
        Vs   )
Elizabeth Haynes   )
Guardian &c.   )

        In accordance with the directions of complts, on
file, this case is dismissed and it is ordered and decreed
that Compts pay the costs in this cause, for which Execution
may issue.

Amos Brimer and   )
Vesta Brimer   )
        Vs   )
Jesse Lemming E.C.   )
Hooper & Thos. H.   )
Calloway & Others   )
Execrs. of Jas.   )
Calloway   )

        This case having been settled by the parties and
complts having assumed the costs, It is ordered that their
Bill be dismissed at their costs.

Rebecca Agnew by her   )
next friend G. Cannon   )
        Vs   )
E.H. Wear, J.O. Cannon &   )
Jno Agnew   )

        Complainant by her solicitor and by leave of Court
filed an amendment to her original Bill.

(P-131)   The court having been annoyed in the transaction
of business by the braying of two Jacks near the court House,
and having directed the Sheriff to request their removal,
which request was disregarded; and the Court having further
directed the Sheriff to bring the owners of said Jacks into
Court; thereupon Thomas J. Caldwell came into Court, and
stated that he was the owner of one of said Jacks and Josiah
Dougherty of the other, and the Court again requested said
owners to remove said animals so that their noise might not
interfere with the transaction of business in Court, and allowed time for Compliance. And the said owners still refusing
to comply with the said request of the Chancellor, the
Sheriff was again directed to bring said Caldwell & Dougherty
into Court, Whereupon it is ordered and adjudged by the Court
that the said Thomas J. Caldwell & Josiah Dougherty for their
said conduct manifesting a contempt of court, be each im-
prisoned forth with, by the Sheriff, and there detained for
the space of twenty four hours.

And, afterwards, it appearing satisfactorily from the affidavit of said Josiah Dougherty that he did not design or intend a contempt of court; but was in good faith intending to comply - he is released, on payment of the costs incurred.

Court adjourned till tomorrow 9 O'clock.

Thos. L. Williams

(P-132)   Tuesday March 19th 1839
            Court met pursuant to adjournment.

On motion R.B. Reynolds Esq was duly qualified as a practising Solicitor & attorney in this court.

Isaac Denton Administrator   )
of Robert Rollins, decd.   )
            Vs   )
Betsy Rollins, widow, and   )
Nancy Jane, William,   )   Final Decree
John, & Fanny Rollins,   )
Children & Minor   )
heirs of said Robert   )
Rollins, decd.   )

This case came on to be finally heard, on the Bill, pro-Confesso, proofs, Interlocutory Decree and the Report of the Clerk and Master, on the 18th day of March 1839, before the Hon. Thomas L. Williams Chancellor &c. And it appearing to the satisfaction of the Chancellor, from the Report of the Clerk and Master, that the tract of land ordered at the last Term of this court to be sold by the Clerk & Master, has been by him sold pursuant to said order, and that Harbard Hutson had become the purchaser of the same for the sum of one hundred and twenty dollars, which sum has been deposited with the Clerk of this Court, subject to the order thereof- Therefore it is ordered, adjudged, and decreed by the court that the title to the East half of the South West Quarter of Section Eleven, of Township Three, of Range two, East of the Meredian Monroe County, Hiwassee District, sold as aforesaid, be divested out of the said widow & heirs of said Robert Rollins, decd. and their heirs and invested in the said Harbard Hutson (P-133)   and his heirs, and that a copy of the Decree be registered in the Register's office of Monroe County.

It is further ordered, that the Clerk & Master be allowed Ten Dollars for his services in executing the order of Court as to the sale of said land, to be taxed in the bill of costs - and that the Clerk and Master, after defraying the costs in this cause pay over the balance of said $120 received for said land, to the complainant, Isaac Denton, administrator and that said minor Defts be allowed six months after mature years to impeach this decree.

William Griffin)
        Vs   )
Jackson Smith   )

On affidavit of complts. Sol. S. Jarnigan, this
case is continued and remanded to the rules for taking testimony on Complainants paying the costs which have accrued
since the filing of Respts answer and By consent of compts
Solicitor, notice to take depositors may be served on him,
for complt.

On affidavit of Respondent it is ordered that Compt.
justify or give new security to prosecute his suit, on or before the first day of the next term of this court.

William Upton & Co.   )
        Vs   )
Carey S. Calloway & Others)

On affidavit of R.B. Reynolds, on behalf of Complts,
this case is continued and also remanded to the rules, on
Complainants paying the costs which have accrued since the
filing of Respts answers.

(P-134)   Tuesday March 19th 1839

Margarette Ellis   )
        Vs   )
Jeremiah M. Ellis)

This day came the complainant into open court and
filed her bill praying for a divorce from the Respondent:
And it appearing to the satisfaction of the court from the
allegations of Complainants Bill that the Respondent has
gone beyond the limits of this State to parts unknown, on
motion of complainant by attorney it is ordered by this court
that publication be made in some news paper printed in the
town of Athens, Tennessee requesting said Respondent to appear
at the next term of this court and answer said bill, otherwise the same will be taken as confessed, set for hearing
exparti and decreed accordingly.

Margarette Ellis   )
        Vs   )
Jeremiah M. Ellis)

On motion of the Complainant, it is ordered by
the court, that Fifty Dollars of the money sought to be en-
joined in the bill in the hands of Aaron Runyan and N.M.
Thomas, be paid by them to complainant without delay; or that
the same be paid to her as soon as collected by the   ,
John Brown Clerk & Master of the Chancery Court at Dand-
ridge, for her support & maintainance and to defray the ex-
penses of this suit, until the further order of this court.
(P-135)
David Sellers   )
     Vs   )
James Adair &   )   Decree
Wm Ainsworth   )

Be it remembered that on Tuesday the 19th day of
March 1839, the foregoing cause came on to be heard by and

before the Honorable Thomas L. Williams Chancellor &c. at
Madisonville on the Report of the Clerk and Master made in
obedience to a decretal order of this court, at the last term
thereof, and the said report not being objected to: - It is
ordered and decreed by the court that the said report of the
Clerk and Master be in all things confirmed - and it is further ordered and decreed by the Court that the Clerk and Master
of this court, expose to public sale to the highest bidder,
the tract of land specified and named in complainants Bill at
the court house door in Madisonville, Monroe County, in the
state of Tennessee, after giving forty days notice of the
time and place of said sale in some newspaper printed in the
Town of Athens, and State aforesaid, by three publications
therein, and that the proceeds of said sale, after payment of
the Costs in this cause, shall be applied by the Clerk and
Master to the satisfaction of the complainants' debt.

Elliot Loyless   )
      Vs   )
Luna Payne and   )
John M. Gibbs   )

        Be it remembered that on Tuesday the 19th day of
March 1839 the foregoing cause came on to be heard and was
heard by and before the Honorable Thomas L. Williams Chancellor &c. at Madisonville, on the report of the Clerk and
Master made in obedience to a decretal order of this Court
at   (P-136)   the last term thereof, and the said report
not being objected to - It is ordered and decreed by the
Court that the said report of the Clerk and Master be in all
things affirmed. And it is further ordered and decreed by
the court that the Clerk and Master of this Court expose to
public sale to the highest bidder, the tract of land specified
and named in Complainants Bill, at the Court house door in
the town of Athens, McMinn County, in the state of Tennessee,
after giving forty days notice of the time and place of said
sale, in some newspaper printed in the town of Athens aforesaid, by three publications therein. And that the proceeds
of said sale shall be appropriated & paid by the Clerk and
Master, after paying the costs of this suit first to satisfy
the debt of the said John M. Gibbs, and secondly to the payment of the debt of the Complainant herein; and the Clerk and
Master will report at next Term how he shall have executed
this decree

John H. Johnston   )
      Vs   )
James Sloane   )
David L. Knox   )
Luke Lea and   )
P.J.R. Edwards   )

        This case having been adjusted between the parties
Complt, by his Solicitor, dismisses his Bill, and assumes the
costs for which let execution issue.

(P-137)   Robert L. Brashere)
                  Vs   )
           Thomas J. Mason   )

      This case coming on to be heard on a motion to
dissolve the Injunction, and the Bill and answer having been
heard and finally considered by the court. It is ordered
and adjudged that the Injunction in this case be dissolved,
on Respondents' giving bond with security to refund, in case
of a final decision against him.

Lewis Ross   )
    Vs   )
H.K. Turk   )

      The order made in this case at last Term, direct-
ing an attachment to issue against Respondent is revived, and
on alias attachment awarded.

R.J. Meigs   )
    Vs   )
H.K. Turk   )

      An alias attachment in accordance with the order
made at last Term in this case, is awarded.

G.W. Churchwill   )
William Woodward & Others   )
          Vs   )
H.K. Turk &   )
Thomas J. Turk   )

      The order made in this case at last Term is con-
tinued, and an alias attachment against said Hiram K. Turk
decreed to issue.
      Court adjourned till tomorrow 9 O'Clock.
           Thomas L. Williams.

(P-138)   Wednesday March 20, 1839
          Court met pursuant to adjournment.

Charles Kelsoe &   )
James Pursley   )
        Vs   )
John Hall &   )
Margaret Hall   )

      The decision of the Clerk & Master in disallowing
the plea filed by Margaret Hall is sustained and the said,
Margaret Hall required to file her answer before, or during
the next Term of the Circuit Court at Madisonville.

      James A. Coffin Clerk and Master of this court
presented the Treasurer's receipt for the State Tax by him
collected for the fiscal year ending Sept. 1; 1838, which is
as follows. and ordered to be entered in the Minutes.

$12.06 of Knoxville October 1st 1838 No. 604

Received of James A. Coffin Twelve Dollars, 06
cents, audited to him by No. 604 and due on account of Revenue by him collected as Clerk of the Chancery Court at
Madisonville from the 1st Sept. 1837 to 1st Sept. 1838.

                                        J.P.N. Craighead Clk.
Signed   for the Treasurer
duplicates   of Tennessee

Mashack Gentry   )
        Vs   )
Allen D. Gentry   )

        On this 19th day of March 1839, came on this cause
for hearing before the Hon. Thomas L. Williams, Chancellor,
upon the Bill of complaint the answer of Respondent, the replication and proofs; and because it appears to the chancellor
that the alligations of Complainants bill or not sustained by
the proof and that he is not entitled to relief. It is therefore ordered, adjudged (P-139) and decreed by the Court
that said bill be dismissed and it is further ordered and decreed by the Court that each party pay his own costs in this
cause.

Samuel Balckburn   )
        Vs   )
Thomas & George   )
C. & M.C. Cope   )   Decree
Reuben B. Allen   )
Enoch Blackburn &   )
George W. Churchwell   )

        On this 19th day of March 1839, came on this cause
for hearing, before the Hon. Thomas L. Williams, Chancellor,
upon the Bill of Complaint, the answers of Respondents,
Thomas & George and of Respondent George W. Churchwell, the
Replication to said answers, the Judgment pro Confesso against Respondents C & M.C. Cope, Reuben B. Allen, & Enoch
Blackburn, the Exhibits and proofs and it appearing to the
satisfaction of the court from the proofs, that on the 31st
day of July 1832 Complainant executed a deed of trust to
Respondent George W. Churchwell, as trustee conveying the two
tracts or parcels of land therein described to secure the
payment of the debts therein specified, to respondents Thomas
& George, Reuben B. Allen, C & M.C. Cope & Enoch Blackburn,
and that it was stipulated in said deed, that if said moneys
thereby intended to be secured were not paid, is one year from
the execution of said deed by Complainant, that said Respondent Churchwell as Trustee was authorized after, advertising
the lands conveyed to him and described in said deed for
twenty days in the Hiwassean, or Knoxville Register, to sell
said lands upon the premises to the highest bidder, and pay
said debts, interest costs &c. And that the said trustee
did on the 21st of September 1833, proceed to sell said lands
at the court house Door in the town of Madisonville, instead
of upon the premises, and bid it off for the benefit of
Respts   (P-140)   Thomas & George and did not the stipulations

of the trust deed, in making said sale. It is ordered adjudged and decreed by the court that said sale be set aside and for nothing held; and that the parties stand respectively in the same situation as if said sale had not been made, that the Credit of eight hundred Dollars given complainant upon the debt of Thomas & George being the amount bid for said lands be set aside, and the court is further pleased to order, that the clerk and master of this court shall proceed to take and state an account of the debts severally Specified in said deed of trust and interest, and also of the payments that have been made by complainant upon the same, to either of the Respondents and ascertain the balance that may be due upon said debts, on either of them and report to the next term of this Court.

Silas Perry)
    Vs)
T.A. Anderson &)
Abel Pearson)

On the hearing of this cause Respondent objected to the reading of the Deposition of James Perry on the ground that he was interested, which objection was sustained by the court & the Deposition requested.

Silas Perry)
    Vs)
Abel Pearson &)   Decree:
Thomas A. Anderson)

Be it remembered that on the 20th day of March 1839 the above cause was finally heard before the Honorable Thomas L. Williams, Chancellor, upon the bill, answers, replication thereto, and proofs. Argument of counsel being heard, and after consideration the chancellor was pleased to order, and does order, adjudge and decree, in as much as Complainants bill is sustained by the proof and be entitled to the relief prayed that the judgment at law stated in said bill be perpetually enjoined and that respondents have no benefit therefrom (P-141) It is further ordered and decreed that defendants pray the costs of this cause in this court, and of the suit at law for which execution may issue. From which decree of the Chancellor Respondents by their Solicitor pray an appeal to the next term of the Supreme Court to be held at Knoxville, on the 1st Monday of July next, they having entered into bond with security to prosecute said appeal according to law.

Jesse C. Moore)
    Vs)
Cookson & Wann)

Complt came into open court and by leave of the Court filed his supplemental Bill praying an injunction whereupon - It is ordered in this cause that an injunction issue restraining the Defts from the use of the timber on the quarter section of land described in the bill except for the purposes of firewood.

Mary Smith and Others)
     Vs)
John, Israel and)
Joseph Smith)

     This case coming on to be heard on the Bill, answers, Replication Plea, proofs and the Report of the Clerk and Master - It is considered by the court that the Plea of the Statute of Limitations constitute no bar to complainants Bill; and, it is ordered and adjudged that the Clerk and Master, after having notified the parties of the time and place of taking the same proceed to take an account in this cause, stating what amounts of money have come to the hands of Respondents testator or to Respondents, and what disburse-
(P-142)   ments or payments have been made by either of them, calculating interest & present said account of next Term.

William M. Biggs)
     Vs)
David Knox)
James Sloane)
John N. Taylor &)
Luke Lea)

     The Demurrer filed in this case by Respondents Knox Sloane & Taylor is sustained, and Complainant allowed to amend his Bill, for which three months are allowed, so as not to delay, and the Injunction is in the meantime continued.

John Beene)
     Vs)
Luke Lea)

     The Demurrer filed in this case is overruled, and Respondents required to answer.

Elizabeth Hill)
     Vs)
James Hill &)
Joel K. Brown)

     It is ordered by the Chancellor that Joel K. Brown the Respt. pay to complt Elizabeth Hill, seventy five dollars, out of the money in his hands, for her maintainance till further order of the chancellor in this cause.

(P-143)
John K. Farmer)
     to)
Nathl. Carey)

     No. steps having been taken in this case for more than two terms - Complts Bill is dismissed and complt. ordered to pay the costs, for which let execution issue.

Joseph H. Smith &)
Martha Smith)
     Vs)

Jesse Melton   )
Saml. Blackburn &   )
Jarrot Stowe   )

        In this case Joseph H. Smith by leave of Court amends his O. Bill.

Thomas Blackburn   )
    Vs   )
Robert Allen & Others   )

        No steps having been taken in this case for more than two Terms, it is ordered that this case be dismissed and that complainant pay the costs, for which let execution issue.

Amos Bond &   )
Marshall W. Cunningham)
Admrs. of Richard A.   )
Bryant   )
     Vs.   )
Catharine Bryant &   )
the heirs at law   )
of Richard A. Bryant   )

        No steps having been taken in this case for two terms of this court, it is ordered that Complts Bill be dismissed and that Complts pay the costs, for which let execution issue.

        Court adjourned till Court in Course.

                       Thomas L. Williams.

(P-144)   September Term 1839

　　　　At a court of Chancery began and held at the
Court house in Madisonville for the 9th Chancery District
in the Eastern Division of Tennessee, on this the 16th day
of September 1839, there was present the Hon. Thomas L.
Williams, Chancellor.

John Hartly   )
　　　Vs   )
George Winton   )

　　　　In this case the death of Respondent George Winton
is suggested.

R. Rothwell   )
　　Vs   )
H. Reynolds   )
W.W. Cunningham &   )
James Gettys   )

　　　　The Rule setting this case for hearing is set a-
side as on affidavit of complainant and Cause remanded to the
rules by consent of parties for four months, so as not to delay.

Joseph Cook   )
　　Vs   )
James McCallen   )

　　　　This case having been compromised by the parties
and then written agreement filed with the Clerk and Master:-
It is accordingly ordered and adjudged that the Injunction
heretofore granted be perpetual that complts Bill be dismissed, and that the costs which have accrued be paid equally by Complainant and Respondent, for which let execution
respectively issue.

　　　　Court adjourned till tomorrow 9 O'Clock.

　　　　　　　　　　　Thomas L. Williams.

(P-145)   September 17, 1839

　　　　Tuesday Sept. 17 - Court met pursuant to adjournment.

James Maddy, Complt   )
　　　　Vs   )   Final Decree
William W. Rose, Respt.)

　　　　This cause coming on to be heard on the 16th day
of September 1839 before the Hon. Thos. L. Williams, sitting
in Chancery upon the bill regularly set for hearing as confessed, and it satisfactorily appearing to the Chancellor from
all allegations in the bill and from an inspection of the pro-
missory note therein complained of the same being under the
hand & seal of the Complainant that Complainant is entitled
to the relief prayed by him - It is therefore considered, ad-

judged and decreed by the Chancellor that the said Respondent
& his agents and all others be perpetually enjoined from all
further proceedings in said suit at law and that said promis-
sory note be surrendered up to be cancelled and the Complainant recover against the Respondent the costs in the action at
law and all costs in this behalf expended; and inasmuch as
Respondent is a non resident; it is ordered that complainant
pay the costs in this case in the first instance, for which
let execution issue.

```
Lewis Moury    )
     Vs        )
Luke Lea       )
```

      On affidavit of Levi Trewhitt Complts Sol this
Case is remanded to the rules, for the purpose of taking the
testimony of the persons   (P-146)   named in said affidavit.

```
John Mee    )
    Vs      )
Luke Lea    )
```

      On the affidavit of Complts this case is remanded
for the purpose of taking testimony therein specified.

```
Benjamin Howard        )
       Vs              )
John J. Humphreys      )
J.H. Porter            )
Samuel Wear &          )
Jos. Donohoo           )
```

      On affidavit of Respondent Humphreys this case
is remanded to the Rules.

```
Lewis Sheppard    )
      Vs          )
Luke Lea          )
```

      On affidavit of Complt this case is remanded to
the rules for the purpose of taking the depositions therein
Specified.

```
Carey S. Calloway &    )
Isaac Denton           )
     Vs                )
Joseph Donohoo         )
```

          Will Upton & Co.
             Vs
          Calloway, Donohoo, Baker & Denton.

      These cases are continued, and the matter is re-
fered to the Clerk and Master to ascertain who has title to
the land Specified in the pleadings & report at next Term.
(P-147)

```
David Sellers         )
     Vs               )        Final Decree
William Ainsworth &   )
James Adair           )
```

This case came on to be finally heard, this September 16th 1839, before the Hon. Thomas L. Williams, Chancellor on the Bill, answer of William Ainsworth, pro Confesso as to James Adair, replication proofs and the Report of sale by the Clk & Master, and it appearing satisfactorily to the Chancellor that the tract of land ordered at last Term of this Court to be sold by the Clk. & Master, has been by him sold pursuant to said order, and that John Henderson has become the purchaser of the same for the sum of Two hundred and twenty five dollars, which sum has been deposited with the Clerk of this Court subject to order thereof; Therefore it is ordered that the Report of sale made by the Clerk & Master be in all things affirmed; and it is further ordered and decreed that all the right and title of D. Sellers the Complainant & of the Respondents William Ainsworth & James Adair or either of them, in and to the South East quarter of The Thirty third section, second Township, Third Range East of the Meredian, be divested out of them and each of them, and vested in John Henderson and his heirs; that the money arising from said sale be applied first to the payment of the costs in this case and that the balance be paid over to Complainant. It is further ordered that said Ainsworth deliver possession of the (P-148) said premises on demand, to said John Henderson & in case he refund that a writ of possession issue and also that a copy of this decree be registered in the register's office of Monroe County. It is further ordered that the Clerk & Master be allowed $10.00 for executing the Interlocutory decree in this cause.

Jacob Fisher   )
        Vs   )
Alexander Thompson &   )   Decree:
Nathaniel Smith   )

This 17th day of September 1839 this cause came on to be finally heard before the honorable Thomas L. Williams Chancellor upon the bill, answer of Nathaniel Smith, replication thereto and a judgment pro confesso as to defendant Alexander Thompson. It appeared to the satisfaction of the Court that on the 14th day of December 1837, in the Circuit Court for McMinn County, Complainant recovered a judgment against defendant Thompson for the sum of five hundred and fifty dollars, and nine dollars and fifteen cents for costs of suit. That to have satisfaction of said judgment a fiere facias was issued upon which the sheriff of McMinn County returned "No Personal property of the defendant to be found in this County, levied on fifty two acres of land, part of the south east quarter of section four, township five, range first west, the north end of said quarter - "

It further appeared that defendant Thompson had purchased said land from defendant (P-149) Smith paid him for it and entered into possession. That the legal title yet remains in defendant Smith upon the foregoing facts the Chancellor was pleased to order adjudge and decree that said tract of land be subjected to the satisfaction of said judgment in favor of Complainant. That the same be sold by the

Clerk and Master of this Court and the proceeds applied
first to the payment of the Costs of this cause, then to the
payment of said judgment, and the residue if any, to the use
of defendant Thompson, and that the Clerk report hereof to
the next term of this court for final decree as to title and
possession.

Augustus W. Elder)
     Vs)   Decree
Gilman Peck)

    This 17th day of September 1839 came on this cause
for final hearing decree, before the honorable Thomas L.
Williams, Chancellor, upon the Bill and judgment pro confesso.
It appears defendant Gilman Peck at the April sessions of the
County Court of Knox. in the year 1832 recovered a judgment
against complainant for one hundred and fifty three dollars
and ten cents for debt and damages, besides costs of suit.
That the instrument upon which said judgment was founded was
procured from complainant by fraud and without consideration.
Upon this the Chancellor is pleased to order and does order
and decree that defendant Peck have no advantage from his
said judgment and that the Collection of the same be and is
hereby (P-150) perpetually enjoined, and that defendant
pay the costs of this cause for which let execution issue,
but this Complainant pay them in the first instance for which
execution may issue against him, and then he may have the benefit of the executions first awarded.

A.N. Armstrong)
    Vs)
John Shook &)
D.L. Knox)
    The Demurrer filed in this case is sustained & the
Bill as to Respt. Shook dismissed, and ordered that complts
pay the costs.

William Griffin)
    Vs)
Jackson Smith)
    The order made at last Term, ruling Complt. to
give security not having been complied with; It is ordered
that complts Bill be dismissed and that Complt. pay all costs
which have accrued, for which let execution issue.

E.B. Loyless, Complt.)
    Vs)
Luna Payne &)   Final Decree
John M. Gibbs, Respts.)
    This cause coming on to be heard, the Report of
sale made by the Clerk & Master is in all things affirmed,
by which it appears that in compliance with the order made
at last Term, he sold the tract of land named in the pleadings at the Court house in Athens where David A. Cobbs became the purchaser for the sum of Two hundred and eighty

five dollars. It is therfore ordered, adjudged and decreed
that all the   (P-151)   right, title and claim of Respondents Luna Payne and John M. Gibbs or either of them in & to
the said tracts of land viz. One hundred and fifty acres of
land, being part of the North West quarter of section fifth,
Fractional Township, south first, Range first, East of the
Meredian; also forty acres of land situated in a square in
the North West corner of the North East quarter of fifth
section, 1st Fractional Township south, Range first, East of
the Meredian, Hiwassee District, be divested out of them and
each of them, and vested in said David A. Cobbs and his heirs,
It is further ordered that the proceeds of said sale be first
applied to the payment of the costs in this case, then to the
payment of the debt due Respt. Gibbs, with the interest thereon; and the balance paid over to complainant that the Interlocutory order and this decree be registered in the Register's
office for McMinn County, and that the Clerk retain $15.00 as
compensation for his services in executing the Interlocutory
order.

Danl. D. Stockton   )
        Vs.   )
Ezekiel Hughs   )
John Rowden &   )
Elijah Rowden   )

     This case coming on to be heard on a motion to
dissolve the injunction & the Bill of Complainant and the
answer of Elijah Rowden having been heard and duly considered. It is ordered that the Injunction heretofore granted
in this case be dissolved, On the said Elijah Rowden entering into bond with good security to refund in case of a final
decision against him.

(P-152)

Nancy C. Mayfield   (
& Others   )
        Vs   )   Cross Bill
Carter Mayfield   )
& Others   )

     The Demurrer filed in this case by Respondents is
overruled.

Samuel Blackburn   )
        Vs   )
C. & M.C. Cope   )
Reuben B. Allen   )
Phillip E. Thomas   )
William G. Thomas   )
& William E. George   )
Merchants, trading   )
under the name   )
of Thomas &   )
George, George   )
W. Churchwell   )
and Enoch Blackburn   )

This 17th day of September 1839 came on this cause for final decree upon the Report of the Clerk and Master, before the Honorable Thomas L. Williams, Chancellor, The exceptions filed by complainant to said Report were overruled and the Report in all things confirmed. By the same it appears, that on the 15th day of May 1839 there was due the said firm of Thomas & George five hundred and twenty five dollars and twenty cents for the payment of which, the tract of land named in complainants Bill is liable under the deed of trust therein refered to in the pleadings. It is therefore ordered and decreed if complainant shall not pay into the Clerk's office, within three months from this time, said sums, for the use of said Thomas & George with interest thereon, then the Clerk and Master shall sell said land, and pay first sum due Thomas & George with the interest   (P-153) thereon, then the costs of nine dollars and three cents as reported by the Clerk, then the sum of two thousand one hundred and twenty two dollars and twenty three cents, the amount reported due Enoch Blackburn on the 15th of May 1839 and secured by the deed of trust, & the residue, if any, paid to the Complainant. It is further ordered and decreed that defendants pay the costs of this cause.

Rebecca Agnew by   )
her next friend (G. Cannon)   )
          Vs   )
E.H. Wear, Jno. Agnew   )
and John O. Cannon   )

One month is by consent allowed Respt. John O. Cannon to file his answer so as not to delay.

William M. Biggs   )
       Vs   )
David L. Knox. J.N.   )
Taylor, J. Sloane &   )
Luke Lea   )

The decision of the Clerk & Master in sustaining the Exception filed to Respt. Taylors answer is sustained by the Chancellor -

Court adjourned till tomorrow morning seven O'Clock.

Thos. L. Williams.

(P-154)   Wednesday Sept. 18, 1839

Court met pursuant to adjournment.

Ex parte - Evelina Cunningham widow of Pleasant T. Cunningham deceased and Sarah Cunningham and Pleasant T. Cunningham heirs at law of said Pleasant T. Cunningham, deceased by their guardian Marshall W. Cunningham.

This 18th day of September 1839 came on the matters of the petition of the before named parties to be decreed upon before the honorable Thomas L. Williams Chancellor upon the petition and the Report of the Clerk and Master. It appears

to the Court that Pleasant T. Cunningham deed in the fall of
1833 or 1834, seized and possessed of the following tracts
of land in McMinn County, in the State of Tennessee, one
tract containing eighty acres, being the North half of the
south east quarter of section twenty four, in township four
and range West of the Meredian in the Hiwassee District and
another tract containing one hundred and sixty acres, being
the North West quarter of Section nineteen, in township four
and range first East of the Meredian in said Hiwassee District.
Said Cunningham left at his decease the petitioners his
widow and heirs at law as the owners of said tracts of land.
That Sarah and Pleasant T. Cunningham two of the petitioners
are minors under the age of twenty one, for each of whom the
said Marshall W. Cunningham has been regularly appointed
guardian. Said petition is filed to have said lands sold,
and it appears by the report of the Clerk and Master that it
is the interest of petitioners to have said lands sold, whereupon the Chancellor is pleased to order & decree that the
Clerk and Master of this Court (P-155) sell said lands to
the highest bidder on a credit of nine and eighteen months,
at the court house door in the town of Athens in said McMinn
County, after giving twenty days notice of the time and place
of said sale, at said Court house door and three other public
places in said county, That said Clerk and Master take from
the purchaser or purchasers bond with approved security for
said purchase money, and that he report thereof to the next
Term of this court for final decree as to title and the deposition of the proceeds of said land.

John Kennedy   )
    Vs   )
E. Boyd, D. Anderson   )
Will Anderson,   )
Malinda Anderson   )
& J. McNair   )

        The exceptions filed by complt to the answers of
William Anderson filed in this case, were taken up by consent
for the consideration of the Chancellor; whereupon the 1st,
2nd and 3rd exceptions are sustained and the 4th and 5th
overruled.
        And the exceptions filed by Complt to the answer
of Erby Boyd, being also considered by consent of parties,
the 1st, 2nd and 3rd are sustained and the 4th refered to the
Clerk & Master and the parties may now proceed in taking
testimony and by consent two months allowed for filing amended answers.

Joseph Donohoo   )
     Vs   )
Charles Gillespie   )
and Others   )
        The decision of the C. & Master in sustaining the
exceptions filed by complt. to Respt. Gillespies answer is
confirmed - and Respondent allowed three months to file his
amended answer by consent.

(P-156)   John Kennedy   )
                vs   )
            Erby Boyd   )
            Daniel Anderson)
            and others   )

The Injunction in this case is dissolved so for as to permit Respondent Boyd to prosecute an action at law for the possession of the premises, to judgment; but not to take out a writ of possession.

John S. Oneal   )
     vs   )
Luke Lea   )

By consent of parties this case is open for taking testimony four months.

Mary Smith &   )
William Smith   )
     vs   )
John, Israel &   )
Joseph Smith   )

This case is refered again to the Clerk & Master & he is directed to ascertain whether the money recd. for the negro girl Aggy was accounted for; and also report as to any credits Respts may be entitled to not heretofore reported.

Samuel Blackburn   )
      vs   )
Thomas & George   )
C & M.C. Cope   )
R.B. Allen   )
Enoch Blackburn &   )
George W. Churchwell)

This day the complainant filed his petition to rehear this cause as to the item of $170 or $175. which was not allowed by the Clerk & Master as a credit to complainant in taking the account. and for which exception was filed to said Report, in not allowing said credit when (P-157) the Chancellor is pleased to order that the cause as to this matter be reheard; that the report as to this item be again refered to the Clerk and Master to take further proof, and examine Complt. and Respt. Churchwell upon oath, touching said alledged payment. But this order is not to interfere with the execution of the decree already made - ordering a sale of the land.

Charles Campbell   )   This is continued for argument
     vs   )   till next Term.
Thos. H. Calloway)
P.J.G. Lea & wife   )   Court adjourned till court in
                                 Course.

                             Thomas L. Williams.

(P-158)   March Term 1840

        Be it remembered that at a court began and held
at the Court house in Madisonville on the 3rd Monday of March
1840 there was present the Hon. Thomas L. Williams Chancellor.

Robert L. Brashare   )
        vs   )
Thomas J. Mason   )
        On affidavit of Complt. this case is continued &
five months allowed for taking further testimony.

Richard Rothwell   )
        vs   )
Humphrey Reynolds   )
and Others   )

        On affidavit of complainant this case is continued
and Complt allowed five months for taking, the deposition of
Williamson B. Rothwell, the person refered to in said affidavit.

Benjamin Howard   )
        vs   )
John J. Humphreys   )
John H. Porter   )
Joseph Donohoo &   )
Saml. Wear   )

        The Chancellor sustains the exception filed by
Respondents Wear & Porter to the deposition of Thomas H.
Calloway, and it is ordered that complainant may retake the
depositions of Thomas M. Humphreys, Robert Stapp & Thomas
H. Calloway and that notice to Respt. John J. Humphreys
shall be good against the other Respondents.
(P-159)

Sarah L. Duggan   )
        vs   )
W.H.H. Duggan &   )
Binona Prichard   )

        The Demurrer filed in this case is overruled; and
Respts allowed one month to file their answer, so as not to
delay.

John Blair Admr.   )
   of S. Skates   )
        vs   )
John Stanfield   )
& Others   )

        The Demurrer filed by Respondents in this case is
sustained, and complainant allowed one month to amend his bill.

William Upton   )
  vs   )
Thomas Hoil   )
Th. J. Caldwell &   )
Saml. P. Hale   )

  This case coming on to be heard on the Bill and
answers of Respt Hoil, on a motion to dissolve the Injunction
and the case having been duly considered - It is ordered
that the Injunction in this case be dissolved, on Respondent
Hoil's giving bond with good security to refund, in case of
a final decision against him.

James A. Coffin Clerk & Master of this court presented the
Treasurer's receipt for the state Tax by him collected for
the fiscal year ending Sept. 1, 1839, which is as follows,
and ordered to be entered on the minutes -
  $34. Nashville 31 January 1840 No. 975

  Received of James A. Coffin Esq. - Thirty four
dollars - - - cents audited to him by No. 975 and due on
account of Revenue by him collected as Clerk of the Chancery
Court at Madisonville from the 1st Sept. 1838   (P-160)
to 1 Sept. 1839.
  Signed Duplicates
    M. Francis Treasurer
    of Tennessee.

  Court adjourned till tomorrow half past 8 O'Clock A.M.

    Thomas L. Williams.

    Tuesday March 17, 1840
   Court met pursuant to adjournment
Exparte

Evelina Cunningham Widow   )
of Pleasant T. Cunningham   )
deceased and Sarah Cun-   )
ningham and Pleasant   )
T. Cunningham heirs   )
at law of said Pleasant   )
T. Cunningham deceased   )
by their guardian,   )
Marshal W. Cunningham   )

  This 16th day of March 1840 came on this cause for
further order before the Honorable Thomas L. Williams Chancellor upon the report of the Clerk and Master, which being
unexcepted to, is in all things confirmed from which it
appears, said Clerk & Master, pursuant to the interlocutory
decree, did on the 14th of October 1839, at the Court house
door in Athens expose to sale the North half of the southeast
quarter of section twenty four, in township four and range
first West of the Meredian in the Hiwassee District also one

other tract of one hundred and sixty acres being the North
West quarter of section nineteen in township four, and range
first West of the Meredian in the Hiwassee District also one
other tract of one hundred and sixty acres being the North
West quarter of section nineteen, in township four, and range
first east of the Meredian in said Hiwassee District at which
said sale Samuel Hale became the purchaser at and for the sum
of nine hundred dollars he being the highest and best bidder
for which said sum the said Clerk & Master   (P-161)   took
from him one note for four hundred and fifty dollars, with
George W. Mayo surety due at nine months, and one other for
the same sum, with the same surety due at eighteen months
In this cause the Court is pleased to order and does order a-
djudge and decree that the right and title of said widow and
heirs be divested out of them, and be vested in the said Samuel Hale to have and to hold to him and his heirs forever a₊s
an estate in fee in the land above described, but that said
purchase money remain a lien upon said lands till paid. It
is further ordered and decreed that the Clerk and Master receive said moneys when due and hold the same subject to the
future order of this court. That he pay the costs of this
cause out of the first of said money that comes to his hands
and also retain thirty dollars for his services in said sale
hereby allowed him. It is further order that a copy of this
decree be Registered in the Register's office of McMinn County.

Jacob Fisher   )
      vs   )
Alexander Thompson &   )   Decree:
Nathaniel Smith   )

          This 16th day of March 1840 came on the above cause
for final decree upon the report of the Clerk & Master before
the Honorable Thomas L. Williams, Chancellor. Said report
being unexcepted to is in all things confirmed from which it
appears that the Clerk & Master of this court, on the 21st
of January 1840 pursuant to the interlocutory decree in this
cause, did sell, (P-162)   at Athens, after the required
notice, fifty two acres of land named in the bill, being the
North end of the southeast quarter of section four, in township five, in range one west of the basis Meredian in the
Hiwassee District in McMinn County, at which said sale Jacob
Fisher, the complainant in this cause became the purchaser
for the sum of six hundred dollars, he being the highest,
last and best bidder, In this cause, the Chancellor is pleased
to order and does order adjudge and decree that all the
right, title and interest said Alexander Thompson and Nathaniel Smith have in and to the said North end of the South east
quarter of section four, in township five in range one West
of the basis Meredian, in the Hiwassee District aforesaid be
divested out of the said defendants Thompson and Smith and
vested in the said Jacob Fisher to have and to hold to him
and his heirs forever as an estate in fee. It is further
ordered and decreed that the said defendants Thompson and
Smith surrender the possession of said land to Jacob Fisher,
the purchaser within ten days after notice of this decree

and if after such notice they fail or refuse to surrender the
possession as aforesaid then that process issue according to
the course of this court to put said purchaser in possession.
It is further ordered and decreed that the Clerk and Master
be allowed the sum of twenty dollars as compensation   (P-163)
for making said sale, that out of the proceeds of said sale,
he retain said sum, pay the costs of this cause, and apply
the residue to the payment of the debt of Complainant Fisher,
as ascertained in the Interlocutory decree, and for the residue of said debt, that Fisher have execution against defendant Thompson. It is further ordered that a copy of this
decree be registered in the Register's office of McMinn County, where the land lies.

Charles Kelso &   )
James Pursley Admrs.   )
         vs   )
John Hall and   )
Margaret Hall   )

        On affidavit of Respt John Hall, the said Respt.
is permitted to file a plea of the examination and determination of the matters charged by Complts. in a Court of law
is bar of complainants Bill. And said Respt. allowed, till
June Rules, for filing said plea.

Soloman L. Stowe &   )
Parella Stowe   )
       vs   )
John Henson & Others   )

        In this case Deft. John Hinson on whom alone proofs
has been served is allowed till next Term to file his answers.
(P-164)

Wm. Upton   )
   vs   )
Saml P. Hale   )
Thos. J. Caldwell   )
Thos Hoyle   )

        By consent of parties, this cause is referred to
the Clerk and Master to take an account of the partnership
and report to the next term of this court the amount of interest each partner had in the contract or contracts; the
amount of the advances of each and what each has paid on
account of said firm and what each received of the profits,
and that all other matters be left open, till the coming in
of said report.

Anthony Davis Complt.   )
   vs   )   Interlocutory Decree:
Jeremiah Hambrich Respt.)

        This 17th day of March 1840 came on this cause
for hearing upon the bill, answer, replication and proof be-

fore the Honorable Thomas L. Williams, Chancellor, where it
appeared to the court complainant was entitled to relief, because the conveyance named in the bill tho absolute upon its
face was money loaned by respondent to complainant, and that
the present is a fit case for an account. It is therefore
ordered and decreed that the Clerk and Master state an account in this cause, showing the amount of money loaned by
defendant to complainant, when loaned, the kinds of money
and the difference (P-165)   between that and every part
of it, and par funds so as to show the amount so loaned in
par funds. That he also show the value of the rents and
profits, if any received by defendant of the motgaged premises and also the amount due defendant for principal and interest, that he report to the next term and have authority
to call before him witnesses in stating said account. All
other matters are reserved till the final decree.

Mary Smith, Guardian &c.   )
and William Smith   )
          vs   )
John Smith, Israel C.   )
Smith and Joseph   )
Smith, Exers &c.   )

          In the chancery court at Madisonville March Term
1840, Be it remembered that on this 17th day of March 1840
this cause coming on to be finally heard upon the Report of
the Clerk and Master and the exceptions thereto made &
filed by the Respondents, before the Honorable Thomas L.
Williams Chancellor and the matter of the Report and Exceptions
being fully considered it has pleased the Honorable Chancellor
to order and he does order, adjudge and decree that the
exceptions aforesaid be overruled that the Report of the Clerk
and Master be confirmed and that the Respondents pay to the
Complainants the sum of ninety three dollars and sixty cents
(P-166)   the amount reported to be due the complainants by
the Respondents as the Executors of their testator William
Smith, deceased, to be paid out of any assets in their hands
or which may come to their hands belonging to the estate of
the said William Smith deceased and also all the costs of
this suit out of the assets for all which execution may issue
as at law. From which decree Defendants pray an appeal to
the next Term of the Supreme Court at Knoxville and to them
it is granted upon their entering into bond with approved
security.

Charles Campbell   )
      vs   )
Thomas H. Calloway   )
et al.   )

          In the Chancery Court at Madisonville March Term
1840.

          Be it remembered that on this 17th day of March
1840, This cause coming on to be finally heard and determined
before the Honorable Thomas L. Williams, Chancellor, upon the

Bill, answers and proofs in the cause, and the Hon. Chancellor
having fully considered thereof is pleased to order and does
order adjudge and decree that the Respondent Thomas H. Calloway surrender the possession and deliver to the complainant
Charles Campbell his minor child Calloway Campbell memtioned
in complainants bill and that said Respondent pay all the
costs in this suit for which execution may issue as at law.
From which decree the Defendant pray an appeal to the next
Term of the Supreme Court at Knoxville, and to them it is
granted on their giving bond with security as required by law.
(P-167)

Samuel Blackburn	)	
vs	)	
Thomas & George	)	
C. & M.C. Cope	)	Final Decree
R.B. Allen	)	
Enoch Blackburn	)	
& George W.	)	
Churchwell	)	

On this 17th day of March 1840, came on this cause
for final hearing before the Honorable Thomas L. Williams,
Chancellor, upon the pleadings of the parties and proofs;
upon the report of the Clerk and Master as to the item of
Credit of $170. or $175, claimed by Complainant, and the exceptions to said report and upon the report of sale according
to the decree made at last term of this court, which latter
report is not excepted to, when the Chancellor is pleased to
order that exceptions to the first report stand over & that
the complainant take the Deposition of James Freeman; that
the report as to the item of $170 or $175 Dollars be again
referred to the Clerk & Master and that he report to the next
Term of this court, & that notice served on respt. Churchwell
be sufficient as to all resp dts. And that the Clerk &
Master having reported that he had in pursuance of the decree
made in this cause at the last term of this court, after
having given forty days notice of the time and place of sale
in the "Hiwassee Patriot", a newspaper printed & published in
the town of Athens, proceeded to sell the lands discribed in
the pleadings at the court house door in the town of Madisonville, Tennessee at public sale, for cash and that at said
sale Samuel Henry bid the sum   (P-168)   of Eighteen hundred
Dollars and became the purchaser. It is therefore ordered,
adjudged and decreed by the court that said report of sale
be in all things confirmed; that all the right & title of
Complainant in & to the lands mentioned in the pleadings &
described as one quarter in the 2nd range East of the Meredian,
2nd Township 31st Section and North East quarter. Grant No.
113 dated 4th of July 1826. One quarter 160 acres 2 range E.
of the Meredian, 2 Township 31st section & the South east
quarter, be divested out of him and vested in complainant &
his heirs forever, subject to redemption according to law, and
that the said Samuel Henry have his writ of possession, and
that the Clerk & Master be allowed the sum of Twenty five

Dollars as compensation for making said sale, and that a copy
of this decree be registered in Monroe County. It is further
ordered that the Clerk and Master retain enough of the money
in his hands to cover the payment claimed of $170 or $175.
And that he pay the costs of this case out of the money due
Thomas and George.

It is ordered that the cause in this court arising
from Bradley County be continued open for taking further
Testimony.

John Kennedy)
    vs)
Erby Boyd &)
Others)

The decision of the Clerk and Master in sustaining
the 4th exception to the answer of Erby Boyd is overruled.

Court adjourned till court in course.

Thomas L. Williams.

(P-169)   September Term 1840

On the 22nd day of September 1840 at a court of Chancery began and held at the Court house in Madisonville for the 9th District in the Eastern Division of Tennessee, there was present the Hon. Thomas L. Williams Chancellor.

A.B. Lee   )
    vs   )
Hugh Smith   )

On motion of Respts Sol. a rule is entered, allowing Respt. to show cause why the Injunction in this case may be dissolved.

Charles Kelsoe and   )
James Pursley   )
        vs   )
John Hall and   )
Margaret Hall   )

The death of Respondent Margaret Hall is suggested

Joseph Dondohoo   )
    vs   )
Chales K. Gillespie   )
and Others   )

On affidavit of Respondent Gillespie this case is continued till next Term and on motion Complts Sol. is remanded to the Rules.   (P-170)

Richard Rothwell   )
        vs   )
Humphrey Reynolds   )
James Gettys & Others   )

On the affidavit of Complainant this case is remanded to the rules for taking further testimony.

John Blair, adm of Joseph
Scates deceased, Complt.
        vs
Eli Cleveland and Others, creditors,
of said Scates, Respts.

By leave of Court Complainant amends his amended Bill so as to make Betsy Scates, widow, and William, James, Joseph C., George W., Betsy Jane, and John Scates, children and heirs of said Joseph Scates, Respondents.

William Upton, Complt   )
        vs   )
Saml. P. Hale, Thomas J.)
Caldwell, and F.L. Hoil   )
Respts.   )

On affidavit of Respt. Caldwell and by consent of
Complainant, this case is again refered to the Clerk and
Master and the parties interested are allowed to furnish ad-
ditional proof.

Jane Austin   )
    vs   )
Jacob Lingerfelt)

On affidavit of Respondent this case is remanded
to the rules for taking further testimony.

A.B. Lee   )
   vs   )
Hugh Smith   )

This case coming on to be heard on the Bill &
answer, on a motion to dissolve the Injunction and the same
having been duly considered, it ordered by the Chancellor that
the Injunction here-tofore granted in this case be dissolved,
(P-171) on the said Hugh Smith entering into bond with
good security to refund in case of a final decision against
him. It is therefore ordered adjudged and Decreed by the
Court that the Respondent on execution of said Refunding bond,
have execution from this Court against complainant A.B. Lee
and J. William, A.J. Hoyal, James Oliphant the securities of
said A.B. Lee in his Injunction Bond for the sum of nine
hundred and forty Dollars and Ten Cents, the balance due on
the judgment at law, (exclusive of costs) together with interest thereon from the 16th day of January 1840 the date of
said judgment.

John Williams   )
Jacob Rodgers & Others   )
      vs   )
Berry & Foute   )

Continued for want of a competent Court.

R.J. Meigs   )   Lewis Ross   )
    vs   ) and   vs   )
H.K. Turk   )   H.K. Turk   )

These causes are continued by Complts. Sol.

Adjourned till tomorrow 8 O'Clock.

Thos. L. Williams

(P-172)   Wednesday September Term 1840

William Upton & Co.   )   Carey S. Calloway   )
     vs   )   & Isaac Denton   )
Carey S. Calloway   ) &   Vs   )
Joseph Donohoo et als.   )   Joseph Donohoo.   )

The death of Carey S. Calloway, a party to these cases is suggested.

Caswell Torbitt and Others, heirs &)
distributees of James Torbitt,)
deceased, Complainants)
      vs)
Robert McReynolds; Maxwell)
Duncan, John Hall and others.)

By consent Two months are allowed Respts Robert McReynolds, Maxwell Duncan, and John Hall so as not to delay.

Sampson H. Prowell,)
Complt.)
     vs)   Final Decree
Luke Lea, Entry Taker,)
Ocoee D.)

Be it remembered that on this 22nd day of September 1840 this cause coming on to be finally heard and determined before the Honorable Thomas L. Williams, Presiding in Chancery at Madisonville, upon bill & judgment pro confesso. and be cause It appears to the satisfaction of the court. by the bill and judgment pro Confesso, that Complainant was in the actual possession of and Residing upon the South East quarter of section Twenty Two, Range first, township Two East of the basis line in the Ocoee district on the 29th day of November 1837, and thereby was vested with the occupaht Right to Enter said quarter section of land and that said Complainant (P-173) in making his Entry through mistake entered the South West quarter of section Twenty Two Range first Township Two East - of the basis line in the Ocoee district and paid in to the office of the Entry taker the sum of three hundred and Twenty dollars.

The court is therefore pleased to order and decree and does order and decree that Respondent correct said mistake by applying the three hundred dollars to the Entry of the south East quarter of section Twenty two Range one Township Two east of the basis line in the Ocoee district that said Respondent as entry taker for the Ocoee district Issue to Complainant a certificate of Entry for the said south East quarter of section Twenty Two. Range one Township Two East; of the basis line in the Ocoee district and that the Complainant pay the costs of this suit for which Execution may issue as at law.

Riley Horn)
    vs)   Interlocutory Decree
John Copeland)

Be it remembered that on this 22nd day of September 1840 this cause coming on before the honorable Thomas L. Williams presiding in Chancery at Madisonville on Bill answer Replication and proof in said cause and because It appears to the satisfaction of the court from the proof in said cause that the assignment of the occupant Right in Complainants bill mentioned was only Intended by the parties as a mortgage to secure to Respondents the money by him loaned and advanced to complainant and that complainant is entitled to the redemption of said land. The honorable court is therefore pleased to order and decree, and does order and decree that the (P-174) Clerk & Master take an account of all the money's that Respondent has advanced to complainant up to the time of the agreement of the occupancy in Complainants bill mentioned together with amount of money by said Respondant paid into the land office to Enter said land and also take an account of the value of all the labors that adds value to the land done by Respondent since the date of said assignment and the amount of lawful interest accruing thereon and also take an account of all the payments made by Complainants to Respondant and Report the same to the next Term of this court and that Respondent pay the costs of this bill and that all other matters and things in said cause is reserved until the coming in of the Master's Report. -

```
Robert S. Brashears    )
        vs             )     Interlocutory
Thomas J. Moser        )     Decree
```

Be it remembered that on this 22nd day of September 1840 this cause coming on to be heard upon bill answers & Replication and because It appears from the bill & answers that complainant and Respondant was partners and the bill prays an account and by consent of parties it is ordered and decreed that the Clerk and Master take an account between the parties that the parties have leave to proceed to take depositions according to the rules of Chancery and read the same before the Clerk and Master and that the Clerk & Master have power to Examine each party upon oath touching the partnership concern (P-175) and report to next Term of this court. And all other matters and things are reserved until the coming in of said report.

```
Daniel D. Stockton     )
        vs             )
Ezekiel Hughes         )
John Rowden &          )
Elijah Rowden          )
```

This case coming on to be heard on the Bill, answer of Elijah Rowden and memorandum of compromise filed with the Clerk, it is ordered that the Injunction as to Elijah Rowden be dissolved, the Bill as to him dismissed, & that Complts pay the costs.

```
John Kennedy Complt.   )
        vs             )
Erby Boyd and others   )
```

On affidavit of Respt Boyd this case is continued, and remanded to the Rules. - And, on affidavit of Complainant, James Berry, Clerk & Master of the Chancery Court at Cleveland is appointed a commissioner before whom Respt. Boyd shall take the deposition of Mrs. Anderson and Nancy Randolph in case he take them at all.

The decision of the Clerk and Master as to the exceptions filed to the depositions of James A. Lea, Sampson H. Prowell, John C. Mullay & Jeremiah Sutton is sustained.

James Maddy)
   vs)
James Pelter et als.)

Leave is given by consent for Respt. Pelters answer to be filed.

The decision of the Clerk & Master as to the exceptions filed to said answer is overruled - said exceptions sustained, and said (P-176) Respondent allowed three months to file his amended answer. In the mean time parties are allowed to take deposition.

Caswell Torbitt)
Charles Kelso &)
John Torbitt)
   vs)
Robert McReynolds)
Maxwell Duncan)
John O. Cannon)
John McGhee et als)

By consent of the parties by their Sols. All exceptions which might be taken to the Competancy of the Court, on account of relationship to J. McGhee, one of Respondents, are waived.

Joseph Smith and wife)
   vs)
Jesse Melton, Jarrot Stowe)
& Saml. Blackburn)

William Grant produced to courts Letters of administration on the estate of Martha Smith deceased, and was admitted as joint complainant with the said Joseph Smith.

Andrew Kerr)
John Kerr)
James & John)
Hope)
   vs)
John Caldwell &)
A. & J. McSpadden)

The Demurrer filed by Defendants in this case is overruled, & they are required to answer the Bill -

Whereupon the answers of Respts John Caldwell and John Mc-
Spadden having been filed, and the Bill and said answers
duly considered; It is ordered that the attachment granted
in this case be dissolved on said Respondents entering into
bond to have said property therein refund to forth coming, on
the final decree, if required or that they pay the debt on
which suit is instituted.

(P-177)
Margaret Ellis)
     vs)
Jeremiah Ellis)

On this 23rd day of September 1840, came on this
cause for final hearing, upon the Bill of Complaint, the
judgment pro - Confesso and the proofs, before the Hon. Thomas
L. Williams Chancellor &c. and because it appears from the
testimony of witnesses examined on oath in open court that
the Respondant Jeremiah M. Ellis had been guilty of adultry
with a certain Milly Treadway as charged in the Bill sub-
siquent to his marriage with complainant & before the filing
of the Bill in this cause, and that complainant had been resident in the State of Tennessee for more than one year,
previous to the filing of said Bill and that complainant has
always sustained an irreproachable character, the Chancellor
is pleased to order, adjudge & decree that the bonds of
matrimony subsisting between complainant and respondant be
totally dissolved, and that complainant be restored to all
the rights and privileges of a feme sole as fully as if said
marriage never existed and the Chancellor is further pleased
to order, adjudge and decree that all the right title and interest which the respondent has to the money in the hands of
John Branner the Clerk and Master of the Chancery Court at
Dandridge and who was appointed receiver in this case be divested out of respondent, and be vested in complainant forever, and said receiver is ordered to pay the full amount in
his hands to complainant except what may be sufficient to
pay the costs of this cause, for her sole and separate use.

And it is further ordered, adjudged & decreed
(P-178) by the court that the costs of this cause be paid
out of the money in the hands of said John Branner. And the
said John Branner is allowed the same commissions for his
services in receiving & holding said money as is allowed by
law to Sheriff upon Executions, to be restrained by him out
of said money.

Elizabeth Hill)
     vs)
James Hill)

Be it remembered that on this 23rd day of September 1840, came on this cause for final hearing upon the
original and amendatory Bill, of complainant, the judgment
pro confesso and the proofs before the Honorable Thomas L.
Williams Chancellor &c and because it appeared to the sat-

isfaction of the Court upon the Testamony of witnesses examined in open Court, that the respondent James Hill had been guilty of adultry with a certain Rachel Looney named in complainants Bill, subsequent to his marriage with complainant and before the filing of the Bill in this cause, and that the complainant had been a resident citizen in the state of Tennessee for more than one year previous to the filing of the Bill, and that complainant is of good moral character. The Chancellor is pleased to order adjudge and decree that the bonds of matrimony subsisting between the complainant & Respondent James Hill be totally and forever dissolved, and that complainant be restored to all the rights and privileges of a feme Sole. And it further appearing to the satisfaction of the Court (P-179) from the proof in the cause that the complainant is entitled to all the property that Respondent has any interest in; it is therefore ordered adjudged and decreed by the court, that all the right, title, claim and interest, that the said James Hill has to a negro woman called Fanny, named in Complainants Bill be divested out of the said James Hill, and vested in the Complainant for her sole use and benefit forever, and that the right to all the household and kitchen furniture named in Complainants Bill or that is now in possession of Complainant be divested out of respondent. And vested in complainant, for her own use and benefit forever. And it is further ordered adjudged and decreed by the court that Joel K. Brown, mentioned in Complts, Bill pay over to Complainant the sum of five hundred dollars mentioned in said bill, for her own use and benefit forever, together with interest thereon from the time the same came into his hands until paid to complainant.

And it appearing to the court that the Respondent is not resident in this County, it is ordered that, in the first instance, Complainant pay the costs of this cause, for which she have a decree against Respondent - for which execution may issue.

Allen D. Gentry   )
        vs   )
Justus Steed &   )
Mesack Gentry   )

Be it remembered that on this 23rd day of September 1840 this cause coming on to be heard and determined before the Honorable Thomas L. Williams (P-180) Chancellor &c on the motion of the Respondents Solicitor to dissolve the injunction upon the Bill and answer of the Respondent Justus Steed, and it appearing to the satisfaction of the court from said answers that the equity of the complainants Bill was denied and obviated it pleased the Hon. Chancellor to order and decree, and he does order and decree that the Injunction obtained in this cause be dissolved, and that the Respondent Justus Steed proceed in his suit at law to judgment; but that no execution issue thereon till further order of this Court.

John Bayless   )
    vs   )
William Bayless)

      Be it remembered that on this 23rd day of September 1840, this cause came on to be heard, before the Hon. Thomas L. Williams Chancellor &c. upon the Bill of Complainant; and answer of Respondent; and it appearing to the satisfaction of the court, that the complainant is entitled to the relief prayed for in his bill; But as it is uncertain what sum said complainant paid to E.L. Matthews guardian of the minor heirs of William Tyler, deceased as security of the Respondent while he was guardian of said heirs and also uncertain what amount Respondent has since paid to said complainant wherefore it is ordered and decreed by the Court that the Clerk & Master take an account and report at the next Term of this court and show how much complainant has paid for Respondent with legal interest thereon (P-181) from the time of the payments respectively and how much Respondent has paid complainant and that all the matters and things touching said mortgage or Trust be reserved until the coming in of said report.

John Mee   )
    vs   )
Luke Lea   )

      Be it remembered that on the 23rd day of September 1840 came on this cause for final hearing upon the bill of Complainant answer of Respondent, replication and proofs before the Hon. Thomas L. Williams Chancellor &c. And because it appears that the Complainants assign George M. Murrell who was an occupant on the South West quarter of section 20 fractional township two, North, Range one, East of the Basis line in the Ocoee District, had not erected a mill on the land mentioned in the Bill of Complaint at the time of the passage of the act of the General assembly of the State of Tennessee entitled "an act to dispose of the vacant and unappropriated lands in the Ocoee District of which said act of assembly Complainant claimed the benefits and privileges guaranteed to occupants who possess quarter sections whereon mills were erected; and because it is further considered if any should be granted it is properly cognizable in the court at common law; It has therefore pleased his Honor to adjudge, order and decree that said Bill of Complaint be dismissed, and also that Complainant pay the costs of this suit, for which let execution issue. From which decision Complainant prays an appeal to the next Term of the Supreme Court, to be held at Knoxville on the (P-182) first Monday of July next; which appeal is granted to Complt, on his intering into bond with Security, as required by law.

Lewis Shepperd)
    vs   )
Luke Lea   )

Be it remembered that on this 23rd day of September 1840, this cause by consent of parties coming on for final hearing before the Hon. Thomas L. Williams Chancellor &c. upon the Bill, answer, and proofs, and it appearing to the satisfaction of the Court that there was no mill erected and in operation on the quarter section mentioned in the Bill of Complaint, at the passage of the Act of assembly, Entitled An Act to dispose of the vacant and unappropriated lands in the Ocoee District, and is therefore not within the purview and meaning of the 6th Section of the aforesaid Act and is therefore not entitled to the relief prayed for; and because it further appears from the proofs in the cause that the Complainant since the filing of his said Bill has entered the aforesaid quarter section of land & obtained a certificate therefor, it is ordered, adjudged and decreed by the court that Said Bill be dismissed, and that Complainant pay the costs of this Cause for which execution may issue as at law.

(P-183)

Sarah L. Duggan   )
     vs   )
W.H.H. Duggan &   )
Benoin Prichard   )

Be it remembered that this cause coming on to be heard on the Bill answers, Replication and proof, before the Hon. Thomas L. Williams, on this 23rd of September 1840 and the matters and things being fully heard and understood, and because it does not appear that the Complainant is entitled to relief, it is therefore ordered adjudged and decreed by the court that said Bill be dismissed & because it appears to the Court that the Complainant is a pauper, it is further ordered by the court that Respts pay their own costs in the first place, and have execution over against the said Complainant, for the same, and that Compts pay the balance of the costs occasioned by the filing of her said Bill for all of which execution may issue.

Allison Frizzell   )
     vs   )
Cannon & Nelson   )

Complt files his bill of Injunction in open Court; and, it is ordered by the Chancellor that the Injunction issue as prayed in said Bill on Complainants entering into bond with security as required by law.   (P-184)

Solomon Stowe and   )
Wife Parella   )
     vs   )
John & Mary Friddle,   )
John B. & Wm. M. Huson,)
Andrew Allen, John   )
Allen and Others   )

Be it remembered that on the 23rd day of September

1840 came on this cause to be finally heard and determined
before, the Hon. Thomas L. Williams Chancellor &c. by consent
of parties - It is ordered adjudged and decreed by the court
that the Negro Sylva mentioned in the Bill remain with Respondent Mary Friddle, for her sole use and benefit, during
her natural life, and that at her death said Negro Woman and
her increase shall be sold at public sale for the best price
that can be obtained, and the proceeds divided equally between Solomon Stowe & wife, Andrew Allen, John Huson and
William M. Huson. It is further ordered and decreed that the
title to the Negro boy Richard be confirmed and vested in
John B. Huson; that the title to Stephen be confirmed and
vested in Andrew Allen; that title to Loo be vested in William M. Huson and the title of Henry in Complainant & wife.
And it is further ordered and decreed that to make up the
portion of the said William equal with the other heirs, that
he have a certain negro boy named Green, and the title is
hereby vested in the said William M. It is further ordered
and decreed by the Chancellor that John B. Huson, Andrew Allen
& Wm. Huson pay the costs of this cause.   (P-185)

Rebecca Agnew by	)	
her next friend	)	The death
G. Cannon	)	E.H. Wear
vs	)	is suggested.
E.H. Wear, Jno. O.	)	
Cannon & John Agnew	)	

Samuel Blackburn Complt.	)
vs	)
Thomas & George,	)
C. & M.C. Cope;	)
George W. Churchwell	)
and Others, Respts.	)

On this 23rd Sept. 1840 came on this cause for
hearing before the Honorable Thomas L. Williams Chancellor
upon the matters refered to the Clerk and Master as to the
payment of $170 alleged to have been made to said Churchwell,
upon the report of the Clerk & Master & the exceptions thereto, and the proofs; and the court being satisfied from the
proofs that Said payment was made: - It is ordered, adjudged
and decreed by the court that the exceptions to said report
be overruled, and that said report be in all things confirmed, and that respts pay the costs, as heretofore ordered.

From which decision Respondents pray an appeal to
the next Term of the Supreme Court to be held at Knoxville,
On the first Monday of July next, and said appeal is granted
on their entering into bond with security as required by law.

It is further ordered that the transcript filed
by the Clerk of the Circuit Court for Monroe Court be copied
as part of the transcript (P-186)

Adjourned till Court in Course.

Thos. L. Williams

March Term 1841

Be it known that on the 15th day of March 1841, at a Court held at the Court house in Madisonville for the 9th Chancery District in the Eastern Division of Tennessee there was present the Hon. Thomas L. Williams Chancellor.

R.S. Brashaur)
    vs)
W.J. Mason)

    The order made at last Term for an account in this Case is revived.

John Beene)   J.T. Oneal)
    vs)   vs)
Luke Lea)   Luke Lea)

          Mowery)   These three cases are continued
           vs)   at next term of this court.
          Luke Lea)

Matthew W. Smith)
Asbery W. Smith)
and Others, Complts)
    vs)
John Cole)
Joshua Wimpry)
Daniel Prince)
and Others)
Respts.)

    It appearing to the Court that no steps have been taken in this case for more than two terms, It is ordered that Complts Bill be dismissed & that Complainants pay   (P-187) the costs for which let execution issue.

James M. Dunn)
    vs)
Wesley McCalister)
& Luke Lea)

    This case coming on to be heard on the Bill answer of Respt. McCalister Replication, and pro- confesso as to Deft. Lea; and it appearing that Complt. is not entitled to relief; It is therefore ordered and decreed that Complainants Bill be dismissed and that complainant pay the costs, for which let execution issue.

A.N. Armstrong)
    vs)
D.L. Knox)

    It appearing to the court that no steps have been taken in this cause for more than two Terms- It is therefore ordered that Complainants Bill be dismissed and that Complainant pay the costs for which let execution issue.

Richard Swafford &   )
Alfred Swafford   )
    vs   )
James B. Leuter   )
Preston Leuter &   )
William Bates   )

       The Rule setting this cause pro Confesso against
Defts Leuter is set aside & one month allowed them to file
their answers.

William P. Allison   )
    vs   )
Calvin H. Leuter &   )
William Bates   )

       The Rule setting this cause for hearing pro- Con-
fesso as to Respts Leuter is set aside, and one month allowed him to answer.   (P-188)

Lewis Ross   )
   vs   )
Hiram K. Turk   )

       No steps having been taken in this case for more
than two terms It is ordered that complainants Bill be dismissed and that in the first instance complainant pay the
costs and have execution over against Respondent for which
let execution issue.

Return J. Meigs   )
    vs   )
Hiram K. Turk   )

       No steps having been taken in this case for more
than two terms It is ordered by the court that Complainants
Bill be dismissed and that Complainant in the first instance
pay the costs; but that he have execution against the Respondent for the same.

       Court adjourned till tomorrow morning ½ past
8 O'Clock.

                Thos. L. Williams.

(P-189)   Tuesday March 16th 1841

      Court met pursuant to adjournment

George W. Churchwell   )
and Others   )
      vs   )
Hiram K. Turk &   )
Thomas J. Turk   )

       Came the Complainants by their Sol. and ordered
the Court that Judgment be rendered against George Henderson
the security in the forth coming bond on file, hearing date
Nov. 8, 1834

Joseph Donohoo)
     vs)
Charles K. Gillespie)

       Be it remembered that on this 15th day of March
1841, Levi Trewhitt solicitor for Complainant & Spencer
Jarnagin Solicitor for Respondent came into Court before the
Honorable Thomas L. Williams presiding in Chancery at Madisonville & filed here in open Court the written Compromise made
by the Complainant and Respondent and which is in the following words and figures to wit. "Joseph Donohoo vs Charles K.
Gillespie in Chancery at Madisonville this cause is compromised,
each party pays one half of the costs - and the title to be
decreed to Joseph Donohoo the Elder and better title Given
under our hands this 12th day of March 1841.

                        Joseph Donohoo
                        C.K. Gillespie

This honor therefore in pursuance of said compromise, and because it appears to the satisfaction of his honor the Chancellor, by the Compromise and the pleadings in said cause
that the complainant Joseph Donohoo (P-190) has the superior and elder and better title to the North West quarter of
section Eleven in Range one, Township Two, West of the Basis
line in the Ocoee District. This honor is therefore pleased
to order and decree and does order and decree that the said
Joseph Donohoo be vested with all legal and Equitable title
in and to the quarter section aforesaid; and it is further
ordered & decreed by the court that the Complainant pay one
half of the costs incurred by this Bill & decree, and that
the Respondent pay the other half of the costs incurred by
this bill & decree for which let executions issue as at law.

Anthony Davis)
     vs)   Decree:
Jeremiah Hambreck)
                       1841
       This 16th day of March/came on this cause for
final decree, upon the Report of the Master, before the Hon.
Thomas L. Williams Chancellor. Said report being unexcepted
to is in all things, Confirmed, from which it appears that
on this 8th day of February 1838 the defendant loaned to
Complainant twenty dollars in United States Bank notes, five
hundred & sixty dollars in Alabama paper, that the discount
on the Tennessee and Alabama paper was at the time nine and
a fifth percent, making the amount borrowed on the 8th day
of February 1838, in par funds five (P-191) hundred and
forty six dollars, and sixty four cents, to secure the repayment of which the mortgage named in the pleadings was taken
upon the North East quarter of section twenty nine and part
of the south east quarter of section twenty, situate in the
second range west of the Meredian, second township in the
Hiwassee District to the payment of which said sum of money,
with the interest thereon said land is liable and subject.
It further appears from said report that there is due at

this time from Complainant to defendant on account of said
loan, for principal and interest the sum of six hundred and
fifty dollars and forty five cents. It is therefore ordered,
adjudged and decreed by the court that Defendant be perpetually enjoined from proceeding at law upon his mortgage
deed to recover possessions of said land; that Complainant
within four months from this time pay into the office of the
Clerk and Master of this Court, for the use of defendant, said
sum of six hundred and fifty dollars and forty five cents
with the accruing interest thereon till paid; and if said sum
of money be not then paid, it is ordered adjudged and decreed
that the Clerk & Master, after thirty days notice in the
Hiwassee Patriot, a newspaper printed in Athens, McMinn County,
sell said tract of land in the said town of Athens for cash,
and out of the proceeds retain twenty dollars for his services,
pay the costs of this cause, and the costs of the action of
Ejectment in McMinn County, and to defendant the said sum due
him, and that said Clerk report hereof at next Term of this
Court. (P-192)

Benjamin Howard   )
        vs   )
Wear, Porter,   )
Humphreys et als.   )

      On affidavit of Complt. this case is continued and
Complt. allowed to take the depositions of Thomas M. Lackrus
& Wife.

John Kennedy   )
     vs   )
Erby Boyd   )
and Others   )

      Spencer Jarnagin, Solicitor for the respondent
Consents and expressly agrees that the agreement between the
agreement between the Complainant Kennedy & John McNair for
the purchase of the Occupant claim in dispute and filed by
Complainant and refered to by him as a part of his said bill
shall be considered as regularly proved and read as proved on
the hearing, and he further agrees that the receipts for money paid on the same as evidenced on the back of the agreement, shall be considered as duly executed by McNair, and
read as if proved regularly, and he further agrees that the
assignment of McNair to Kennedy of his occupant claim to the
same, shall be considered as proved and read as such in Consideration of which Complainant waives the benefit of the
Continuance to establish these facts, this day granted by
the Court.

                       Spencer Jarnagin Sol.
                        for defendants
    16th March 1841   John Kennedy
                         Plff. in the
                          above cause.

(P-193)

John Blair, Adm.   )
  vs   )
Cleveland & Others)
& Elizabeth Scates)
and Others   )

   In this cause the answer of Elizabeth Scates the Widow of Joseph Scates being filed in which she claims her dower in the lands of which her husband Joseph Scates died seized & possessed, and the Court being satisfied that she is entitled to dower, the court is pleased to order and decree that Charles Kelsoe, Jessee Butler, John Knox, Street Lane, John Holstein, be commissioners to lay off dower to said Elizabeth in all the lands or houses & lots her husband Joseph Scates died seized & Possessed, and report to next Court.

William Hale   )
  vs   )
Thomas J. Caldwell)
Wm. Upton, Wm. A.)
Upton, Samuel   )
P. Hale   )

   This case coming on to be heard before the Hon. Thomas. L. Williams, Chancellor on the pleadings and proof, and it appearing to the Chancellor that Complainant has not sustained the allegations of his Bill - It is ordered adjudged and decreed that his Bill be dismissed and that Complainant pay the costs, for which let execution issue.

William Upton & Co.)
  vs   )
Denton, Donohoo,)
and Baker   )

   Complts filed their Bill of Revenue against the widow & heirs of Carey S. Calloway. (P-194)

John Hooper   )
 vs   )
James M. Greenway)   Decree
& V.A. Harris   )

   This case coming on to be heard before the Honorable Thomas L. Williams Chancellor, on the Bill, answer of Respondent Greenway, Replication proofs and pro Confesso as to Deft Harris, and it appearing to the Chancellor that Complainant is not entitled to the relief prayed in his bill, It is ordered, adjudged and decreed by the court that complainants Bill be dismissed; that the Injunction heretofore granted be dissolved, and that Execution issue from this Court against Complainant John Hooper and Jonathan Thomas his security in the injunction bond for the sum of one hundred and ninety six dollars and two cents, the amount of the judgment at law, together with ~~the sum of seventeen dollars and sixty four cents~~ interest from the 16th day of September 1839, the date of said judgment till paid, and also for the sum of nine dollars cost of said suit at law.

It is further ordered that Complainant Hooper pay the costs in this cause, for which let execution issue.
(P-195)

Richard Rothwell)
    vs)
Humphreys Reynolds)
Marshall W. Cunningham)
and James Gettys)

Be it remembered that on this 16th day of March 1841, this cause coming on to be heard and determined before the Honorable Thomas L. Williams, Chancellor upon the Bill answers and proofs - after argument of Counsel and mature deliberation of the Court. It is ordered, adjudged and decreed that the Complainants Bill as to the Respondent Reynolds be dismissed; and it appearing that the sale made by the Trustee to Reynolds was not made at the place designated in the Deed of Trust, it is further ordered that the sale made by the Trustee Marshall W. Cunningham to Humphrey Reynolds and the deed made by said Trustee to the Respondent Gettys, be set aside- It is further ordered and decreed that the Clerk and Master take an account of the sums of money due by the Complainant to the Respondent Gettys- together with the interest thereon accruing from the time the same became due till the taking of the account, and ascertain, if any, what portion has been paid by the complainant and when paid- It is further ordered, adjudged and decreed that the Clerk & Master, after giving forty days previous notice in the Hiwassee Patriot a newspaper published in the town of Athens, McMinn County of the time and place of sale, proceed to sell in the Town (P-196) of Athens to the highest bidder for ready money, the two several tracts of land mentioned in the Deed of Trust to wit, the North east quarter of the thirty fifth section, first township, West of the Meredian, second range, Hiwassee District, and the south East quarter of the twenty sixth section, first township, second, range West of the Meredian Hiwassee District, and that said Clerk and Master make report of what he has done to the next term of the Court. It is further ordered that the costs of this suit be first paid out of the proceeds of the sale of said lands and the balance of said proceeds be applied to the payment of whatever may be ascertained to be due the Respondent Gettys.

John Queener & Others)
    vs)
George W. Queener &)
James C. Queener)

In this cause on motion Respondents Counsel it is ordered that the sealed packet accompanying the Respondents answers and purporting to be the last will and testament of

John Queener Sen. decd. be redelivered to the Respondents for the purpose of having the same proved &c.

James A. Coffin Clerk & Master presented the receipt of the Treasurer for the revenue by him collected for the last fiscal year which is as follows viz - (P-197) $16.94 Nashville March 16th 1841 No. 11.

Received of Jas. A. Coffin Clerk of the Chancery Court Madisonville Sixteen Dollars ninety four Cents audited to him by No. 1071 and due on account of revenue by him collected from Sept. 1, 1839 to 1 Sept. 1841.

Miller Frances
Treasurer of
Tennessee

Signed Duplicates - By V.M.

Campbell, Cashier.

Court adjourned till tomorrow Morning 8 O'Clock.

Thos. L. Williams.

Wednesday March 17, 1841
Court met pursuant to adjournment.

William Upton   )
    vs   )
Thomas J. Caldwell &)
Samuel P. Hale   )

On affidavit of William Upton, Complt., this case is again refered to the Clerk and Master, and each party is reguired to appear before the Clerk & Master on taking the account and answer interrogations and also to produce whatever papers & vouchers touching said partnership may be in their possession.

G.W. Churchwell & Others   )
    vs   )
Hiram K. Turk &   )
T.J. Turk   )

The motion made on yesterday in this cause is continued till next Term.
(P-198)

John Bayless   )
    vs   )
William Bayless)

It being suggested by Respondents Sol. that the negroes mentioned in the Deed of Trust refered to in the pleadings are not slaves for life, the chancellor directs the Clerk & Master to Report at this Term what Claim Respondent has to said negroes.

Isaac A. Miller   )
& Nicholas Swan   )
    vs   )
David M. Harlin   )
Silas Perry, Hannah   )
Perry & J. Tucker   )

      Complts by their sol. J.O. Cannon dismisses their Bill as Respondents Perry & Tucker.

The Pidgeon (a Cherokee))
      vs   )
Gideon Morgan &   )
K.L. Hanks   )

      No steps having been taken in this cause for more than two terms, it is ordered that Complainants Bill be dismissed, at his costs, for which let execution issue.

William W. Cowan   )
    vs   )
Lewis Ross, R.J.   )
Meigs & Luke Lea   )

      This case coming on to be heard on the Bill, Answers, Replication and proofs before the Honorable Thomas L. Williams, Chancellor, and the case having been maturely considered and it appearing to the Court that the Compt. is not entitled to relief; It is   (P-199)   ordered adjudged and decreed by the Court that Complainant pay the costs thereby incurred, for which let execution issue.

John Bayless   )
    vs   )   Decree
William Bayless   )

      Be it remembered that on this 17th day of March 1841, this cause coming on to be finally heard, The Hon. Thomas L. Williams Chancellor, presiding upon the Report of the Clerk and Master, heretofore ordered to be taken in this cause, which is unexcepted to, and for reasons appearing to the satisfaction of the Court, it is therefore ordered, adjudged and decreed, that said report be in all things confirmed, and it further appearing to the Court, from the Report of Clerk and Master, that there is yet due from Respondent to Complainant the sum of Three Thousand Nine hundred and five dollars, and forty six cents. The Chancellor is therefore pleased to order, and does order, adjudge and decree, that the several tracts or parcels of land mentioned in the deed of Trust given to Complainant by Defendant, and all the interest the defendant has in the negroes mentioned in the Deed of Trust and their issues as reported by the Clerk and Master, and all the other property mentioned in said Deed of Trust which can be found, be sold, by the Clerk & Master in the Town of Madisonville,Tennessee, or so much thereof as will together with the cost of this suit,

upon a Credit (P-200) of six months, the purchasers
giving bond and security for the purchase money upon the
Clerk & Master first having advertised said sale at least
thirty days at the Court House door in the town of Madisonville, Tenn. It is further ordered that the purchase money
remain a lien upon the land till paid.

And it further appearing from the Report of the
Clerk and Master, that the negroes mentioned in said deed of
Trust and their issue, are to be free at the death of Sarah
Bayless, the wife of defendant; It is therefore further
ordered, adjudged and decreed by the Court that the purchaser
or purchasers of said negroes, at said sale, shall give bond
and security to the Clerk & Master in an amount that shall
be approved of by him, not to remove said negroes out of the
State of Tennessee without the execution of which bond, the
purchaser shall not to be vested with title to said negroes.

Court adjourned till tomorrow morning 8 O'Clock.

Thos. L. Williams

(P-201)   Thursday March 18th 1841.

Robert H. McEwin, Exr.   )
Elizabeth McEwin, Exr.   )
        vs   )
Henry Matlock   )
J. McPherson & Others   )

The death of Elizabeth McEwin Complt. is suggested
by J. Jarnagan Esq. Complts Sol.

Jane Austin   )
    vs   )   Decree:
Jacob Lingerfelt   )

March 18, 1841, This Case Coming on to be heard
before the Hon. Thomas L. Williams Chancellor upon the Bill,
Answer, Replication and proof and argument of Counsel having
been heard, it is considered by the Court that Complainant
is not entitled to relief; It is therefore decreed by the
Chancellor that Complainants Bill be dismissed, and that
Complainant pay the costs, for which let execution issue.
From which decree Complainant prays an appeal to the next
Term of the Supreme Court to be held at Knoxville on the
First Monday of July next, which appeal, for reasons satisfact-
ory to the court is granted without requiring bond and se-
curity for the same.

John Blair, admr.   )
of Joseph Scates, dec.   )
        vs   )
Eli Cleveland and   )
Others   )

By consent of parties, it is ordered adjudged and decreed by the Honorable Chancellor that the Clerk and Master take an account in this cause and ascertain who are (P-202) Creditors of Complainants intestate, and the amount due to each; the amount of the assets which came to the hands of the administrator, or that should have come to his hands; that he also ascertain the amount of the reality of which the said Joseph Scates died seized and possessed, and that he have power to examine the parties on oath by interrogations. And it is further ordered and decreed that the Complainant John Blair sell the two negroes mentioned in the pleadings within forty days from this time, and that he give at least twenty days notice of the time & place of sale in the Hiwassee Patriot, published in Athens, Tennessee.

John Key adm of)
    A. Pogue)
      vs)
George C. Harris)
and Others)

      This cause coming on to be heard before the Hon. Thomas L. Williams Chancellor presiding on the 18th March 1841, he is pleased to order and decree that the Clerk and Master take an account of the estate of the said Alfred Pogue deceased, both real and personal, and that he also ascertain the amount of the debts due from said estate and to whom, what has come to the hands of the administrator as well as what should have come to his hands, and that he report to the next Term of this Court. (P-203)

William M. Biggs)
    vs)
David L. Knox & Others)

      On affidavit of Complainant this Case is Continued till next Term, and Complainant allowed to take the Deposition of T. Hartly Crawford - on Complainants paying the costs of said Continuance.

Nancy Mayfield)
Wm. Mayfield & Others)
      vs) Cross Bill)
Jesse Mayfield)
Thos. B. Mayfield)
& Others)

      Complts by leave of court filed their amended Cross Bill.

      Court adjourned till tomorrow 8 O'Clock.

            Thomas L. Williams.

    March 19th 1841. Friday.

    Court met pursuant to adjournment.

James W. Netherland)
     vs)
Stephen Smith and)
Nathl. Smith)

       This case coming on to be heard on this 19th day
of March 1841, before the Honorable Thomas L. Williams,
Chancellor, on a motion to dissolve the Injunction in this
case, and the Bill and Answer of Respondent Stephen Smith
having been heard and considered, It is ordered by the Court
that the Injunction be dissolved on Respondents entering into bond with good security to refund in case the final decision should be against him, (P-204) and that on the
execution of such Bond the Clerk of this Court issue execution against Complt for the sum of one hundred and forty
two dollars and forty eight cents, with interest from the
date of the judgment at law, and also for the amount of the
costs at law.

Andrew Taylor)
    vs)
Edward Delozier &)   Decree:
John Mee)

       Be it remembered that this cause came on to be
finally heard and determined before the Honorable Thomas L.
Williams Chancellor presiding in Chancery at Madisonville
the 19th day of March 1841, Upon the Bill answer of John Mee,
Replication, and Judgment pro confesso as to Respt. Delozier
and because it appears to the satisfaction of the Court by
the Judgment pro- confesso entered in this cause as to Delozier, that he was guilty of the fraud Charged in Complainants Bill. His Honor is pleased to order and decree, and
does order and decree that the Judgment at Law be perpetually
enjoined, and that the Respondents pay the costs of both the
suit at law and the costs of this Bill & decree, for which
an execution may issue.

Joseph H. Smith &)
Wm Grant)
      vs)
Jesse Melton, J.)
Stow & S. Blackburn)

       The death of Respt. Blackburn is suggested.
(P-205)

Joseph H. Smith &)
William Grant, adm.)
     vs)   Decree:
Jesse Melton &)
Jarrot Stow.)

       This cause coming on to be finally heard and de-
termined on the 19th day of March 1841, before the Honorable
Thomas L. Williams Chancellor presiding, on the Bill, Answer,

Replication, proof and the Report of the Clerk & Master; and it appearing that Respondent Stow has heretofore been one of the administrators of his father Abil Stow and that he had received into his possession the personal effects of said Abil, and thereby became bound and liable to discharge the real estate of the said Abil from all incumberance; and it further appearing that Respondent Stow at the time of his being removed from the administration had in his hands, and which remains unaccounted for, and for which a decree was extered on the 27th March 1835, $130.56, and it also appearing that Jesse Melton had been appointed Administrator de bonis non of said estate and had in his hands unaccounted for, and for which there was a decree of this court on the said 27th March 1835 $448.34 - That of the last named sum respondent Stow had borrowed on the 18th day of June 1832. One hundred and five dollars and secured the repayment thereof to the administrator Jesse Melton by the Mortgage deed exhibited with Complainants Bill, making in all received by the said Jarrot Stow over and above his distributive share of said estate the sum of $235.56 and it further appearing that Complt.   (P-206) Joseph H. Smith had laid out and expended in discharge of certain incumberance which were upon the real estate of the defendants intestate at the time of his death and which by law they were bound to have discharged the sum of $376.88 for which complainant Smith with other things had the decree aforesaid. It is therefore ordered adjudged and decreed that in case the defendant Stow shall not within four months from this date pay the one hundred and five dollars secured by the mortgage and the interest thereon from the 18th June 1832 till paid; and also the sum of one hundred and thirty dollars & fifty six cents, the amount of Complainant Smith's decree rendered the 27th March 1835 with interest till paid; and also the sum of Ten dollars and seventy seven Cents Costs of said suit for which Complt Smith has a decree against Respt. Stow; then and in that Case the Clerk and Master shall proceed to sell the land mentioned in the Mortgage deed at the Court House door in the Town of Madisonville, giving forty days previous notice in the Hiwassee Patriot a Gazette printed in Athens, Tenn. for Cash; the proceeds of said sale to be applied first to the payment of the costs of this cause, then to the payment of the money secured by said Mortgage deed and enterest thereon, and then to the decree aforesaid- the balance if any to be paid over to said Stow.
(P-207)

John Kennedy	)
vs	)
Erby Boyd	)
Daniel Anderson	)
William Anderson	)
Malinda Anderson	)
John McNair	)

Upon the trial of this cause it was agreed in open Court by the parties, that the survey of the land in dispute was made between February & April 1837 said ad-

mission to be made a part of the record & Considered as
evidence on the hearing.

Samuel Parks   )
    vs   )
Will Bryson &   )
L. Taylor   )

      By consent of parties & Leave of the Court the
parties are permitted to Copy their grants and the Copy of
the same to go up to the Supreme Court as evidence instead
of the Originals read upon the hearing of the cause in this
Court.

John Kennedy   )
    vs   )
Erby Boyd,   )
Daniel Anderson   )   Decree:
William Anderson   )
Malinda Anderson   )
& John McNair   )

      On this 19th day of March 1841, Came on this cause
for hearing before the Hon. Thomas L. Williams Chancellor,
upon the Bill of Complainant, the answers of Respondents
Erby Boyd, Daniel Anderson, William Anderson, and Replications
thereto, and the answer of John McNair & replication and Judgment pro Confesso, against Malinda Anderson, and the proofs.

      And because it appears to the Chancellor from the
proofs that John McNair was in the actual possession of and
residing upon the North East quarter of section 33 in Fractional Township 2. South, in Range 2, East of the basis line in
the Ocoee District before and at the passage (P-208) of
the "Act to dispose of the lands in the Ocoee District, and
that the said John McNair had thereby acquired a right to
enter the same as an account in the entry Taker's office of
said district, and that he did, on the 5th day of November,
1838, assign said occupant claim, to said quarter section of
land to the Complainant John Kennedy; and it further appearing to the Chancellor from the proof, that William Anderson
was not in actual possession of and residing upon said quarter
section of land at and before the passage of said act. It is
therefore ordered, adjudged and decreed by the Court, that
the Entry and Grant of Respondent Boyd, made and obtained as
assignes of said William Anderson for said quarter section of
land, be declared Null and Void as against the Complainant;
that all the right, title, interest, claim & demand of the
respondents, or either of them in and to the said quarter
section of land be divested out of them and vested in Complainant John Kennedy – That the Clerk and Master of this
Court proceed to take and state an account of the rents and
profits of said land with the annual interest which have been
received by the Respondents Boyd, D. Anderson, & William Anderson or either of them since the 5th day of November 1838,
and that he deduct the amount of rents so received by Res-

pondents from the amount Respt. Boyd paid the state for said land or from the accruing interest thereon if sufficient, and show if any what is the balance due said Boyd, which balance is to be paid him by Complainant in such funds as were paid (P-209) by Respondent Boyd. And further that he take an account of the permanent improvements and repairs which have been made on said land, and for which he shall be allowed such sum as they may have added to the permanent value of said land, and report to the next Term of this court.

And it is further ordered adjudged and decreed by the Court that the Respondents Erby Boyd, William Anderson and Daniel Anderson pay the Costs of this cause.

It is further ordered that possession of said land be surrendered to Complainant, reserving a lien thereon for whatever may be ascertained to be due said Boyd, and if possession be not surrendered, that process issue according to the Costs of this court.

From which decree of the Chancellor Respondents pray an appeal to the next Term of the Supreme. Court to be held at Knoxville on the first Monday of July next, which appeal is granted on their entering into bond & security according to law.

James Maddy   )
    vs   )
James Pelter &   )
Jarnagin & Bradford   )

This case coming on to be heard on a motion to dissolve the Injunction heretofore granted and the Bill and answers of Respt. Pelter having been duly considered, It is ordered by the Court that the Injunction be dissolved, that Respt be allowed to proceed to judgment on his suit at law; but that no execution issue until (P-210) he give bond and security to refund in case of a final decision against him.

A.B. Lee   )
  vs   )
Hugh Smith   )

Be it remembered that on this 19th day of March 1841 this cause came on to be finally heard and determined before the Honorable Thomas L. Williams Chancellor presiding upon the Bill, answer, Replication & proofs and it appearing that the Complainant is entitled to relief by having the title to the lot mentioned in the pleadings decreed to him, and it also appearing that a portion of the consideration money which was to have been paid by the Complainant for said lot has not yet been paid. The Chancellor is pleased to order and decree that the Clerk and Master of this Court, take an account in this cause and ascertain the amount due from Complainant to Respondent for said lot and the interest thereon, and that he report to the next Term of this Court.

G.L. Hawkins   )
    vs   )
A.D. Gentry &   )
Others   )

        In this case an Injunction is ordered to stay Waste according to the prayer of Complt. in his petition presented at this term.
(P-211)

Samuel Parks   )
    vs   )
Larkin Taylor &   )
Will Bryson   )

        This case coming on to be heard on the Bill Answers Replication & proof, and the case having been duly considered, and argument of Counsil heard, and it appearing that the Complainant is not entitled to the relief prayed; It is ordered adjudged and decreed that Complainants Bill be dismissed and that Complt. pay the Costs, for which let execution issue.

        From which decree of the Court Complainant prays an appeal to the next Term of the Supreme Court to be held at Knoxville on the first Monday of July 1841, which appeal is allowed by the Chancellor without security for the Costs of the same.

Samuel Parks   )
    vs   )
J.F. Jones   )
J.F. Cleveland   )
Luke Lea &   )
Francis M. Lea   )

        This case is continued till next Term for further argument- and on affidavit of G.W. Parks agent for Complt. An Injunction is granted restraining Respts Jones & Cleveland from committing waste on the land in dispute till the further order of the Court.

Thomas Green   )
    vs   )
Jane Hannah   )
Elisha Green   )
Walter Carouth et als)

        Complt by his Sol. dismisses his Bill as to Respts Lea, Carouth, & Elisha Green.

(P-212)   Court adjourned till Court in Course.

                Thomas L. Williams.

September Term. 1841.

Monday Sept. 20, 1841

At a court of Chancery began & held at the Court House in Madisonville for the 9th Chancery District in the Eastern Division of Tennessee, there was present the Hon. B.L. Ridley.

The Circuit Court being still in session, Court adjourned till tomorrow eight O'Clock.

Bramfield Ridley.

(P-213)   September Term Tuesday Sept. 21, 1841.

Court met.

The Hon. B.L. Ridley Chancellor, presiding.

John K. Farmer   )
        vs   )
Nathaniel Carey   )

No steps having been taken in this case for more than two terms it is ordered to be stricken from the docket; and that Complts pay the costs which have been accrued, for which execution may issue.

John McGhee   )
        vs   )
John Lyon   )

This case is ordered to be stricken from the docket for want of prosecution no steps having been taken for more than two terms. It is further ordered that Complt pay the costs.

Thomas L. Williams   )
        vs   )
Thomas Crutchfield   )

No steps having been taken in this case for more than two terms, it is ordered to be stricken from the docket at Complts costs.

William Ainsworth   )
        vs   )
John Davis   )

No steps having been taken in this cause for more than two terms, it is ordered to be stricken from the docket and that complainants pay the costs for which let execution issue.   (P-214)

R.L. Brasheres   )
        vs   )
Thomas J. Mason   )

This cause coming on to be heard on the Report of

the Clerk & Master and it appearing from the affidavit of
Complts & also from the exception filed by his sol, that the
Case should be remanded to the Clerk and Master; it is ordered that the order heretofore made directing an account to
be taken be revived and that the Clerk and Master report at
next Term and that the parties have leave to take testimony
generally.

John Key adm   )
of A. Pogue   )
    vs   )
George C. Harris   )
and Others,   )
Creditors   )

  The order heretofore made directing an account to
be taken is continued, and the Clerk & Master directed to
Report at next Term.

Thomas B. Mayfield   )   Nancy Mayfield &
and Others   )   Others
  vs) O Bill)   &   vs) Cross Bill
Nancy Mayfield   )   Thomas B. Mayfield &
and Others   )   Others

  It appearing to the Chancellor that the Cases
stated above should be Consolidated it is ordered that they
be prepared for trial & heard together.

  Court adjourned till tomorrow 8 O'Clock.

        Bramfield Ridley

(P-215)   Wednesday Sept. 22nd 1841

  Court met pursuant to adjournment

Gregory F. Hawkins   )
    vs   )
Allen D. Gentry & Others)

  This case is by consent of the parties Continued
for taking further testimony.

Caswell Torbett & Others   )
heirs of James Torbett dec.   )
    vs   )
Robert M. Reynolds   )
Maxwell Duncan & Others   )

  This Case is by consent continued for taking further testimony on both sides.

Cowan Dickinson & Co.)
    vs   )
R.D. Blackstone   )

On affidavit of Perry Dickenson one of the firm of
Cowan Dickenson & Co. Complts are permitted to answer their
bill in accordance with said affidavit, so as to include in
their bill a note due for Defendant for $148.97 dated Feb.
28th 1838 due six months after date.

Anthony Davis   )
     vs   )
Jeremiah Hambrick   )

On the 16th of March 1841 this cause Came on for
final decree on the report of the Master, when it was decreed
that defendant be perpetually enjoined from proceeding at law
upon the mortgage deed named in the pleadings to recover
possession; that Complainant within four months from the date
of said decree pay into the office of the Clerk of this Court
for the use of defendant the sum of six hundred and fifty
dollars and forty five cents with the accruing interest thereon till paid, which said sum with   (P-216)   the costs of
the suit at law and in this court were paid by the Complainant.   It is therefore now ordered, adjudged and decreed by
the court that the title to the land named in the pleadings ,
as conveyed to the defendant by said mortgage be divested
out of him, and be and is hereby vested in the Complainant
in the same condition as if said Mortgage deed had never
been executed, and it is further decreed that the Complainant pay the costs of this entry.

John Blair, adm. of Joseph
Scates, deceased
          vs.
Eli Cleveland, John Stanfield
and others Creditors and
heirs at law of Joseph
Scates, deceased.

Be it remembered that on this 22nd day of September 1841 the above cause came on before the Hon. Broomfield
Ridley presiding at Madisonville on the report of the Clerk
and Master, and it appearing from said report that the Complainant has received and now has in his hands belonging to
said estate, Cash amounting to about six hundred and fifty
dollars and also the following discribed notes on good and
solvent persons to wit:

```
One on Geo. Chesnut & Wm.
Hudgeons Prin.  81.05    Int.   9.78        -    $ 90.83
    do  "  A. Bacum Prin.      49.00
                        Int.    5.06        -      54.06
    do   Wm. Reynolds Prin.    23.00
                        Int.     .20        -      23.20
    do   Wm. Reynolds Prin.     2.72
                        Int.     .34        -       3.06
    do   B. Hickman    Prin.   20.00
                        Int.    2.16        -      22.16
    Do   John F. Calloway        -                 14.89
    Do   James Roy               -                  5.12
```

(P-217)	One note on	Andrew Allen	for	6.30
"	" "	J.H. Johnston -		7.65
"	" "	Henry Chestnut -		29.63
"	" "	Jackson Duncan -		20.45
"	" "	Wyly Blair	-	141.17
"	" "	John Blair		7.21
"	" "	John Blair & H.Blair for		41.35
"	" "	Robert Allen	"	7.25
"	" "	Elizabeth Scates & securities -		1080.57

The Honorable Chancellor is therefore pleased to order and decree that the administrator pay over to the Clerk and Master, in one week after he receives a copy of this order, the money in his hands which is of said estate viz the six hundred and fifty dollars so represented, and because it is uncertain whether it was received by the administrator in currency or money, the court is pleased to order that the Clerk and Master ascertain of the administrator by interrogatories to be answered on oath in what he received of said money and if it shall appear that the money which he has on hands is that which he received in the Course of his administration and that it is Currency, then the Clerk and Master shall receive of the said administrator the currency so received; but if it shall appear that it has been received in money, the administrator shall deposit with the Clerk & Master of this court the cash received whether in Currency or money, and the Clerk shall proceed as soon as practicable to make a pro- rata distribution of said money among the creditors of said estate. The Chancellor further orders and decrees that the complainant hand over to the Clerk of this court the notes before mentioned and it is hereby made the duty of the Clerk & Master to proceed (P-218) without delay to the Collection of said notes. And because it appears to the Court that there were certain negroes belonging to the estate whose hire has not been accounted for, the Chancellor orders that the Clerk & Master ascertain and Report to the next Term of this Court, what was the value of said hire from the granting of administration up to the sale of said negroes by the decree of the Court. - And that he report to next Term touching the things mentioned in the decree.

Wm. White Sen.   )
David White &   )
Wm. White, Jun.   )
   vs   )
John F. Gillespy   )

This case coming on to be heard on the Bill & answer on a motion to dissolve the Injunction and because it appears that the equity of the Bill is fully answered; it is ordered that the Injunction heretofore granted be dissolved on Respondents entering into bond with security to refund in case of a final decision against him and that Respondents have execution against Complainant and Benjamin White, security in the Injunction Bond for Three hundred and twenty one dollars & seventy five cents with interest from the 17th of June 1841 the date of the judgment at law.   (P-219)

John Bean	)		Lewis Mowry	)
vs	)	And	vs	)
Luke Lea	)		Luke Lea	)

      Because it appears to the Court that the decision of the case of John L. Oneal against Luke Lea which has gone to the Supreme Court by appeal will greatly affect the principle involved in the two above stated causes - It is ordered by the Court that these two causes stand continued for said decision.

Samuel Samples	)
vs	)
Joel Kelly	)

      This case coming on to be heard on the Bill, answer Replication & proofs, and it appearing to the Court that Complts is not entitled to relief; It is ordered by the court that Complainants Bill be dismissed and that Complainant pay the costs for which let execution issue.

(P-220)

John L. Oneal	)
vs	)
Luke Lea	)

      This cause coming on to be heard on this 22 day of September 1841 before the Hon. Broomfield Ridley Chancellor &c. Upon the Bill, answers, Replication proof and argument of Counsel and it appearing to the Satisfaction of the Court that the mill described in Complainants Bill was not erected and in operation at the time of the passage of the act of the Legislature of Tennessee entitled an act to dispose of the vacant and unappropriated lands in the Ocoee District passed 29 Nov. 1837. Non bona fide commenced at that time and therefore not within the preview and meaning of the 6th Section of Said Act and not entitled to the relief prayed in his bill, it has pleased the Chancellor to order adjudge and decree and he does decree that Complainants bill be dismissed and that he pay the costs of this cause for which an execution may issue as at law.

      From which decree Complainant prays an appeal to the next Term of the Supreme Court to be held at Knoxville on the first Monday of July next, and said appeal is granted, Complainant having entered into bond with security according to law.

John Hambright
and Others
    vs

Malissa Hambright)
and Others)

This case is remanded to the Rules; The order appointing a guardian ad litem be rescended, and it being admitted that a guardian has been appointed & is ordered that process issue against the regular guardian.
(P-221)

Elliott Peck adm of)
Gilbert H. Peck dec.)
  vs)
The Creditors of)
Gilbert H. Peck, dec.)

The complainant in this cause having filed his Bill of Complt charging that the assets of the Estate of Gilbert H. Peck decd. in his hands as administrator of Said Estate, are insufficient to pay the debts, and that the Estate real and personal of the Said exceeds the value of Five hundred dollars; and praying that all persons may be enjoined from Commencing or prosecuting all suits at law against Said Estate; and that all Creditors and others interested in said Estate may be made parties to Said Bill to prove their demands and to have an account taken thereof & to decree whatever they may be entitled to receive; and further praying that the administration of Said Estate may be transferred from the County Court of Hamilton County to this Court, and an account taken of the personal estate & assets of Said Intestate. It has pleased the Honorable Chancellor to order and direct, and he does order and direct the Clerk & Master to make publication in some newspaper published in Athens, McMinn County, requiring all Creditors and Others interested in Said Estate to file and prove their respective demands against Said estate; that the Clerk & Master take and State an account thereof; That the Clerk & Master issue an order directing all proceedings on said estate to be transferred from the County Court of Hamilton County to this Court; that he take and state an account of the personal estates (P-222) and assets of Said Intestate and that he report what he has done in the premises to the next term of the Court-

John Queener & Others)
  vs)
Queener & Queener)

On the affidavit of George Inley this case is remanded to the Rules for taking further testimony.

John L. McCarty Exr.)
  vs)
Nelson B. Grubb)

In this case publication having been made, and Complainants Bill being taken pro confesso, and the cause having been regularly set for hearing, and coming on to be examined and determined by the Hon. Chancellor it is order- ed and decreed by the Court that the same be refered to the Clerk & Master; that he take an account and ascertain the Amount due Complainant - that he have leave to call before him if necessary and examine witnesses and hear testimony, and report to the next term of this court.

Jesse C. Moore)
    vs   )
Luke Lea)

      On affidavit of Complt this case is remanded to the rules for taking the depositions of Anderson Fitzgerald and John Gee - (P-223)

William Hale)
    vs   )
Eliza White, adm.)

      This case coming on to be heard on the Bill & an- swer, on a motion to dissolve the Injunction heretofore granted; It is ordered by the Court that said Injunction be dissolved except as to the sum of ninety six dollars and thirty three cents.

      Court adjourned till tomorrow 8 O'Clock.

            Broomfield Ridley

      Thursday Sept. 23rd, 1841
      Court met pursuant to adjournment.

Samuel Parks)
    vs   )
Jesse F. Jones)
Jesse F. Cleveland)
Luke Lea and)
P.J.R. Edwards)

      Be it remembered that on the 22nd day of September 1841, the death of Complainant was suggested in open Court before his Hon. the Chancellor, and by consent of parties this cause is revived in the name of Ruth Price, Almira Price & husband James Price, Jane Langdon & her husband Thomas Langdon, George W. Parks, Thomas J. Parks, Richard Parks, Calvin Morgan Parks, William Parks, Polly Ann Parks, Robert Parks, Samuel Houston Parks, the heirs at law and devisers of said Samuel Parks, deceased, Thomas J. Parks, Richard Parks, Calvin Morgan Parks, William Parks, Polly Ann Parks, Robert Parks, Samuel Houston Parks, Minors under Twenty one years of age by their Testamentary Guardian being in open Court, agreeing thereto, and there (P-224) upon this Cause was by consent set down for hearing.

George W. Pars, Almira Price
and husband James Price,
Jane Langdon & Husband
Thomas Langdon, Ruth Price,
Thomas J. Parks, Calvin Morgan
Parks, Polly Ann Parks, Robert
Parks and Samuel Houston
Parks, Richard Parks, William
Parks and John Parks heirs
at law and devisers of
Samuel Parks, deceased.
            vs
Jesse F. Jones, Jesse F. Cleveland,
Luke Lea, Frances W. Lea &
Pleasant J. R. Edwards,

      This cause coming on to be finally heard & de-
termined before his honor Broomfield Ridley presiding in
Chancery at Madisonville this 22nd day of September 1841
Upon bill answers replication and proofs in this cause and
because it appears to the satisfaction of his Honor the
Chancellor, that the Plaintiffs Testator paid into the Entry
takers office the sum of Eight hundred dollars for the purpose of Entering the North East quarter of section Twenty
one Range one Township one west of the Basis line in the
Ocoee District but through mistake, said entry was made upon the North East quarter of section Twenty one Range one
Township One East of the basis line in the Ocoee District,
which said last mentioned quarter is of little or no value;
and was not intended to be Entered and because it further
appears to the satisfaction of the Court (P-225)   that
Respondents Jones and Cleveland entered the said North East
quarter of section twenty one West of the Basis line before
the filing of this Bill & because the Plaintiffs have not a
right to a decree against the Respondents Jones & Cleveland
for the recovery of the land intended to be entered as
aforesaid and because the complainant has prayed for general
relief in his bill; that said money has been enjoined in the
hands of the Entry Taker- His honor is therefore pleased
to order and decree and does order, adjudge and decree that
the said Respondent Luke Lea refund to the said Plaintiffs
George W. Parks and William W. Cowan the testamentary Guardian of the said Plaintiffs the sum of Eight hundred Dollars
so paid into the Entry Takers office aforesaid, provided
said Entry Taker had not paid over the money before the
service of the process issued in this cause, or provided he
may have so much money in his hands, belonging to his office;
that all right and title that the said Plaintiffs may have in
and to the said North East quarter of section Twenty one
Range one, Township one, East of the Basis line be divested
out of the said Plaintiff and vested in the state of Tennessee - That Plaintiffs pay the costs of this suit, and that
Execution issue therefor as at law.

James Maddy   )
 vs   )
James Pelter   ) Decree:
Spencer Jarnagin &)
James F. Bradford)

    This 22nd of September 1841 this cause came on for
final decree before the Hon B.L. Ridley, Chancellor, (P-226)
upon the Bill, answers of defendant Pelter, replication thereto, and pro- confesso as to defendants Jarnagin & Bradford -
It appeared to the satisfaction of the Court that the allegations of Complainants Bill were devised by the answer and
not sustained by proof, and that complainant is not entitled
to the relief he has prayed, upon which it is ordered and decreed by the court that the Bill of Complainant be dismissed,
and that he pay the costs of this cause for which an execution
may issue as at law.

Thomas J. Caldwell &)
David Caldwell   )
  vs   )
Jesse Kerr   )

    On motion of Respondent it is ordered by the Court
that the Injunction granted in this case be dissolved, and it
is further ordered adjudged and decreed by the Court, that
Respondent Jesse Kerr, recover of Complainants and Charles
Donohoo, their security for the Injunction the sum of Two
hundred and fifty dollars fifty two cents the amount of the
two judgments at law, together with the further sum of Twelve
dollars and sixteen cents, interest on said Judgment up to
this term, for which execution may issue on Respondents giving bond & security to the Clerk & Master, to refund said
money in the writ of a final Decree against him.

O.G. Murrell &   )
M. Humphreys   )
  vs   )
George Bush   )

    No steps having been taken in this cause for more
than two terms, the Bill is dismissed at Complts costs for
which execution may issue. (P#227)

William M. Biggs   )
  vs   )
David L. Knox,   )
James Sloan   )
and John N. Taylor)

    This 23rd of September 1841 this cause came on for
hearing and decree before the Honorable B.L. Ridley, Chancellor,
upon the Bill, answers, Replications thereto and proofs.
The Court is satisfied that Complainant was not entitled to
enter the fraction named in his Bill under the provisions of

the act of assembly passed the 29th day of November 1837,
entitled "An act to dispose of the lands in the Ocoee District as an occupant, but that defendants had a right to enter the same as had been done as occupant enterer, and that
Complainant is not entitled to the relief he has prayed.
It is ordered and decreed that complainants Bill be dismissed and that Complainants pay the cost for which execution
may issue.

And. Kerr, John Kerr   )
James Hope & John Hope   )
        vs   )
Alfred McSpadden   )
John McSpadden   )
& John Caldwell   )

   Complts by their Sol. dismisses their Bill and
assumes the costs, for which let execution issue.   (P-228)

Thomas Green Complt   )
        vs   )
Jane Hannah widow of
Joseph Hannah, deceased,
Mary Hannah, Margurite
Hannah, James Hannah,
& Columbus Hannah, heirs
at law of said Joseph
Hannah.

   Be it remembered that this cause coming on to be
heard after the Bill, answers, replications and proofs taken
in the cause before his honor Broomfield Ridley, presiding
in Chancery at Madisonville on this 23rd day of September
1841. And because It appears to the satisfaction of his
honor that the Complainant is not entitled to the relief
prayed because he has no Equity in his cause and was not a
mile occupant as prescribed by the act of assembly his honor
is pleased to order and decree and does order and decree that
Complainants bill be dismissed and that he pay the costs of
this suit for which an execution may Issue as at law.

Berry Fry   )
   vs   )   Decree-
Betsy Fry   )

   Be it remembered that on this 23rd day of September 1841 this Cause came on to be finally heard and determined before the Hon Broomfield Ridley Chancellor presiding at Madisonville on the Bill pro- confesso and proofs,
and the matters and things being heard and it appearing from
the proof that the defendant had been   (P-229)   guilty of
adultery since her intermarriage with Complainant, the Court
thereupon orders and decrees that the bonds of matrimony now
subsisting between Complainant and his wife, Betsy Fry be
dissolved and for naught held and that he be restored to all
rights and privileges of a single man. It is further order-

ed and decreed that Complainant pay the costs in this cause in the first instance and have a decree over against Respondent.

Cowan Dickenson & Co.)
       vs
R.D. Blackstone & Co.)

     This 23rd September 1841 it is ordered by the Chancellor that the sheriff of McMinn County sell the Jacks hired on by him in this cause, after ten days notice upon a credit of six months, the purchaser giving bond and security for the purchase money to said sheriff, who shall file with the Clerk of this Court the security by him taken on said sale, but in as much as the bond taken by said sheriff Upon the service of the Attachment is not warranted by law; it is further ordered by the court that the Clerk of this Court ascertain the amount of the necessary charges for keeping said property and to whom due and to report the same to the next term, and that said sheriff take into his possession said Jacks wherever they may be found.
(P-230)

Gideon Morgan)
    vs)
Arthur H. Henly)
and Others)

    This case coming on to be heard on the Bill and answers of Arthur H. Henly on a motion to dissolve the Injunction and because it appears that the equity of the Bill is answered, and devised in said answers It is ordered that said injunction be dissolved on Respondents entering into bond with security to refund in case of a final decision against them. And that Respts recover of Complt. and Parker Hood his security the sum of forty five dollars debt with interest from July 27, 1827 and $1.25¢ costs at law.

Gideon Morgan)
    vs)
Spencer Jarnagin &)
Archibald Bacum)

    This 23rd of September 1841, this cause came on before the Honorable B.L. Ridley, on a motion to dissolve the injunction granted, and because it appears that the equity of the Bill is answered and devised by the answers of Respondents- It is ordered and decreed that said Injunction be dissolved, and that defendant Jarnagin for the use of defendant Bacum recover of Complainant and George W. Torbett his surety in the Injunction Bond the sum of Two hundred and twenty seven dollars and ninety one and two thirds cents the amount of the judgment at law with the further sum of $4.74 interest thereon up to this time, for which an execution may issue as at law.

(P-231)
George Schorn)
    vs)
Jacob Fisher)
Augustus Fisher &)
Henry Rider)

    On this 23rd day of September 1841 This cause
coming on to be heard and determined before the Honorable
Broomfield Ridley, Chancellor &c on the Bill & answers and
the motion of Respondents solicitor to dissolve the Injunction in this cause Because it appears from the answers that
the Equity of the Complainant Bill be devised. It is ordered by the Court that the Injunction be dissolved. It is
further ordered & decreed that the Complainant and Augustus
W. Elder his security in the Injunction Bond pay to the Respondents the sum of one hundred fifty dollars the amount of
the judgment mentioned in the pleadings together with the
further sum of Eleven dollars and twenty five cents the interest accrued thereon up to this date, for all which an injunction may issue as at law upon the Respondents giving
bond and security to refund if upon the final hearing a decree
shall be rendered against them.

James W. Netherland)
    vs)
James P. Thompson)
Administrator of)
Thomas Hopkins, dec.)

    On this 23rd day of September 1841, this cause
Coming on to be finally heard and determined before the Hon.
B.L. Ridley Chancellor &c. Upon the Bill and pro confesso
heretofore taken against the Defendant, and   (P-232)
After argument of counsel and mature deliberation of the
Court. Because it appears from the Complainants Bill that
the consideration of the Writing obligatory mentioned in
Complainants said Bill had failed. It is ordered adjudged
and decreed that the judgment at law recovered as charged
in said bill upon the said writing obligatory be perpetually
enjoined; And it is further ordered that the defendant James
P. Thompson pay the costs of this suit and the costs of the
suit at law out of any assets in his hands of the estate of
the said Thomas Hopkins, decd., to be administered.

Joseph H. Smith for)
himself & William)
Grant, adm.)
    vs)   Final Decree
Jesse Melton, Jarrot Stow)

    This cause coming on to be heard and finally de-
termined, on the report of the Clerk and Master, before the
Hon. Broomfield Ridley Chancellor presiding at Madisonville,
on the 23rd day of September 1841, and said Report being un-

excepted to, it is in all things confirmed, and it is further
ordered, adjudged and decreed by the court that all the
right, title interest and demand that Respondent Stow the
mortgager, and also all the right, title interest and demand
that the mortgages had or had of and to the premises mentioned in the mortgage deed viz - one hundred and twenty acres of
land   (P-233)   being part of the North West quarter of Section thirteen, fourth township, and first range East of the
Meredian Monroe County, bounded as follows, beginning at the
North West Corner of said quarter, thence East on the section
line one hundred and twenty poles, thence south one hundred
and sixty poles along Barters line to the Quarter section line,
thence west on said line one hundred and twenty poles to a
stake on the section line three poles nineteen links south
of Middle Creek thence North with the section line to the beginning, be divested out of them and vested in William Terry
and his heirs in fee, the said William Terry being the purchaser for the sum of four hundred and twenty five dollars,
at the sale of the Clerk and Master, made in pursuance of
the decretal order in this cause; and it is further ordered
that Jarrot Stow deliver possession to the said William Terry
Upon demand thereof; And upon his refusal that the said
William Terry have a writ of possession according to the
Course of this court. It is further ordered that the Clerk
and Master be allowed Twenty Dollars for his services in the
sale of said land, and that he obtain the costs of this cause
out of the monies in his hands; and that he pay over to complainant Smith the sum of Three hundred and fifty four dollars
and forty two cents the amount of his claim as mentioned in
the decretal order and interest thereon up to this day and
that he pay the remainder if any over to the said Jarrot Stow.
It is further ordered that a copy of   (P-234)   this decree
be registered in the Register's office of Monore County.

William Coker &   )   Petition -
Robt. McAdams   )

        The petitioners presented to the Court their pe-
tition praying an order for the sale of Certain negro slaves
mentioned in said petition; and because it appears to the
Hon. Chancellor that division of said negroes cannot be made
equally among the heirs of petitioners intestate - he is
pleased to order that petitioners sell said negro slaves,
viz. Susan, March, Rachel, Richard & Anderson to the highest bidder on a twelve months Credit, and that they give
twenty days notice of the time and place of sale in some
newspaper published at Athens, & Report to the next Term of
this Court. And it is further ordered that the Complainants
pay the costs of this cause, Out of the assets of their intestate in their hands.

Allison J. Frizzell   )
        vs   )
Robert Cannon &   )
Lawrence P Nelson   )

Be it remembered that on this 23rd day of September 1841; this cause came on to be finally heard and determined before the Hon. Broomfield Ridley Chancellor presiding at Madisonville on the bill, answers and replications; and because it appears that the Complainant is not entitled to relief; the answers being fully responsive to the Bill and Complainant (P-235) having produced no proof in support of the Allegations of his Bill: - The Chancellor is pleased to order and adjudge that and does order that the injunction be dissolved, the Bill dismissed, and that complainant pay the costs for which let execution issue.

```
A.B. Lee      )
     vs       )
Hugh Smith    )
```

Be it remembered that on this 23rd day of September 1841 this cause came on to be finally heard on the Report of the Clerk and Master and it being unexcepted to is in all things confirmed. The Chancellor is pleased to order and does order adjudge and decree that the legal title to the lot mentioned in the pleadings being lot No.16 in the town of Philadelphia in Monroe County Tennessee be divested out of Respondent Smith and vested in Complainant A.B. Lee and his heirs. And it is further ordered that a Copy of this decree be registered in the registers office of Monroe County- And it is further ordered that Respondent and Complainant each pay one half the costs of this cause for which let execution issue.

```
Jane C. Douglass, widow of
Jonathan Douglass Decd.
          vs
Harriet Hogshead, Alexander
Hogshead, Mary E. Hogshead,
Joseph R. Douglass, DeWitt
Douglass, Mary E. Douglass,
Oscar E. Douglass and
Theodore Douglass, and
John Ramsey Guardian ad
Litem & John Stanfield
and Robert Sneed adm
with the will annulled
```

(P-236)   Be it remembered that on this the 23rd day of September 1841, this cause came on to be heard before the Hon. B.L. Ridley Chancellor presiding at Madisonville on Complainants petition and because it appears to the court now here, that the regular notice has been given and that the petitioner is entitled to relief - The Chancellor is pleased to order and decree that Complainant be allowed dower out of the real estate of which the said Jonathan Douglass died seized and possessed lying and being in the County of Monroe on the waters of Pond Creek and that the sheriff of Monroe County is hereby ordered and directed to summon five free

holders and go upon the premises and lay off and allot to
the complainant dower out of the said seven hundred and
forty acres of land aforesaid and that they report to the
next Term of this Court.

John Wilson   )
Henry Hatten   )
     vs   )
Thomas Latimore   )

     This 23rd day of September 1841, this cause came
on before the Hon. B.L. Ridley chancellor on a motion to
dissolve the Injunction obtained by Complainants. The Bill
and answers were not read & heard & because the court is
satisfied the equity of complainants Bill is fully answered,
it is ordered & decreed that said injunction be dissolved,
that Respondents recover of Complainants and James M. Broyles
their security the sum of one hundred and three dollars and
eighty cents, the amount of the judgment at law and the
further sum of fifty two and a half cents interest upon said
judgment up to this time all of which an execution may issue
as at law on Respondent giving bond with security to refund
if so ordered on final decree.
(P-237)

Jonathan Thomas   )
     vs   )
Johnston Minton &   )
Theophelus Smith   )

     This 23rd of September 1841 this cause came on
before the Honorable B.L. Ridley, Chancellor, upon the exceptions to the answers of Johnston Minton and on a motion
to dissolve the Injunction granted to Complainant. The Court
is pleased to order and does order and decree that the exceptions to Defandant Mintons answers be dissolved, that
said injunction be dissolved and that Defendant Johnston
Minton recover of Complainant and Anthony Davis, his surety,
the sum of four hundred and forty seven dollars, sixty nine
cents, the amount of the judgment enjoined, and also the sum
of eleven dollars and nineteen cents interest on said judgment up to this time, for all of which an execution may issue as at law upon Defendant Minton entering into bond with
surety to refund if the final decree be against him.

James K. Farmer &   )
James Gettys   )
     vs   )
Dempsey Carey   )

     This 23rd of September 1841, this cause came on
for hearing before the Honorable Broomfield Ridley, upon
the Bill and answers, by the consent of the parties for decree. It appeared to the Court that in December 1837, Complainant James K. Farmer sold to Defendant Carey certain
Town property in the Town of Athens, in the County of McMinn

being the lot on which said Farmer's house, his former residence stands, except his medical office and the ground he
had sold to Robert Frazier; also his back lot just back of
his residence and back of Isaac Crows or what was then Isaac
Crow's - and also the fourth of the lot that Isaac Crow then
lived on, being the part adjoining the property of said
Farmer, which he purchases from said Crow and on which his
kitchen was for the consideration of eleven hundred dollars,
one hundred paid, and the residue secured by three notes for
three hundred and thirty three and a third dollars each. On
the 14th of December 1837 Farmer executed and delivered to
defendant Carey a title bond for said property. Some of said
notes became the property of Complainant Gettys by assignment
from Farmer. Aside from said notes Carey became indebted to
Complainant Gettys in the sum of three hundred, and twenty
five dollars, & he was surety for Carey to Reeders &co. for
one hundred dollars. To secure said sum of three hundred and
twenty five dollars. & to indemnify for said suretyship,
Carey assigned and transfered to Gettys said title bond on
the 24th of December 1839. That of the original purchase
money, for which said property is liable, there remains due
a considerable sum, and due to said Gettys for which Farmer
appears responsible as indorser so the amount due said Gettys
is six or seven hundred dollars as alledged, and for which
said property is liable and pledged and that defendant Carey
is unable to pay the same without a sale of said property -
In this cause the Chancellor is pleased to order and decree
that the   (P-238)   same be refered to the Clerk and Master
to state an account showing the amount due by Carey to Gettys
or Farmer and for which said property has been made liable
that said property be sold to pay and discharge whatever may
be found to be due, and that the same be sold on a credit of
twelve and eighteen months at the Courthouse in Athens,
or forty days notice in some newspaper printed in said Town
the purchaser paying twenty dollars in money and securing the
residue by bond with security to said Clerk, and that said
Clerk report hereof at the next term for further order and
decree.

Robert H. McEwin surviving
Executor of John McEwin,
deceased.
          vs
Henry Matlock, John McPherson,
Elizabeth McPherson widow of Burton McPherson, deceased
Alexander McPherson, Thomas Johnstons, and his wife Mary
formerly Mary McPherson, Wesley Whitten and his wife Sarah,
formerly Sarah McPherson, Henderson Small and his wife
Eliza, formerly Eliza McPherson, Ann McPherson, Rufus Mc-
Pherson, Sarah Elizabeth McPherson and Isabella McPherson,
heirs at law of Burton McPherson, deceased.

          This 23rd day of September 1841, came on this
cause for hearing before the Honorable Broomfield L. Ridley.
Upon the Bill and judgment pro confesso as to all the defend-

ants regularly entered. It appeared to the Court that on the 9th day of February 1825, Burton McPherson deceased became (P-239) indebted to the personal representatives of John McEwin deceased in the sum of one hundred and fifty one dollars, and to secure said sum, on the day and year aforesaid, with John McPherson his surety executed to Elizabeth McPherson executrix, Robert H. McEwin and Matthew Stephenson executors of the last will and testament of John McEwin deceased, such personal representatives and of whom the said Robert H. McEwin is the surviving Executor their two notes under seal, payable twelve months after date, one for eighty dollars and the other for seventy one dollars, upon said notes there is now due for principal & interest the sum of two hundred and ninety two dollars fifty one and a half cents to said surviving executor Robert H. McEwin. It further appeared that about the year 1824, Burton McPherson purchased of defendant Henry Matlock a part of the south West quarter of section twenty three of Township third, in range first West of the Meredian live in the Hiwassee District, now in McMinn County, being that part on the East sides of the Creek Containing one hundred acres more or less, and took from said Matlock a title bond That Burton McPherson had paid said Matlock for said land the amount of the purchase money, who still holds the legal title. Burton McPherson to indemnify his said surety John McPherson, and to secure the amount due complainant assigned said title bond to said John McPherson that the amount due complainant might be paid out of the proceeds of said land. That after this Burton McPherson died intestate, (P-240) Upon whose estate no administration has ever been granted, and that he had no estate except what interest he might have in said tract of land. That after John McPherson received said title bond to enable him to pay the amount due complainant he removed from Tennessee to the state of Missouri without making any deposition of said lands or paying the amount due Complainant, except declaring said land was sufficient to pay the amount due complainant. Upon these facts the court is of opinion said tract of land should be subjected to the payment of the amount due Complainant as herein before stated. It is therefore ordered, adjudged and decreed that the Clerk & Master of this Court, after forty days notice in some newspaper printed in Athens, Tennessee and ten days notice at the Court house in Athens sell at said Court house said tract of land to the highest bidder upon a credit of twelve and eighteen months, upon the purchaser giving bond and security to said Clerk and Master for the purchase money after paying twenty dollars for the use of said Clerk and Master, and the costs of this cause, then the residue to be secured as above stated.

It is further ordered that the Clerk & Master report hereof at the next Term for further order & direction.

William Upton   )
      vs   )
Samuel P. Hale &   )
Thomas J. Caldwell   )

This cause coming on to be heard on the Report of the Clerk and Master, to which no exceptions have been filed; and Complt having presented an affidavit for (P-241) remanding said case to the nilis (the Decree of the Chancellor having been pronounced) It is ordered that said cause be remanded to the Clerk and Master and that the orders heretofore made directing an account be revived and it is further ordered that complainants pay the costs of this case which have accrued up to this time - for which let execution issue.

John Bayless   )
   vs   )
William Bayless   ).

       This case coming on to be heard on the Report of Sale made by the Clerk and Master and it appearing that the Complt who purchased the negroes refund to therein has not yet executed Bond with security as required, No further order is now made than that the Clerk be allowed fifty dollars for executing the Decree rendered at last term which together with the costs of this cause are to be paid by Complt out of proceeds of said sale.   .
(P-242)

Richard Rothwill   )
   vs   )
Marshall W. Cunningham   )   Final Decree
& James Gettys   )

       Be it remembered that on the 23rd day of September 1841, this cause coming on to be finally heard and determined before the Hon. Broomfield Ridley Chancellor &c upon the Bill, answers, Replication and proofs report of the Clerk and Master and the exceptions to said report, after argument of counsel and mature deliberation of the Court: - It pleased the Honorable Chancellor to order that the exceptions to the report of the Clerk & Master be overruled and that said report be in all things confirmed. It is further ordered and decreed that Complainants Bill as to Marshall W. Cunningham be dismissed; and because it appears from the report of the Clerk and Master that on the 30th day of August 1841 pursuant to the interlocutory decree in this cause did take and state an account by which it appears that the Complainant Richard Rothwill is indebted to the Respondent James Gettys in the sum of five hundred and nine dollars and sixty one cents, It is ordered, adjudged and decreed that the said Complainant Richard Rothwill pay to the said Respondent James Gettys the said sum of five hundred and nine dollars and sixty one cents And because it appears further from said report of the Clerk & Master that on the 18th day September 1841 pursuant to the aforesaid (P-243) Interlocutory decree in this cause he did after having given the required previous notice in the Hiwassee Patriot sell at public sale at the Court house door in Athens the tracts of land described in the pleadings in this cause to wit. two quarter sections of land situated in the County of McMinn and state of Tennessee being the North

East quarter of section Thirty fifth in Township first and
Range second West of the Meredian; & the South East quarter
of Section twenty sixth in the first township and Second
range west of the Meredian Hiwassee District in McMinn County at which said sale James Gettys the Respondent aforesaid
became the purchaser for the sum of five hundred and sixty
dollars he being the highest, last and best bidder. It has
pleased the Honorable Chancellor to order adjudge and decree
and he does order adjudge and decree that all the right, title,
interest and Claim the said Complainant Richard Rathwill
hath in and to the said North east quarter of section thirty-
fifth, in township first, range second, west of the Meredian,
and the South East quarter of Section twenty sixth in first
Township and second Range West of the Meredian Hiwassee District, McMinn County be divested out of the said Complainant
Richard Rathwill and vested in the said James Gettys to have
and to hold to (P-244)   him and his heirs forever as an
estate in fee and that the said James Gettys have his writ of
possession as at law. It is further ordered and decreed that
the Clerk and Master be allowed the sum of twenty five dollars
as Compensation for making said sale; that out of the proceeds of the sale he retain said sum, pay the costs of this
cause and apply the residue to the payment of the debt due
the Respondent James Gettys as aforesaid as ascertained by
the Report of the Clerk and Master aforesaid.

It is further ordered that a copy of this decree
be registered in the Register's office of McMinn County where
the said lands lie.

It is further ordered and decreed that the Judgment at law mentioned in the pleadings be perpetually enjoined.

From which decree of the Chancellor Complainant
prays an appeal to the next Term of the Supreme Court to be
held at Knoxville on the first Monday of July next which
appeal is granted on the Complainant entering into bond with
security as required by law. And on application being made
for time to procure security, the Chancellor is pleased to
allow the Complainant one month, during which time he may
execute said appeal bond. (P-245)

Robert McAdams and Others
        vs
Legrana Henderson, Guardian of
Sarah McAdams.

The petition in this Cause coming on to be heard,
the Chancellor is pleased to order & decree that William
Bayless, Nicholas S. Peck and James Vaughn be appointed commissioners to go upon the lands mentioned in the Complainant's
bill viz- One hundred and sixty acres in the County of Monroe
being the quarter section on which the said McAdams lived at
the time of his death also four other tracts in the same
County to wit the South West quarter of the ninth Section,
third Township Third Range East of the Meredian Containing

one hundred and sixty acres, also one other tract of one
hundred and sixty acres in the third Range Fourth Fractional
Township thirteenth section and the South East quarter East
of the Meredian, also one other tract of one hundred and
fifty five acres being the North East Fractional quarter of
the twenty second section in the Third Township and Third
Range East; also Eighty acres in the third Range, third Township, fourteenth Section, West half of the South West quarter
all in the neighborhood of Tellico Plains in the County of
Monroe, Hiwassee District. Also forty acres of the North east
corner of the South West quarter of Section fifteen, Township
one, Range one East of the basis line -   (P-246) Also
forty acres the South east corner of the North West quarter
of Section fifteen, township one, Range one East, also forty
acres the North East Corner of the North West quarter of
Section ten, Township one, Range one East and Eighty acres
the West half of the South East quarter of Section thirty six,
Fractional Township Two North, Range one East of the basis
line all in the County of Bradley, Ocoee District, also two
other tracts in the County of Polk viz Forty acres in the
North East Corner of the South East quarter of Section three,
Fractional Township three, Range five East of the basis line
and forty acres the North West Corner of the south West fractional quarter of Section two, Fractional Township, Third
South Range five, East of the basis line Ocoee District, and
make partition and division among the petitioners towit:
Robert McAdams, John McAdams,Isaac McAdams, Tibler McAdams,
William Coker & Wife and Respondent Sarah McAdams, heirs at
law of John McAdams deceased, of the lands aforesaid which
have descended to them and that they make report to the next
Term of this Court and because the Guardian of Sarah McAdams
has not answered leave is given him to file an answer at the
next Term if he shall deem it proper

          Court adjourned till Court in Course

                              Broomfield Ridley

(P-247)   Monday March 21St 1842.

        At a court of Chancery held at the Court house in
Madisonville on the third Monday being the 21St day of March
1842, there was present presiding the Hon. Thomas L. Williams,
Chancellor.

John L. McCarty Ex-   )
ecutor of John Walker   )   Supplemental
        vs   )   Bill
Betsy Walker   )   vs
                                    Morgan & Hanks

        These cases are continued to await the decision
of the suit at law, which has gone to the Supreme Court.

Joseph Donohoo   )
& Others   )
        Vs   )
Heirs of AndW Miller   )

        No steps having been taken in this case for more
than two terms, it is ordered that Complainants Bill be dismissed, at their costs, for which let execution issue.

Thomas Henderson   )
        vs   )
W.C. Roadman &   )
G.D. Edgar   )

        No steps having been taken in this case for more
than two terms, the Chancellor is pleased to order, adjudge
and decree that said Bill be dismissed for want of prosecution and it is further ordered, adjudged & decreed by the
Court that the Injunction granted in this cause be dissolved
that Respondent William C. Roadman, recover of Complainant,
and William P.H. McDermott, and Andrew L. Henderson his securities for the Injunction the sum of Five hundred & eighty
six dollars & (P-248) fifty cents, the judgment at law,
together with the further sum of one hundred and twenty three
dollars - and sixteen cents, the interest on said judgment
from its rendition to this day, making in all the sum of
seven hundred and nine dollars and seventy two cents, and
also the costs of the suit at law and of this court, for all
which execution may issue. It is ordered that this Dismissal
be without prejudice.

George W. Churchwell   )
& others   )
        vs   )
Hiram K. Turk &   )
Thos. J. Turk   )

        This case for want of prosecution is ordered to
be dismissed, at the costs of Complainants, for which let
execution issue.

D.D. Stockton   )
    vs   )
E. Hughes &   )
J. Rowden   )

       No steps having been taken in this case for more than two terms it is ordered to be stricken from the docket at Complainants costs for which let execution issue.

       Court adjourned till tomorrow morning 9 O'Clock.

            Thos. L. Williams

(P-249)   Tuesday March 22nd 1842

Barckley McGhee   )
J.J. Walker & Wife &   )
Jane McGhee   )
    vs   )
Nancy McGhee   )
& the heirs of   )
Alexander McGhee   )
& John McGhee   )

       This day came the parties by their solicitors & waived all exceptions to the Competency of the Hon. Thomas L. Williams, Chancellor presiding in this case.

Rebecca Agnew by   )
her next friend   )
Guilford Cannon   )
    vs   )
E.H. Wear, John O.   )
Cannon & John Agnew   )

       Be it remembered that on this 21st day of March 1842, This cause coming on to be finally heard and determined upon the Bill, answer of E.H. Wear & John O. Cannon & Replications thereto, the pro- confesso as to John Agnew, the Bill of Revivor as to Robert Wear, Guardian of Lucretia P. Wear now deceased and pro- Confesso thereto, and the proofs in this cause, After argument of Counsel and mature deliberation of the Court. Because it appears to the Satisfaction of the Court that the House & Lot No. 10 in the town of Madisonville, mentioned in the pleadings was not sold at the Court house door in the town of Madisonville as directed in the Deed of Trust mentioned in the pleadings, but was sold to Respondents E.H. Wear and James W. Lea at a place different from that prescribed in said deed of Trust: It is therefore ordered, adjudged and decreed by the Court that the said sale of said house & Lot No. 10 aforesaid, and the deed therefor to the said E.H. Wear and James W. Lea be Set aside, anulled and held for naught and void. It is further ordered adjudged and decreed by the Court that the Judgment in Ejectment mentioned in the pleadings as obtained in the Circuit Court of Monroe County by the said James W. Lea and E.H. Wear against

said John Agnew be perpetually Enjoined and that the said
Robert Wear Administrator of the Estate of the said E.H.
Wear pay the costs of the action of Ejectment and the Costs
of this court out of the Effects of Estate of said (P-250)
E.H. Wear in his hands to be administered for which execution
may issue as at law.

Jesse C. Moore   )
        vs   )
Luke Lea, Entry Taker   )

   This cause coming on this 22nd day of March 1842
to be heard before the Hon. Thomas L. Williams Chancellor &c
upon the Bill answer & Replication and because it appears
satisfactorily to the court that there was a mill erected
and in operation on the quarter sect. mentioned in the pleadings at the time of the passage of the act of Assembly Entitled an act to dispose of the lands in the Ocoee district
passed 22nd Nov. 1837 and that therefore he is not within
the equity of the Statute. Nor Entitled to the relief he
seeks. The Chancellor is therefore pleased to order & decree
that the bill be dismissed and that complainant pay the
costs of this cause for which an Execution may issue as at
law. And on motion of Complainant an appeal is granted him
to the Supreme Court to be held at Knoxville on the 1St Monday of July next upon his giving security according to law
for which he is allowed one month.

John L. McCarty Ex^r   )
of Allen B. Grubb   )
        vs   )
Nelson B. Grubb &   )
Joseph Rogers   )

   This 22nd day of March 1842 this cause came on
for final decree upon the report of the Master before the
Honourable Thomas L. Williams Chancellor, the Report being
unexcepted to is in all things confirmed from which it
appears that Complainant paid out as Executor of Allen B.
Grubb in settling the Estate of his testator the sum of
three thousand Six hundred and forty seven dollars, thirty
five and a fourth cents, for principal and Interest. And
that he Received by way of reimbursement from Nelson B.
Grubb the only heir of said Allen B. Grubb for principal
and interest, the sum of three thousand three hundred and
Eighty seven dollars and thirty seven dollars and thirty
Cents leaving a balance due the Complainant from the Estate
of said Allen B. Grubb of two hundred and sixty dollars and
five and a fourth cents on the 22nd of March 1842. It also
appeared that Allen B. Grubb died seized and possessed of
lots No. 40,79,82 (P-251) 109,111, 13 and 6 in the town
of Calhoun in the County of McMinn, Tennessee, in the plan
of said town, that ought to be subjected to the payment of
said sum of two hundred and sixty dollars, five and a fourth
cents; The Chancellor orders and decrees that said town lots

be sold in Calhoun by the Clerk of this Court after forty
days notice in some newspaper printed in Athens, to the
highest bidder, and out of the proceeds pay the costs of
this Cause and then pay the said sum of two hundred and
sixty dollars five and a fourth cents to said John L. McCarty
and the Residue if any pay to said Nelson B. Grubb, and that
said Clerk & Master report hereof to the next Term.

Gregory F. Hawkins   )
        vs   )
Allen D. Gentry & Others   )

        On affidavit of Respts A.D. Gentry this case is
remanded to the rules for taking further testimony. (P-252)

Robert H. McEwin Ex.   )
and Elizabeth McEwin   )
Executrix of John McEwin   )
decd.   )
              vs   )
Henry Matlock, John   )
McPherson, Alexander   )
McPherson, John   )
McPherson, & his wife   )
Mary, Wesley Whitten   )
& his wife Sarah,   )
Henderson Small &   )
his wife, Eliza, Ann   )
McPhersons, heirs   )
at law of Burton   )
McPherson, deceased,   )
Rufus McPherson,   )
Sarah Eliza McPherson,   )
Elizabeth McPherson,   )
and Isabella McPherson,   )
Children of Richard   )
McPherson, deceased,   )
Who was an heir   )
of Burton McPherson,   )
deceased.   )

        This 22nd of March 1842, this cause came on before
the Honorable Thomas L. Williams Chancellor, for further decree upon the report of the Master, which report being unexcepted to is in all things confirmed from which it appears
that the said Master, on the 5th day of March 1842 did on
the terms prescribed by the interlocutory Decree in this
Cause proceed to sell the land specified in said decree, and
at and upon said sale George L. Gillespie and Robert N. Mc-
Ewin became the purchasers of said land at the price of Two
hundred dollars, they being the highest bidders, that twenty
dollars of said purchase money was paid, and the Residue
secured, as directed in Said decree. The court now orders
and decrees that all the right and title said defendants and

Each of them have in and to the said land mentioned in said
interlocutory decree being a part of the south West quarter
of section thirty three of Township third, in Range first,
West of the Meredian in the Hiwassee District, being that
part on the East side of the Creek, containing one hundred
acres be divested out of them and Each of them, and be vested
in the said George L. Gillespie and Robert N. McEwin. Said
purchasers as an estate in fee. That a copy of this decree
be registered in the Register's office in the County of McMinn
and that said defendants surrender possession of said land to
said purchasers and on refusal that process issue to put them
in possession. (P-253)

Thomas J. Caldwell   )
et al   )
        vs   )
Jesse Kerr   )

        On the affidavit of Complainant, Thomas J. Caldwell
this case is remanded to the rules for taking testimony.

Charles Wilson, Complt   )
        vs   )
Nathaniel Smith &   )
Wm. Morgan, Respts   )

        The death of Complts is suggested, and the suit
revived in the name of the heirs of said Complainant Charles
Wilson, viz. Elizabeth Wilson, the widow, and Isaac, James
& Uriah H. Wilson, Mary Winkle & her husband Joseph Winkle,
Elijah, John, Malinda, Elender, Rosannah, Sarah Jane &
Elizabeth Wilson, all of whom are children & heirs of said
Charles Wilson, decd. (except the said Joseph Winkle) Com-
plainants.

Thomas Crutchfield   )
        vs   )
Thomas N. Clark Jr. Adm.   )

        This case coming on to be heard on the Bill of
Complainant & Respondents, answers, on a motion to dissolve
the Injunction, and the case having been considered by the
Court; it is ordered that the Injunction be dissolved as
to the amount of Two thousand dollars of the judgment at law,
and that it continue in force as to the balance; and that a
procedendo be awarded. (P-254)

Theophelus Smith   )
        vs   )
Jonathan Thomas   )

        This case coming on to be heard this March 22nd
1842, on the Bill & answer on a motion to dissolve the Injunction heretofore granted, and the case having been considered It is ordered that the Injunction be dissolved, and

that the Respondent Jonathan Thomas recover of Complainant &
James Spencer his security for the Injunction the sum of two
hundred and twenty eight dollars and fifty cents, with interest from the 9th day of September 1841 title paid, for
which let execution issue upon the said Respondent executing
a Bond to refund in case of a final decision against him and
that a procedendo be awarded for the collection of the costs
at law.

Gideon Morgan   )
     vs   )
James S. Bridges)

       This exception filed by Complt. to the answer of
Respt coming on to be heard by consent, the Chancellor sus-
tains the 1st. and 3rd exceptions, and overrules the balance
of said exceptions. Three months are allowed Respondent to
file his amended answer, and it is required that he within
that time deposit with the Clerk & Master the Books of account belonging to and connected with the partnership refered to in the pleadings 4th Exceptions suspended till
next Term.   (P-255)

Thomas B. Mayfield   )
William Mayfield   )
and others heirs   )
at law of Jesse   )
Mayfield   )
       vs O. Bill   )
Nancy Mayfield   )
Samuel Mayfield   )
Jesse Mayfield   )
and Others,   )
widow and heirs   )
of Pearson Mayfield   )
deceased, who was   )
a son of Jesse   )
Mayfield deceased   )
       and   )
Nancy Mayfield, Widow   )
and the heirs at law   )
of Pearson Mayfield, decd.)
     vs. 3 Cross Bill)
Thomas B. Mayfield   )
William Mayfield &   )
Others, heirs at   )
law of Jesse Mayfield,   )
deceased.   )

       This 22nd day of March 1842 these two causes came
on for hearing before the Honorable Thomas L. Williams Chancellor upon the Bills answers Replications and proofs which
when all read and understood and argument of Counsel heard
It appears to the Court that Jesse Mayfield the ancestor of

the complainants and Respondents, died in the County of Mc-
Minn, in the state of Tennessee, about the 29th of September
1833 intestate, leaving a considerable real and personal
Estate, not involved to be divided. That Complainants and
Respondents are the heirs at law of said Jesse Mayfield, decd.
and the representatives of such, and entitled to said Estate,
That Thomas B. Mayfield and David A. Cobb were appointed by
the County Court of said McMinn County, administrators in the
estate of Jesse Mayfield, deceased; The Court is satisfied
from the proof in these causes that the tract of land of one
hundred and sixty acres on Conasauga Creek in said McMinn County upon which Pearsen B. Mayfield resided at the time of
his death and upon which his widow and sons of his Children
have resided since, belonging to and was a part of the real
estate of the said Jesse Mayfield deceased, at the time of
his death, and which descended to his heirs at law, and was
not the property of said Pearson B. Mayfield, deceased. And
the Chancellor doth so adjudge. It further appeared to the
Court that the whole of the estate of said Jesse Mayfield deceased was divided by consent among his heirs at laws both
the real and personal Estate, that such   (P-256)   consent
was given by Nancy Mayfield widow of Pearson Mayfield, deceased, and Guardian of his Children, and the Court not being
satisfied as to her power is pleased to order and decree
that these two cases be refered to the Clerk & Master to Examine and Report whether said division was equitable and just
and if the part or portion alloted to the widow and heirs of
Pearson B. Mayfield, deceased was a just part or portion due
them of the estate of said Jesse Mayfield, deceased, after
bringing into   all advances made by Jesse Mayfield deceased to his Children all other matters not here decreed are
reserved to the final hearing The clerk will also report
how much money was paid by Pearson Mayfield for the Conosauga
tract of land & how much by Jesse Mayfield.

Robert L. Brashers   )
        vs   )
Thomas J. Mason   )

          This 22nd day of March 1842 came on before the
Honorable Thomas L. Williams, Chancellor, this cause for
final decree upon the interlocutory order, heretofore made
and the Report of the Clerk and Master. said report was excepted to but the exceptions disallowed and the report in
all things confirmed. It appears that Complainant and Respondent were partners in a tavern kept in the state of
Georgia. The Report shows that Complainant advanced to said
firm the sum of two hundred and twenty four dollars, seventy
nine and a half cents and that Responded advanced to the same
the sum of three hundred and forty five dollars eighty nine
and a half cents. That upon a final settlement of said
partnership concern, the Complainant is in arrears and justly indebted to respondent in the sum of one hundred and
twenty one dollars and ten cents, exclusive of the notes on
which suit was brought at law as specified in the pleadings

in this cause from these facts the Chancellor is satisfied that Complainant is not entitled to any relief in this Court and therefore orders and decrees that Complainants bill be dismissed, and that he pay the costs of this cause and that Respondent Recover against him the said (P-257) Sum of one hundred and twenty one dollars and ten cents for all of which an Execution may issue as at law.

William Lowry)
    vs)
John G. Glass for)
the use of Siter)
Price &Co.)

      This 22nd of March 1842 this cause came on before the Honorable Thomas L. Williams, Chancellor upon a motion to dissolve the injunction heretofore granted. And issued in the same upon the Bill alone, which being read and understood by the court and because it appears to the satisfaction of the Chancellor that Complainant should not have an injunction for the whole amount specified in his bill. It is ordered and decreed that said injunction be dissolved for the sum of twelve hundred dollars. That said John G. Glass for the use of Siter Price & Co. recover of said William Lowry and Hilton Humphreys his security in the injunction bond filed in this cause the said sum of twelve hundred dollars for which an execution may issue as at law.

John K. Farmer &)
James Gettys)
    vs)
Dumpsey Carey)

      This 22nd of March 1842 this cause came on for final decree upon the interlocutory decree and the report of the Master before the Honorable Thos. L. Williams Chancellor said report was not excepted to and is in all things confirmed from which it appears that the amount due complainant James Gettys on the 5th of March 1842 from the respondent Dumpsey Carey and for the payment of which the land described in the bill was ordered to be sold, was six hundred and sixty nine dollars and forty eight cents. That the Clerk and Master did on the 5th day of March 1842 after giving forty days notice of the time and place of sale, sell at the Court house (P-258) door in Athens, on the Credit and terms prescribed in the Interlocutory decree in this cause, the land described in the pleadings to wit. Certain town property in the town of Athens, in the County of McMinn being the lot on which said Farmer's house the former Residence of said Farmer stands, (except his medical office) and the ground he sold to Robert Frazier also his back lot just back of his residence and back of Isaac Crow or what was Isaac Crows and also the fourth of the lot that Isaac Crow lived upon being the part adjoining the property of Farmer which he purchased from said Crow and on which his kitchen was. At which sale the

said James Gettys became the purchaser of said property for
the sum of one hundred dollars, he being the highest and
best bidder. Upon these facts the Chancellor is pleased to
order and does order and decree that all the right and title
to said property, now in said John K. Farmer or Dumpsey Carey
be and is divested out of them and vested in said James Gettys
as an Estate in fee, that the costs of this cause be paid
out of the proceeds of said sale and that the possession of
said lands be surrendered to said Gettys and on refusal that
process issue to put him into possession. It is further decreed by the Court that said Gettys name leave to proceed at
law against said Dumpsey Carey for the residue of the debt
due said Gettys-

   Court adjourned till tomorrow morning 8 O'Clock.

       Thomas L. Williams.

(P-259)   Wednesday March 23rd 1842

   Court met pursuant to adjournment.

Richard Swafford &   )
Alfred Swafford   )
   vs   )
Elizabeth Leuter & Preston)
Leuter & William Bates   )

   Be it remembered that on this 22nd day of March
1842 this cause coming on to be finally heard and determined
on the Bill and answers. Replications and proofs. After
argument of Counsel and mature deliberation of the Court and
because it appears to the Satisfaction that the Complainants
are entitled to the relief prayed for in their said Bill. It
is ordered, adjudged and decreed by the court that all the
right, title interest and claim which the Respondents James
B. Leuter and Preston Leuter have in and to the South West
quarter of section Eleven, Fractional Township four, Range
Second, West of the Meredian Hiwassee District be divested
out of the said James B. Leuter and Preston Leuter and vested
in the said Complainants Richard Swafford and Alfred Swafford
in fee simple; and because it is uncertain what deduction
should be made in the purchase money for said land by reason
of the failure of the said James L. Leuter to comply with his
agreement with complainants. It is ordered by the court that
the Clerk and Master enquire into that matter and report, if
any, what deduction should be made to be credited on the
note of five hundred dollars alledged in the Bill as in the
hands of the Respondent William Bates. It is further ordered
by the court that the Clerk and Master pay to the Respondent
Wm. Bates administrator of said James L. Leuter on said note
the sum of three hundred and 63$\frac{50}{100}$ --- dollars the sum deposited with him by complainants, after deducting therefrom
the costs of this suit. And further report whether there is
any and what balance of the purchase money remains unpaid.

(P-260)

Jonathan Thomas   )
    vs   )
Johnson Minton   )
& Thophilus Smith   )

        Be it remembered that on this 22nd day of March
1842 this cause coming on to be heard and determined by the
Court upon the Bill, answers replications and proofs. Because it appears to the satisfaction of the court that the
Complainant and Respondents were partners as charged by Complainant and that their partnership accounts have not been
settled. It is ordered by the court that the Clerk and
Master take and state an account between said parties in
which he shall ascertain and state how much capital stock was
paid into the concern by each party how much of the partner
ship Effects had been received by each party how much had
been paid by each on account of the partnership concern how
much, if any each party is indebted to the concern and if
anything how much either party is debted to the others on
the partnership account and to make a report to the next court.

Robert McAdams; John McAdams,
Isaac McAdams, Sebba McAdams,
William Coker & Wife Miria
Coker, formerly Miria
McAdams, Complainants
        vs
Sarah McAdams Respondent
& Legrand Henderson,
Guardian of said Sarah.

        Be it remembered that on this 22nd day of March
1842 this cause came on to be finally heard and determined
before the Hon. Thomas L. Williams, Chancellor for the Eastern Division of Tennessee, on the report of Nicholas S. Peck,
James Vaughn & William Bayless, Commissioners appointed at
the last Term of this Court, by an Interlocutory decree then
made in this   (P-261)   cause requiring the said Commissions
to make partition of the land decended to the complainants
and the Respondent Sarah McAdams as heirs at law of their
ancestor, John McAdams, deceased, and it appearing from the
said report that the said Commissioners After having been
duly sworn, did divide and make partition of said land as
follows (viz) "the undersigned after making full examination
of each tract, and putting an estimate on each, we make partition and allotment in the following manner to wit. the
quarter section on which John McAdams lived at his death
being the North West quarter of Joseph Phillips reservation
lying on the East side of Tellico River, estimated at nine
hundred dollars we give and grant under said decree said
quarter to Sebba McAdams, now Sebba Lynn and Sarah McAdams
& make the river the dividing line. Sebba to have eighty
acres more or less on the West side of the river. Sarah
to have the East side, eighty acres, more or less- We give

to John McAdams eighty seven acres in the north of the south
West quarter of section nine. township third, Range third,
East of the Meredian divided by an East and West line across
said quarter, the whole of said quarter being estimated at
Eight hundred dollars, we give to Isaac McAdams the balance
of the said quarter section, being seventy three acres, the
south part of said quarter valued at three hundred and sixty
five dollars We also give to the said Isaac McAdams forty
acres, the North West Corner of the South West Fractional
quarter of Section two, Fractional Township third, south
Range five, East of the Basis line, Ocoee district Polk County
worth one hundred dollars. We give to Robert McAdams one
hundred & sixty acres worth two hundred dollars, the south
East quarter of (P-262) Section thirteen, township third,
Range third, the North East quarter of Section twenty two.
Township third, Range third, East, one hundred and fifty five
acres worth one hundred and fifty dollars. Also the West
half of the south West quarter of Section fourteen third
township, third Range East, worth fifty dollars, lying in the
neighborhood of Tellico Plains, Monroe County. We give to
William Coker and wife Miria Coker formerly Miria McAdams, in
right of his wife the said Miria, Eighty Acres, West half of
the south East quarter of Section thirty Six. Fractional
Township, Second North, Range first, East of the basis line
Ocoee District, worth one hundred dollars, also the North East
Corner of the south quarter of Section fifteen, Township
first Range first Worth Sixty dollars. Also the North East
Corner of the North West quarter of Section Ten, Township
first, Range first, Range first, East all in the County of
Bradley containing forty acres worth seventy dollars, also
forty acres in the County of Polk in the North East Corner
of the South East quarter of Section third, Fractional township three Range five East of the Basis line Polk County, worth
one hundred and Twenty six dollars - making the partition as
equal as seems to us reasonable and in making the partition
equal we say that Lyas Lynn & wife pay to Robert McAdams
fourteen dollars, Sarah McAdams pay Robert fourteen dollars,
and Isaac McAdams pay to the said Robert eight dollars,
making the said Robert's portion worth four hundred and
thirty six dollars, that Isaac McAdams pay William Coker &
wife twenty dollars and the said Isaac pay John McAdams one
dollar, making the above named eleven tracts of land equal
(P-263) between the said heirs as named in said decree,
signed, William Bayless, Nicholas S. Peck and James Vaughn,
and sworn to before N.J. Spilman, Exq. and the said report
being unexcepted to is in all things confirmed and the Chancellor is pleased to order and decree and does order and decree that the title to the above described lands be vested
in each in severally according to the report of the Commissioners, and that they and their respective heirs each hold and
have the respective lots of land as laid off and alloted to
them by the commissioners aforesaid, and that they no longer
hold as joint tenants but that each have an indefrasable in-
heritance in fee simple in the respective pieces of land alloted to them; and it is further ordered and decreed by the

Chancellor that the costs of this cause be paid by the Complainants and Respondent in equal proportion, all being interested in the partition of the lands for which execution may issue as at law, and the Commissioners are allowed each two dollars per diem and that this decree be registered in the Register's office of Monroe, Polk, & Bradley Counties.

Jesse C. Moore   )
    vs   )
Silas M. Wann   )
Joseph Cookson   )
David Melton &   )
James Johnston   )

    This case coming on for hearing this 23rd day of March 1842 before the Hon. Thos. L. Williams, Chancellor presiding upon the Bill, amended Bill, answers, Replication and proofs; and the case having been maturely considered; Because it appears satisfactorily to the Court that Complainant is not entitled to relief, it is ordered, adjudged & (P-264) decreed that Complainants Bill be dismissed, and that Complainant pay the costs of said cause for which let execution issue.

    From which decision Complainant prays an appeal to the next term of the Supreme Court to be held at the Court house in Knoxville, on the 1st Monday of July next; which appeal is granted to him without the requirement of bond and security for said appeal.

Mary C. Jones   )
    vs   )   Final Decree:
Calvin T. Jones)

    Be it remembered that on this 23rd day of March 1842 the above cause came on to be finally heard and determined before the Hon. Thomas L. Williams Chancellor presiding at Madisonville, on Bill, publication, pro- Confesso and proofs, and because it appears to the court that defendant had wilfully and maliciously deserted and abandoned the petitioner more than two years before the filing of her said bill and that during all the time from thence up he has continued to absent himself and remain separate and apart from his said wife, the petitioner. The Chancellor is therefore pleased to order and decree and does order and decree that the bonds of matrimoney now subsisting between the petitioner and her husband the respondent be dissolved and annulled and that the said Mary C. Jones be restored to all the rights and priviledges of a feme sole, & that the Complainant pay the costs of this cause for which Execution may issue as at law and have execution over against Respt. for the same.
(P-265)

John Rogers   )
    vs   )
Francis A. Patten)

Be it remembered that on this 23rd day of March
1842 this cause came on before the Hon. Thomas L. Williams,
Chancellor, presiding at Madisonville on Bill answer & pro
Confesso as to Jacob H. Brown And it appearing to the Chancellor that Complainants and the respondents were partners
in the purchase and sale of Clocks, and that each were to receive an Equal share of the profits after defraying all expenses, and that Twenty one dollars per month was to be paid
to Complainant and a like sum to respondent Brown after defraying the other expenses incident to the purchase & sale of
said Clocks, during the time they should be engaged in the
selling the Clocks & collecting the money. The Chancellor
is therefore pleased to order an account and ascertain the
number of Clocks furnished to Complainant and respondent
Brown and at what price that he ascertain what number of the
Clocks were accounted for to Respondent Patton & if they did
not, what were said Clocks worth at a fair price Let him ascertain the amount of the Expense of the sale of said Clocks
& the length of time that Rogers & Brown were Engaged in the
sale thereof. The amount of money which they accounted for
to Patton. The amount of the monthly pay which either Rogers
or Brown or both were entitled to under said partnership and
that he strike a balance and report to next Court.

William Hale   )
    vs   )
Eliza White, Admx.   )

        By consent of the parties by their Sols. this case
is remanded to the rules for taking testimony.
(P-266)

Caswell Torbett &   )
Others heirs &c   )
of J. Torbett, decd.   )
    vs   )
John Hall & Others   )

        On affidavit of Respts John Hall this case is re-
manded to the rules for taking testimony - and said Respt. is
allowed to take the deposition of his co-defendant Robert Mc-
Reynolds subject to all legal exceptions. And it is ordered
that said Respt. Hall pay the costs of this Term.

Charles Kelsoe &   )
James Pursley   )
    vs   )
John Hall   )

        This case is dismissed for want of prosecution at
the costs of the Complainants for which execution may issue.

William White and   )
Other Complts.   )
        vs   )
John F. Gillespy, Respt.)

Be it remembered that on this 22nd day of March 1842 this cause came on to be finally heard and determined before the Hon. Thomas L. Williams, Chancellor presiding at Madisonville on Bill, answers, Replication and proof, and the matters & things therein contained being seen & considered the Chancellor is pleased to order and decree and does order and decree, because the equities of Bill are devised by the answers and not made out by the proof, that the Complainants Bill be dismissed, and that they pay the costs of this cause for which execution may issue as at law.
(P-267)

Fannie Grimmet	)	
vs	)	Petition for
Hannah Grimmet	)	Dower.
and Others	)	

Be it remembered that on this 22nd day of March 1842, this cause came on to be heard and determined on petition and pro- confesso, and it appearing that Samuel Grimmet, late of Monroe County departed this life leaving the petitioner, his widow, that at his death he was seized and possessed of Eighty acres of land in said County being the land on which he the said Grimmet died, And it further appearing that the said petitioner was entitled to have dower out of the said Eighty acres of land; the Chancellor is therefore pleased to order and decree that the sheriff of said County of Monroe summon a Jury according to the acts of Assembly in such cases provided to go upon the premises and lay off and allot to the petitioner dower out of said Eighty Acres of land, and that he have the report of the said Jury at next Term, of this Court, with a return of his proceedings thereon.

Jane C. Douglass, Complainant
            vs
Harriet Hogshead & Others,
Respondents.

Be it remembered that on this the 22nd day of March 1842, this cause came on to be finally heard and determined before the Honorable Thomas L. Williams, Chancellor, presiding at Madisonville, on the Report of the Jury summoned by the Sheriff in (P-268) pursuance of the Interlocutory order made at the last Term of this court, and it appearing from said Report that said Jury have allowed the Complt. thirty acres of the quarter section of land on which she resides including the dwelling house &c. situated as follows, towit: - Beginning on the quarter section line forty poles East of the South West Corner of said quarter section: thence running North sixty poles; thence East eighty poles, thence south sixty poles, to the quarter section line thence West with said line to the beginning; also that she be allowed a tract of land supposed to be one hundred acres known by the name of the Murray tract; also that she be allowed thirty acres of the quarter section, lying West of said Murray tract, as follows- Beginning at the North East Corner of said quarter,

thence running West thirty poles, thence south one hundred
and sixty poles, thence East thirty poles to the south East
Corner of said quarter, thence North one hundred and sixty
poles to the beginning, with all the appurtenances thereto
belonging- signed James Witten, Thomas Vernon, John Lotspeich,
Alexander Biggs and Charles Owens and the said report being
unexcepted to, is in all things confirmed, and it is ordered,
adjudged and decreed by the Chancellor that the said Jane C.
Douglass have the land and appurtenances thereto during her
natural life for her dower out of the seven hundred and forty
acres of land of which her husband the said Jonathan died
seized and possed. It is further ordered and decreed by the
Chancellor that the Complainant pay the costs of this cause,
(P-269) and that the jury be allowed the sum of two dollars
each, and that the sheriff be allowed the sum of five dollars
for his services in the premises and that execution issue
therefor as at law.

Queener, Ward & Inley   )
        vs   )
Geo. W. & John C. Queener   )

        This case having been Compromised by the parties
as is admitted by their solicitor at their respective costs;
it is ordered that the said case be stricken from the docket,
and that each party pay their own costs for which let
execution issue as at law.

Wilson & Hatten   )
        vs   )
Thomas Latimore   )

        This case is remanded to the rules, as an affidavit
of the Complainants.

State of Tennessee	State of Tenn.
by L. Frazier atty gen	by Atty. Gen.
vs	vs
Joseph Routh & Others	G. Morgan
	& F.G. Gregor

State of Tennessee   )
        vs   )
McCaslin & F.H. Gregory   )

        In these cases five months are allowed Respondents
to file their answers so as not to delay their trial.

Grady & Herbert.	Hyatt, McBurney & Co.
vs	vs
McReynalds &	McReynolds,
Uptons	Upton, & Grady.

Beach, Power & Bozee   )   H.W. Conner & Co.
        vs   )   vs
McReynolds, Upton   )   McReynolds
& Grady   )   Upton, et als

(P-270)   In the four last stated cases two months are allowed Respondents to answer, so as not to delay.

P.B. Anderson   )
        vs   )
J. McKinn Jr. & Son   )

  This case coming on to be heard on the Bill, on a
motion to dissolve the Injunction, after argument of Counsel
the motion was overruled.

Barckley McGhee   )
Joseph J. Walker   )
& wife Rachel   )
and Jane McGhee   )
        vs   )
John M. McGhee   )
Nancy McGhee   )
& John McGhee   )
Guardian &c   )

  This cause coming on to be heard this 22nd day of
March 1842 before the Hon. Thomas L. Williams, Chancellor &c
upon the bill of Complt. and answers of Respondents and it
appearing to the satisfaction of the Court that Alexander
McGhee had died intestate seized and possessed of a large
real Estate in the Counties of Blount and Monroe and leaving
and leaving a widow Nancy McGhee and Barckley McGhee Rachel
Walker and Jane McGhee heirs at law of full age and John,
Thomas Lyles, & Mary Jones McGhee minor heirs, of whom John
McGhee is the regularly appointed guardian, and it also
appearing that said intestate at his death was jointly possessed as tenant in Common with said John McGhee of a large
real estate, and it also, appearing to the satisfaction, of
the Chancellor that it is necessary and proper and to the
advantage of the parties in interest that partition Should
be made between said John McGhee and the heirs at law of
said intestate and between the respective heirs of said intestate so that each may hold is severalty and to assign and
lay off dower in said lands to said to said widow Nancy Mc-
Ghee, It has therefore pleased the   (P-271) Chancellor
to order and decree that Robert Wear Arthur H. Henley, S.S.
Glenn, John P. Hardin, and John B. Tipton are appointed
surveyors, be and they are hereby appointed Commissioners
by and with the assent of all the parties in interest, to
make partetion of the real estate mentioned in the pleadings
between the parties, and it has pleased the Chancellor further to order and decree that said Commissioners first proceed to partition & divide the following lands described in

the pleadings as owned and possessed jointly by John McGhee
and said intestate, to wit, one tract containing 498½ acres
and twelve poles granted to Barcklay McGhee the elder by
Grant No. 813 Dated the 28th of September 1809 also one
tract containing 49 acres, lying between Joseph Tedfords
survey and Barckley McGhee's survey: Also one tract known as
the cup tract, lying on the waters of Crooked Creek Containing about three hundred acres all of which are in the County
of Blount. Also the following tracts lying in the County of
Monroe, Hiwassee District one tract containing 151 Acres
Conveyed to M.W. McGhee by the old Bark of Choto, a Cherokee,
by deed dated the 2nd day of June 1823; also the moiety of a
tract of 489 Acres Conveyed by the heirs of the old Bark of
Choto to John & Matthew W. McGhee, by deed dated the 10th of
December 1825 three fourths of which belongs to said John and
one fourth to the heirs of said intestate the above deeds
covering the lands known as the Barks reservation, also jointly one tract of 640 acres known as Andrew Taylor's reservation,
and designated as such on the map of the Hiwassee District;
also a tract of 95 Acres granted to M.W. McGhee by Grant
dated the 15th of August 1827, No. 549;   (P-272)   Also a
tract of 160 Acres granted to M.W. McGhee by Grant No. 1857
dated 26th of October 1830, Also a tract of 80 acres granted
to M.W. McGhee by Grant No. 492 dated the 5th of July 1827,
also a tract of 640 acres, granted to M.W. McGhee by Grant
No. 1844 dated 26th of October 1830, also a tract of 80 acres
granted to M.G. McGhee by Grant No. 1859, dated 26th of
October 1830; also a tract of 84 acres, granted to M.W. Mc-
Ghee by Grant No. 1850, dated 26th October 1830, also a tract
of 80 acres Granted to M.W. McGhee by Grant No. 1851, dated
26th Oct. 1830, also a tract of 120 acres granted to M.W.
McGhee by Grant No. 1852, dated 26th of October 1830, also
a tract of 80 acres Granted to M.W. McGhee by Grant No. 1853,
dated 26th of October 1830, also a tract of 320 acres Granted
to M.W. McGhee by Grant No. 1845, dated 26th Oct. 1830, also
a tract of 80 acres granted to M.W. McGhee by Grant No. 1846,
dated 26th October 1830, also a tract of 160 acres granted
to M.W. McGhee by Grant No. 1847, dated the 26th October 1830,
also a tract of 208 acres Granted to M.W. McGhee by Grant No.
148, dated 26th October 1830, also a tract 339 acres granted
to M.W. McGhee by Grant No. 1849, dated 26th of October 1830,
also a tract of 40 acres granted to M.W. McGhee by Grant No.
1854, dated 26th of October 1830, also a tract of 160 acres
granted to M.W. McGhee by Grant No. 1855 dated 26th of
October 1830, Also a tract of 160 Acres Granted to M.W. McGhee
by Grant No. 1856 dated 26th of October 1830, also a tract
of 160 acres   (P-273)   granted to M.W. McGhee by Grant No.
1858 dated 26th of October 1830, also a tract of 158½ acres
granted to M.W. McGhee by Grant No. 1869, dated 26th Oct. 1830,
also a tract of 44 acres Granted to M.W. McGhee by Grant No.
552, dated 15th of Aug. 1827, also a tract of 160 acres granted to M.W. McGhee by Grant No. 493 dated 5th July 1827, also
a tract of 160 acres granted to M.W. McGhee by Grant No. 2125;
dated 9th July 1831, and it further appearing to the Court
that the widow of said intestate Nancy McGhee is entitled to

Dower in all the lands of which Said Intestate died seized
and possessed and it further appearing that said Respt. Nancy
had Elicited in her answer to take her dower in the tracts
of lands described in the bill as follows (viz) one tract
containing 472 acres, two roads & 4 chains, One tract containing 564 Acres 2 Roads and 7 Chains, also a tract containing 437 Acres & 7 Chains also a tract Containing 639
Acres 1 Road & 12 poles lying adjoining being the same where-
on said Respdt. Nancy now resides so as to include the Mansion
house. It has therefore pleased the Chancellor to order, adjudge and decree that said Commissioners proceed and assign
to said widow, her dower in the lands so elicited so as to
make her interest equal to one third of the Real Estate of
which said intestate so died seized and possessed . And it
further appearing that said intestate was seized and possessed
of the following other described tracts of land and Town lots
in the County of Blount (viz) lots No. 69 & 76 in the Town
of Maryville and designated as such in the plan of said Town
embraced in a deed from John & Matthew W. McGhee to said intestate bearing date the 27th June 1822 also, a tract or
pacel of land Containing 48 acres   (P-274)   1 Road & 16
poles granted by the State of Tennessee to Barckley McGhee
the Elder by Grant No. 809 and devised by the granter to
Mathew W. McGhee and by him to said intestate, also a town
lot in the town of Louisville containing one acre Conveyed to
said intestate by John Gillespy by deed dated 30th of January
1837. Also the following lots in the Town of Maryville and
designated as lots No. 19,20,21,22,23,24,25,26,27,28,29,30 &
73 in the plan of said town also a tract of land known as the
Torbett place containing Containing, about 225 acres Conveyed to said intestate by deed from Nathaniel Torbett bearing
date the 16th of January 1829. The Chancellor is further
pleased to order, adjudge & decree that said commissioners
after having made partetions of the lands jointly held by said
John McGhee & said intestate and after having assigned to the
said widow of said intestate her dower shall proceed to partition and divide the residue of the lands herein mentioned
among the heirs at law of said intestate setting apart to
each an Equal portion in severalty according to quality and
value and that they report thereof to the next term of this
Court.

Gideon Morgan   )
      vs   )
A. Bacum & S. Jarnagin   )

          On motion of Respondent A. Bacum by his solicitor
and it appearing to the Chancellor that the dissolutions of
the Injunction in this cause an Error was committed in entering the decree against Complainant, and it appearing from
the papers on file in this case, that the amount of Respondents A. Bacum's Judgment as at law was two hundred & thirty
six dollars and six cents, rendered on the 17th of May 1841
(P-275)   And the Decree in this Court assuming through mistake that said judgment was for but the sum of $227.91½

making an error of eight dollars and fifteen Cents against Respt. Bacum. The Chancellor is therefore pleased to order that the said Decree be corrected, and that the said Bacum have execution against the said Morgan and his security Parker Hood for the sum of Eight dollars and fifteen cents with interest from the 17th May 1841 till paid.

March 23, 1842

Cowan, Dickenson & Co.   )
          vs   )
R.D. Blackstone &   )
    - Inman.   )

Motion to set aside the sale of property of the Deft. R.D. Blackstone levied on to satisfy the debt of Complts, and sold under an order of the last Term of this Court.

Upon the affidavits of John H. Crozier and John McGhee presented on this motion. Because it appears to the satisfaction of the Court that the sale made by the sheriff of McMinn County of the two Jackasses levied on by him as the property of the Defendant R.D. Blackstone was fraudulent and void, and in violation of the rights of the parties in this cause, and it also appearing that notice has been served by the Complainants on two of the purchasers, William Lowry and Erby Boyd of one of said Jackasses that said sale was illegal & void. It is therefore ordered by the court that said sale be set aside and for nothing held; and it is further ordered by the Chancellor that the Clerk and Master of this Court issue an order to the purchasers William Lowry, Erby Boyd (P-276) and James Vaughn of the two Jackasses aforesaid forthwith to deliver the same into the possession of the Clerk and Master of the Chancery Court at Madisonville, Monroe County, and it is also ordered by the court that the Bonds given by the aforesaid purchasers for the purchase money be cancelled; and it is also further ordered that the Clerk and Master of this court expose the aforesaid two Jackasses to public sale at the Court house door in the town of Madisonville, Monroe County giving twenty days notice thereof, on a credit of six months; the purchaser giving bond & security therefor; and that a copy of this order be served upon the aforesaid purchasers.

Isaac A. Miller &   )
N.B. Swan   )
          vs   )
D.M. Harden   )

This cause coming on to be heard and determined on the Bill & Pro- Confesso as to Respt. for the matters & things therein contained being seen and understood and it appearing that complainants and the Respt. were partners in merchandise and that the Complts made large advances to Respt, which are unaccounted for, The Chancellor is therefore pleased to order and decree and does order & decree that an

account be taken by the Clerk & Master of this court in which
he is directed to ascertain the advances made by either of
the parties the amount of the profits of the concern, what
debts are yet due from the partnership, the amount of payments
made to either of the partners, and on what account- What
there is yet remaining on hands, and in   (P-277)   whose
possession of the effects of said partnership, and that he
report to the next Court, with the balance struck.

John Blair admr.   )
        vs   )
Creditors & heirs of   )
Joseph Scates decd   )

       This cause coming on upon the Report of the Clerk
& Master and because it appears from said Report that said
Joseph Scates was the owner, at his death of 80 acres of
land on Paint Rock Creek in the County of Roane, and it also
appearing that it will require a portion of the real estate
of the said Joseph, deceased to pay the debts of the said
estate; and it further appearing that the above named land
can be sold with the least injury to those interested in
said estate. The Chancellor is pleased to order and decree,
that the Clerk and Master of this Court sell said land in
the Town of Philadelphia, Monroe County, on a Credit of six
months, first giving forty days notice in some newspaper
published in Athens, McMinn County, of the time & place of
sale and make report to next Court.

M.M. & G.M. Hix   )
        vs   )
Heirs of C. & C.R. Hix   )

       Be it remembered that on this 23rd day of March
1842 this cause came on to be heard & determined upon the
Hon. Thomas L. Williams, Chancellor, on the petition and
pro- Confesso and it appearing to the Chancellor   (P-278)
that Charles Hix had in the year 1836 departed this life,
leaving the following heirs, to wit. the Complainants and
Albert G. Hix, Charles R. Hix, Narcissa Hix, Elizabeth C.
Hix and Wesly Hix his heirs at law; that the said Charles
Hix at his death was seized and possessed in his own right
of the following real estate, which decended to his heirs at
law aforesaid, to wit, One hundred and sixty acres of land
in the Hiwassee District, second range East of the Meredian,
third township, twenty ninth section & the south West quarter
of said section, and one other tract of one hundred and sixty acres situate in the District aforesaid second Range,
East of the Meridian, third Township, twenty ninth section,
beginning at the North West corner, also one hundred & sixty
acres in the same district second Range East of the Meridian,
Third Township, thirteenth section, and the south West
quarter of said section, also forty acres situated in the
thirteenth section third Township, Range second, East, and

being the southeast quarter of said section; that the said lands are as yet undivided, except ninety acres of one of the 160 acre tracts which was given by the said Charles Hix in his lifetime to the said Albert G. Hix, as his part of his father's real estate, and it further appearing that Charles R. Hix since the demise of his ancestor Charles Hix had departed this life intestate leaving Eliza E. and Wesley J. Hix his heirs who are entitled in right of their (P-279) father Charles R. Hix to be distributive share of the said Charles Hix real estate, and also that Albert G. Hix had departed this life leaving Sarah A. and Cynthia M. Hix his children and heirs at law, to all of whom guardians have been appointed and it further appearing that the Complts had been regularly appointed administrators of Charles R. Hix, and that the estate of the said Charles R. Hix, deceased, is not of value sufficient to pay the debts of said estate The Chancellor is therefore pleased to order & decree and does order and decree that John Scruggs, John Griffith and John Coltharp be appointed commissioners to go upon the premises and make petition of the real estate, of the said Charles Hix deceased, among the heirs of the said Charles and their representatives having regard to the land given to Albert G. Hix, by his father the said Charles Hix, and the Chancellor further orders and decrees that the Clerk and Master of this Court take an account of the personal estate of the estate of Charles R. Hix, deceased, and ascertain the amount thereof; And the amount of the indebtedness of said estate, and report the same to next court.

William Upton   )
     vs   )
Thomas J. Caldwell &   )
Samuel P. Hale &   )
Thos. L. Hoyl   )

On this 23rd day of March 1842, came on this cause for final hearing before the Hon. Thomas L. Williams, Chancellor &c. Upon the Bill, answers, Replication & proof (P-280) and Report of the Clerk & Master, which is not excepted to, and because it appears to the court from the proofs that Complts Thomas J. Caldwell and Samuel P. Hoyl are jointly liable to pay to Respt Thomas L. Hoyl the amount of his judgment, It is ordered, adjudged and decreed by the Court that said Bill as to him be dismissed. And it appearing to the satisfaction of the Court from the Report of the Clerk and Master that Respondent Samuel P. Hale had advanced to the firm the sum of $1254.22 Cents over and above what he had received from said firm, it is ordered adjudged and decreed by the Court, that Respondent Samuel P. Hale, recover of William Upton the Complt. the sum of $418.47½ cents the one third of said sum and that Samuel P. Hale recover of the said Thomas J. Caldwell the sum of $418.47½ cents, the one third of said sum, and it further appearing to the satisfaction of the Court from the Report of the Clerk & Master that Respondent Thomas J. Caldwell had received from said firm the sum of

$1646.75 cents over and above what he had advanced to said
firm, and that William Upton the Complt had received from
said firm the sum of $62,12½ ¢ over and beyond what he had
advanced to said firm. It is ordered, adjudged and decreed
by the Court that William Upton recover off of the said
Thomas J. Caldwell the sum of $569.62 the one third of the
receipts by them over and beyond their advances, and that
said Samuel P. Hale recover off of the said Thomas J. Caldwell the sum of $569.62 the one third for all which execution
may issue. And it is further ordered, adjudged   (P-281)
and decreed that William Upton, Samuel P. Hale and Thomas
J. Caldwell pay the costs of this cause that have not heretofore been decreed to be paid by Complt.

John Henderson adm. &c   )
            vs   )
Joseph R. Henderson   )

        On this 23rd day of March 1842 came on the above
cause before the Hon. Thomas L. Williams, Chancellor &c. &
because it appears to the Court that it is necessary to take
and state and account in this cause By consent of parties
it is ordered by the Court that the Clerk and Master proceed
to take and state an account, and ascertain first, what
amount of assets from every source came to the hands of Respondent; or which by reasonable diligence might have come to
his hands, belonging to the estate of Andrew Henderson, decd.

        Secondly - What amount of debts are due and owing
by the said Andrew at the time of his death.

        Thirdly - What amount has been disbursed by Res-
pondent, in a due Course of administration, and to whom paid-
including necessary expenses and costs incurred in the execution of his trust, and on what account.

        Bourthly - What of the real estate of the said
Andrew has not been sold under the will.

        Fifthly - What amount is now in the hands   (P-282)
of said Respondent, belonging to said estate, and what amount of debts is owing to Respt. that belongs to said estate;
by whom owing and how is the same secured and report to the
next Term of this court.

W.R. Utter   )
    vs   )
D.W. McReynolds   )
and Others   )

        By leave of court Complt. files his amended Bill;
and by consent Respts are allowed two months to answer, so
as not to delay.

```
W.C. Baldwin          )      McBrides
and Others            )         vs
     vs               )      Grady, McReynolds
Grady, McReynolds &   )        et al.
Others                )
```

In the above two last stated cases two months are allowed Respts in which to file their answers, so as not to delay.

```
J.M. Greenway     )
      vs          )
John Hooper       )
```

The deft who had been arrested on a Ca. Sa. appeared and presented a schedule of his property and took the oath presented by act of assembly whereupon he was discharged. And it is ordered that the Sheriff proceed to sell the property embraced in said schedule, so far as the same is subject to execution sale.

Court adjourned till Court in Course.

Thomas L. Williams.

(P-283)   Monday September 19, 1842

          Be it remembered that on this the 19th day of
September 1842, at a Court of Chancery began and held at the
Court house in Madisonville there was present the Hon.
Thomas L. Williams, Chancellor &c.

Orvill Rice   )
     vs   )
Samuel G. Jameson   )
& J.B. Fitzgerald   )

          Two months are allowed Respt. Jameson to file
his answer, so as not to delay hearing.

Barckley McGhee   )
Jane McGhee   )
J.J. Walker & Wife   )
& others   )
        vs   )
Nancy McGhee &   )
Others, heirs of   )
Alex. McGhee, dec.   )

          By consent of the parties by their solicitors the
death of Complt. J.J. Walker is suggested - and in like
manner the death of Respt. Thos. Lyles McGhee is suggested
which is admitted.

Saml. Bell   )
     vs   )
Enoch Blackburn   )
Saml Henry & Others   )

          Complt is allowed to amend his bill so as to
make Mary Upton & her husband N.B. Upton, Respondents.

William Hale   )
     vs   )
Eliza White, Exr.   )

          This case coming on to be heard on this the 19 day
of Sept. 1842, on the Bill, and answer- the case having been
regularly set for hearing by Respts Sol. It is ordered and
decreed by the court that Complts Bill be dismissed, the Injunction (P-284) dissolved as to the ninety six dollars
for which it was heretofore retained; that Respt recover of
Complt and Joseph Johnston his security in the Injunction
Bond the sum of ninety six dollars with interest from the 22
nd day of Sept. 1841 till paid.

Robert Frazier   )
Ann Blackwell   )
J.E.S. Blackwell &   )
Adaline A. Blackwell   )
        vs   )

Julius W. Blackwell   )
John McKinn Jr. & son   )

On motion of Complts sol. the death of Ann Blackwell one of the Complts is suggested.

John Beene   )
    vs   )
L. Lea Entry Taker &c.   )

This cause coming on to be heard on this the 19th Sept. 1842 on the Bill and answers and proofs and having been duly Considered; It is ordered that Complainants Bill be dismissed and that Complainant pay the costs of this cause, for which let execution issue.

From which decree Complainant prayed an appeal to the next Term of the Supreme Court to be held at Knoxville Tenn. which appeal is granted on Complainants entering into bond with security as required by law.
(P-285)

Lewis Mowery   )
    vs   )
Luke Lea   )

This case coming on to be heard on this the 19th day of September 1842 on the Bill, answers Replication and proof, and the case having been by the Court fully considered It is ordered adjudged and decreed that complainants Bill be dismissed and that Complts pay the costs of said cause for which let execution issue.

From which decree Complt. prayed an appeal to the next Term of the Supreme Court to be held at Knoxville on the 1St Monday of July next, which appeal is granted on Complts entering into Bond with security according to law.

Jonathan Thomas   )
    vs   )
Johnston Minton   )
and Others   )

By leave of court Jonathan Thomas filed his supplemental Bill against Johnston Minton and Harrington Cole, and subs copies & Injunctions are ordered to issue according to the prayer of said Supplemental Bill on said Thomas giving bond and security for the costs which may accrue.

Caswell Torbett   )
& Others   )
      vs   )
John Hall   )
Robt. McReynolds   )
& Others   )

The parties by their Solicitors waive all exceptions which might be taken as to the Competing of the Hon. Th.

L. Williams Chancellor presiding.

(P-286) Barckley McGhee, Rachel Walker
and Jane McGhee.
                    vs
Nancy McGhee, widow, and
John McGhee and Mary
Jones McGhee, heirs of
Alexander McGhee, John McGhee
in his own right and
as guardian of John McGhee
& Mary Jones McGhee, infants.

        On this 19th day of September, 1842, Came on the
above cause for final hearing before the Hon. Thomas L. Williams Chancellor &c. Upon the Bill of Complainants, the answer of Respondents and the Report of the Commissioners
Appointed at the last term of this court to assign to the
said Nancy McGhee, dower out of the real estate of her late
husband, Alexander McGhee, and also to make partition of the
real estate which was held jointly by the said Alexander Mc-
Ghee & John McGhee, between the heirs at law of the said
Alexander McGhee and the said John McGhee, and also to make
partition among the heirs of the said Alexander McGhee, of
all the real estate which has decended to them from the said
Alexander McGhee, and which report is not excepted to: And
is in the words and figures following.

Barckley McGhee   )
Joseph J. Walker & wife   )
Rachel & Jane McGhee   )
        vs   )
John McGhee, Nancy   )
McGhee, & John   )
McGhee, Guardian   )

        The undersigned having been appointed commissioners
in this case by the honorable Court of Chancery and Two of
them Robert Wear and John B. Tipton, Surveyors, have after
being duly qualified proceeded to the execution of the duties
assigned them in the Decree of said Court of date the 22nd
March 1842 and submit the following as a Report of thier proceedings We have proceeded to the survey of (P-287) lands
held by John McGhee & Alexander McGhee as tenants in common,
and first the tract said to contain 498½ acres and 12 poles,
Granted to Barckley McGhee the elder by Grant No. 813 with
the Contiguous tract of 49 acres lying between Barclay Mc-
Ghees and Joseph Tedfords surveys and consolidating them into one found it to contain 515 acres after throwing off Twenty
four acres which had been given for a compromise with Joseph
Wear, senior from the east end. This we have divided between
John McGhee and the heirs of Alexander McGhee agreeable to
the following boundaries, To wit, That part assigned to the
heirs, Beginning at a small Cedar Bush on the West bank of
Pistol Creek where line No. 19 of the original survey crosses

the same Thence with the lines of said Tract North eighty
seven east, thirty and tenth chains to a stake, then North
two and a half West eight chain to a stake, North fifty
four east, forty six Chain to a post oak by the Gnat Road
North fifty three and a fourth east, thirty six chain to a
stake, North forty nine east, sixty six and three tenth
Chains to a stake by the Branch, South sixty three and a half
West forty five and one tenth chain to a hickory, South sixty
one and a half West, thirty two and five tenth chain to a
Hickory, south thirty seven West, one hundred and twenty
Chain to a Black oak, North thirty seven and a half, West
Twenty four and nine tenth chain to a Post Oak, North Fifty
six and a half West thirty nine chain to a rock, South sixty
nine West, three and two tenth Chain to a Walnut stump south
fifteen West six and five tenth chain to a stake, North fifty
(P-288)   six and a half West three chain to the middle of
Pistol Creek, thence down the middle of the same to a large
White Oak at the head of the spring, thence North Twenty and
a half West three and one tenth chain to the Beginning, containing three hundred and seven acres- The other part of the
said tract, beginning at the same Cedar Bush on the bank of
the Creek, thence South Twenty and a half east, crossing the
Creek, three and one tenth Chain, to a white oak at the spt
spring, thence thence up the middle of the Creek to where the
upper line of the Tedford Track conveyed to John McGhee,
crosses the same, thence with the land of Tedfords North fifty
six and a half West ninety nine and five tenth chain to a
stake, North seventy three and a half West, fifty three
Chain to a stake, Then with Robert Thompson North Ten East
nine and five tenth Chain to a post oak south seventy three
and a half east six chain to a stake, north sixty four and a
half east, eight and three tenth chain to a stake, North
sixty seven and a half east, 10 chain to a stake, North forty three and three fourth east, fourteen & three tenth chain
to a stake, North fifty six & a fourth east. Twenty six and
six tenth Chain to a stake, North thirty six and three fourths West, fifteen and two tenth Chain to a pine stump, North
forty nine and a half east, seven and four tenth chain to a
stake, then with the seminary land & Samuel Pride south
thirty seven and three fourths east, sixty five and one tenth
Chain to a black oak stump, North seventy five east, twelve
and six tenth chain to a stake, Then south Eighty eight three
fourths east fourteen and five tenths Chain to a stake. North
eighty five east Ten and six tenth (P-289) Chain to a stake,
North Eighty seven east fifty Chain to the Beginning containing Two hundred and eight acres to John McGhee- We next proceeded to the survey of the cup tract on Crooked Creek estimated at about Three hundred acres but which on actual survey
proved to contain four hundred and forty seven acres, bounded
as follows to wit, Beginning at a hickory saplin corner with
David Cup, thence with his lines south thirty three west,
eleven and five tenth chain to a Hickory saplin, south thirty
two and a half east, Twenty nine and five tenth Chain to a
stake, thence with the land of the heirs of Wyatt Elliot.

North fifty five and a half East, Ten and five tenth Chains to a Hickory, thence with the same and Martin Rorax South thirty three and a half west, forty Chain to a stake, thence with the land of Rorax South one east twenty two chains to a stake thence with the heirs of Abraham Wallace south eighty nine West forty chain to a stake, then south thirty six and a half West sixteen chain to a large poplar, then south thirty ~~six and a half West sixteen chain to a large poplar, then~~ West one hundred and seventeen Chain to a stake North nineteen West Two and seven tenth chain to a stake South thirty nine and three fourth west Twelve and eight tenth Chain to a large black Oak, Corner to the track originally surveyed for Pates Heirs, thence with the Lines of Dearmond North thirty six and a fourth West fifty five and eight tenth Chain to a stake, North twenty Two West Ten and five tenth Chain to a stake, North thirty five West, twenty one and five tenth Chain to a stake, thence with the lines of Jonathan Wear, North forty one and a half East Seventy and eight tenth Chain to a (P-290)   Spanish Oak Saplin, North thirty five and a fourth east, forty seven and five tenth Chain to a Hickory Saplin, North five West, five and six tenth Chain to a stake North twenty seven and three fourth West, ten Chain to a Black Gum North fifty and a half east Thirty eight and one tenth Chain to a stake, North thirty eight and a fourth east, thirty nine and two tenth Chain to a Hickory saplin then with David Cup North seventy five and three fourths east nineteen and four tenth Chain to a stake thence with same North sixty six and a fourth East twenty nine and six tenth Chain to the beginning-This we have assigned to John McGhee. We next surveyed a tract of land located on Nine Mile, held in joint tenancy but not mentioned in the Decree, being part of a tract of land granted to Barclay McGhee the elder by Grant No. 163 for 612 Acres 2 roads 14 poles, bounded as follows, to wit. Beginning at a black oak the fourth corner of the Original survey and Corner with the Original Surveys of Andrew Jackson and John Ewing thence with Ewings line North sixty one and three fourths West. Eighty four and eight tenths chains to a Stake on the Top of a Hill, thence with the Original Surveys of Scott and McClerkin North fifty and three fourths east ninety nine and six tenths Chain to a stake thence with McClerkin South forty seven and a half east thirty eight and six tenths chains to a stake, south (P-291) seventy three and a fourth east fifty one and four tenth chain to a Stake, thence leaving the old line and running with the land of Saml. Henry South thirty seven West one hundred and eleven Chains to a stake in line No. 3 of the Original survey, thence with the same North Twenty Seven and a half west thirty one Chain to the Beginning Containing two hundred and twenty eight acres, which we have assigned to the heirs of Alexander McGhee Completing the division in the County of Blount between John McGhee and the heirs. We then surveyed the moiety of the old Bark Tract of 489 Acres Conveyed by the Heirs of the Old Bark of Choto to John and Matthew McGhee and have assigned to John McGhee his half of that tract at the lower end of the survey beginning

at a Hackberry on the River Bank three North fifty five east
fifty five Chain to a stake near two Gates on the Unicoy Road,
thence east forty seven and a half Chain to a stake in a line
with the 151 acre survey from Old Bark to M.W. McGhee thence
with the same south fifty one East twenty three Chain to a
stake, thence leaving said line south seventy seven chain to
a stake in a line of the Barks Original survey thence with the
same west fifty six chain to a stake. Then leave the line
of the old Bark's Original survey running so as to include a
tract of ten acres 1 road ten poles decreed to M.W. McGhee
from Samuel Wear on the 25th of November 1834, which we have
added to equalize the division to wit. from (P-292) the
last stake mentioned above, South twenty four West sixteen
and three tenth chain to a stake Thence with the land of
Charles Donohoo Jr. North seventy two west fifty one chain
to a bunch of Hackberries on the Bank of the River. Old
Barks beginning corner, thence up the meanders of the river
fifty nine Chain to the beginning making two hundred and
thirty four acres in The residue of the Tract of 489 acres
we have thrown into the common Stock of the undivided lands
in Citico, which we have proceeded to divide between John
McGhee and the Heirs of Alexander McGhee in the following
manner To wit to John McGhee the lower part of Citico, beginning at a Hackberry on the Bank of the river corner with
the 234 Acre Tract assigned to said John McGhee then with the
same North fifty five East fifty five Chain to a stake near
the two gates on the Unicoy Road thence east forty seven and
five tenth Chain to a stake in the line of the 151 acre survey
from Bark to M.W. McGhee thence with the Heirs North forty
two East eighty five chains to a small locust and Sasafrass,
on the river Bank, thence down the meanders of the river
four hundred & twenty two chain to the beginning. This Division includes part of the Bark reservation part of the Taylor
reservation and twenty two acres of Grant No. 552 for 44 Acres,
Also ninety five acres of Grant No. 549 for ninety six acres
(P-293)   and the whole of Grant 550 for 100 acres the last
of which was held by John and A. McGhee as tenants in Common
though not mentioned in the decree altogether comprising the
amount of five hundred and ninety three acres, (593) we have
assigned to John McGhee the following out lands, to wit One
Tract of Twenty two acres North of Tennessee River, Granted
to M.W. McGhee by Grant No. 552 for 44 acres half of which is
included in the flat land of the lower division of Citico on
the South Side of Tennessee, one tract of eighty acres granted to M.W. McGhee by Grant No. 492, one tract of one hundred
and sixty acres Granted to M.W. McGhee by Grant No. 493, one
tract of one hundred and sixty acres, granted to M.W. McGhee
by Grant No. 1847. One tract of one hundred and thirty acres
granted to M.W. McGhee by Grant No. 1849 for three hundred and
thirty nine acres, two hundred and nine acres of which is
assigned to the heirs. One tract of one hundred and twenty
acres granted to M.W. McGhee by Grant No. 1852. One tract of
eighty acres granted to M.W. McGhee by Grant No. 1853, one
tract of forty acres granted to M.W. McGhee by Grant No.
1854. One tract of one hundred and sixty acres granted to

M.W. McGhee by Grant No. 1855. One tract granted to M.W. McGhee by Grant No. 1856 for one hundred and sixty acres. One tract of one hundred and sixty acres granted to M.W. McGhee by Grant No. 1857. One tract of one hundred and fifty acres Contained in Grant No. 1858 to M.W. McGhee for one hundred and sixty acres of which was added to Samuel Wear's land by a Decree of the Chancery Court, dated 25th November 1834, One tract of land of one hundred and sixty acres Granted to M.W. McGhee (P-294) by Grant No. 1868. One tract of one hundred and sixty acres Granted to M.W. McGhee by Grant No. 2125. One tract of forty acres granted to M.W. McGhee by Grant No. 3265, not included in the Decree. One tract granted to Joseph Milligan for one hundred and sixty acres by Grant No. 2778, Conveyed to John McGhee right in M.W. McGhee, one tract of eighty acres granted to M.W. McGhee by Grant No. 3266 divided 80 acres to each between J. McGhee and the heirs making of the out lands assigned to the lower division two thousand twenty two acres.

Then we assigned to the heirs the upper division of Citico, being part of the Bark and part of the Taylor reservations, Consisting of five hundred & sixty three acres, bounded as follows, beginning at a small locust and sassafras on the River Bank Corner with John McGhee, running south forty two west with the upper line of John McGhee eighty five Chain to stake south fifty one east twenty three chain to a stake, south seventy seven Chain to a stake, west eighteen Chain to a stake, thence leaving McGhees line and running with the lines of the Taylor Reservation south four East twenty four Chain to a stake, North eighty six east eighty Chain to a stake, North four West thirty seven Chain to a stake, North eighty six east one hundred and ninety four Chain to a stake on the bank of the river corner with Gideon Morgan, then down the meanders of the river two hundred and sixty four Chains to the beginning. Of the out land we assign to the upper division of Citico the following to wit One tract of six hundred and forty Acres Granted to M.W. McGhee by Grant No. 1844, also one tract Granted to M.W. McGhee by Grant No. 1845 for three hundred & twenty acres, one tract (P-295) of eighty acres granted to M.W. McGhee by Grant No. 1846 One tract of two hundred and eight acres granted to M.W. McGhee by Grant No. 1848 known as the Goodfields, also one tract of two hundred and nine acres being part of Grant No. 1849 to M.W. McGhee for three hundred & thirty nine acres, One hundred and thirty of which is assigned to the lower division, one tract of eighty four acres Granted to M.W. McGhee by Grant No. 1850, one tract of eighty acres Granted to M.W. McGhee by Grant No. 1851, one tract of eighty acres Granted to M.W. McGhee by Grant No. 1859, one tract of one hundred fifty eight and a half acres Granted to M.W. McGhee by Grant No. 1869. One tract of eighty acres Granted to M.W. McGhee by Grant No. 3266, for one hundred and sixty acres, divided between the upper and lower tracts of the citico general division making $1939\frac{1}{2}$ acres of the upper division - We have assigned the out lands held under the Grants enumerated so

as to afford timber to the Convenience of each tract, taking
into view the facilities for hauling and the outlets they
offer. These lands have been entered apparently for the
timber and are of much the same quality throughout. There
is a balance of 829 Acres in favor of the lower division in
the assignment of these out lands which is made up by giving
eighty five acres more of timbered land to the upper tract
within the reservations than the lower division includes.
The next in order is the widow's dower which we have laid off
within the four tracts of the home place named in the Decree,
having first confered with her and received her assent and
Concurrence which accompanies this report, Beginning at a black
Oak at the great road the fifth Corner of Grant No. 205, thence
with the lines of the same North sixty two east twenty four
and seven tenth Chains to a black oak, North fifty four east
forty nine (P-296) And five tenth to a stake North fifty
two east thirty five Chain to a Hickory Saplin, North forty
three East ninety five and eight Tenth Chains to a Spanish
Oak, South thirty eight, east four chains to a Post Oak.
South forty Seven East Seventy Chain to a Stake Second Corner
to Grant No. 228 thence with the lines of the same South forty
seven East Sixty nine Chain to a Pine, South twenty five East,
Seventy eight & seven tenth Chain to a Pine South three and
four tenths Chain to a Stake South forty six and a fourth
West one hundred and thirty and two tenths Chains to a stake
Corner to Grant No. 230. Thence with the lines of the same
South thirty one west Seventy three Chains to a stake, then
South seventy West ninety five Chains to a small Post Oak at
the great road leading from Maryville to Louisville thence
along the same road to the Beginning, So as to include the
Mansion House, out houses and Stables, Comprising an amount
of 1352 Acres which does not exceed one third of the Real
Estate we now proceed to partition and divide the residue of
the real estate which we have done agreeable to the decree
according to Quality and value. To wit. To Jane McGhee the
residue of the home place After separating the widow's dower,
beginning at a Small Post Oak on the road leading from Maryville to Louisville the third corner of Grant #230 and corner
with the Dower land, thence South Sixty two West ninety four
And five tenth Chains to a small black Oak Corner with Grant
No. 231 thence with the (P-297) lines of the same North
twenty nine West, one hundred and ninety seven and eight
Tenth Chains to a Stake, North forty one East Sixty nine
Chain to a black Oak Corner to Grant No. 205 thence with the
lines of the Same North twelve West, two and three tenth
Chain to a black Oak, North fifty three east, thirty nine
Chain to a black Oak by the road Corner to the dower land on
road leading from Louisville to Maryville, thence with that
road to the post Oak at the beginning making seven hundred
sixty one and a half acres included in this tract. To which
we add lot No. 24 and twenty five in The Town of Maryville
and find that she has to pay Rachel Walker fifty cents. To
Barclay McGhee fifty cents to John McGhee Jun. five dollars
& fifty Cents. To Mary Jones McGhee one dollar - in all $7.50
Cts. which this share pays out to equalize the division To
Barclay McGhee we assign the East end of the Tract near Maryville on the waters of Pistol Creek, Containing three hundred

and seven acres, and the nine mile Tract of two hundred & Twenty eight acres the Courses and distance of which are already set forth in this report, in the first & second divisions between John McGhee and the Heirs: to this we add two lots in the town of Maryville Nos. 69 and 76 and say that Jane McGhee pays to him fifty cents.

To Rachel Walker the widow of Joseph Walker we assign Three lots in the Town of Maryville, Nos. 28,29 & 20 the (P-298) two first on the main street with all the buildings thereon, also one Tract of land near the Town Containing forty eight acres 1 road 4 Chains granted to Barclay McGhee by Grant No. 809 dated 28th September 1809, also a piece or parcel of land containing Two acres 1 road 3 Chains Conveyed by Charles Donohoo to Barclay McGhee Senior by Deed dated 24th January 1816. adjoining the 48 acre Tract and lying on the main road from Maryville to Madisonville not mentioned in the decree and say that Jane McGhee to Rachel Walker fifty cents.

To Thomas L. McGhee we assign one lot of land in the upper division of Citico Consisting of one hundred and sixty one acres bounded as follows,Beginning at a birch on the bank of the river Corner with Mary J. McGhee thence with her division South thirty two and a half West fifty two chains to a forked black oak in the Road, thence south sixty six West, Seventy eight Chains to a Stake, Corner of the Taylor Reservation, thence with the line of the same North eighty six east, One hundred and ninety four Chains to a stake at the Bank of the river, Corner with Gideon Morgan, thence down the meanders of the river one hundred & eighteen chains to the Beginning with the following out lands annexed to wit: One tract of forty nine acres out of the Grant No. 1849, being the south East fractional quarter of section 18 in One (P-299) Tract of one hundred fifty eight & a half acres granted by Grant No. 1869, 5th Range East, 2nd Fractional Township North East fractional quarter of section 18 in One Tract of Two hundred and eight acres Granted by Grant No. 1848, known as Goodfields in one Tract of eighty four Acres, Granted by Grant No. 1850. One Tract of 160 Acres out of Grant No. 1844 being the South West quarter of Section 30, 2nd Fractional Township, range 5th East. One Tract of eighty acres granted by Grant No. 3266 being the East half of the South West quarter of Section 36, 2nd Fractional Township, Range 4th East in.

To Thomas L. McGhee we also assign the tract of land known as the Torbet tract of Two hundred and twenty five acres in Blount County, Conveyed by Nathaniel Torbett to Alexander McGhee by deed dated the 16th January 1829. And we award that he pay to Mary Jones McGhee seventy four dollars & fifty cents.

To Mary J. McGhee we assign a lot of land in the upper division of Citico Containing one hundred and eighty four acres bounded as follows, beginning at a birch on the Bank of the river Corner to Thos. L. McGhee, thence with his

line   South thirty two and a half West fifty two Chains to a
forked black oak in the road, then south sixty six West,
seventy eight Chain to a stake on the range line corner to
Taylor's reservation, thence with the same south four East
thirty seven Chain to a stake South eighty six West, eighteen
Chains to a stake,   (P-300)   then leaving said line North
eighty Chain to a stake, then North twenty five east sixty
three Chain to a small Walnut on the Bank of the River Corner
with John McGhee, Jr. then up the meanders of the river ninety
six Chain to the beginning.

        To this lot we attach the following out lands - One
tract of one hundred and sixty acres part of Grant No. 1849
being the southeast quarter of Section 7, 2nd Frac. Township
Range 5 East One Tract of Eighty Acres Granted by Grant No.
1851 - One Tract of one hundred and sixty acres part of
Grant No. 1844 being the South West quarter of Section 19 2nd
Frac. Township Range 5th East ﹦ one Tract of one Hundred and
sixty acres part of Grant No. 1844 being the North West
Quarter of section 31st 2nd Frac. Township Range 5th East.
We assign also to Mary J. McGhee Two lots in the Town of Maryville Nos. 19 & 30 and say that she receive from Jane McGhee
One Dollar and from Thos. Lyle McGhee seventy four dollars &
fifty Cents To John McGhee Jr. We assign one lot of land in
Citico, bounded as follows, beginning at a small Walnut on
the Bank of the river Corner with Mary J. McGhee, Thence with
her line south twenty five West sixty three Chains to a stake,
then South eighty Chains to a stake in the line of the Taylor
reservation thence with the same south eighty six West sixty
two chain to a stake, North four west twenty (P-301) four
Chain to a stake, Corner to John McGhee senior thence with
his line North seventy seven Chain, North fifty one West,
twenty three Chain to a stake, North fifty two East, eighty
five Chain to a small sassafras and Locust on the river Bank
Corner with John McGhee senior, thence up the meanders of
the river forty nine Chain to the Beginning including Two
hundred and eighteen acres - .

        This lot has the following out lands. One tract
of eighty acres granted by Grant No. 1846, one Tract of one
hundred sixty acres part of Grant No. 1844 being the North
West quarter of section 30, 2nd Frac. Township, Range 5th
East, one Tract of Three hundred and Twenty Acres Granted by
Grant No. 1845 - To John McGhee Jun. we assign the Town lots
Nos. 21,22,23,26,27, and one lot in the Town of Louisville
and say that he receive from Jane McGhee five dollars and
fifty cents. Given under our hands this 6th day of August
1842.

                          Robert Wear   )
                          Alex. H. Henly)
                          S.S. Glen   )   Com.
                          John P. Harden)
                          John B. Tipton)

It is therefore ordered, adjudged and decreed by the Court
that said report be in all things Confirmed that the title
to the tract of land laid off and assigned in said report to

Nancy McGhee, widow of Alexander McGhee (P-302)   be vested
in the said Nancy as her dower for and during her natural life;
That all that portion of lands designated in said report as
having been laid off and assigned to John McGhee Sen, be divested out of the heirs of said Alexander McGhee and be vested in the said John McGhee and his heirs forever: That the
title to all that portion of land alloted to Barclay McGhee
as designated in said report be divested out of the said John
McGhee, Sen, and the heirs of Alexander McGhee and be vested
in the said Barclay McGhee and his heirs forever. That the
title to all that portion of land laid off and assigned to
Rachel Walker formerly Rachel McGhee & Sr. designated in said
report be divested out of John McGhee and the heirs of Alexander McGhee and be vested in the said Rachel Walker and her
heirs forever; that the title to all that portion of the lands
laid off and assigned to Jane McGhee & so designated in said
report be divested out of the said John McGhee Sr. and the
heirs of said Alexander and be vested in the said Jane McGhee
and his heirs forever. That the title to all that portion of
the lands laid off and assigned to John McGhee Jr. and so designated in said report be divested out of the said John Mc-
Ghee Senr. and the heirs of said Alexander and be vested in
the said John McGhee Jr. and his heirs forever, that the title
to all that portion of the lands laid off and assigned to
Mary Jones McGhee and so (P-303)   designated in said report be divested out of the said John McGhee Sr. And the heirs
of said Alexander and be vested in the said Mary Jones McGhee
and heirs forever.

        And it further to the satisfaction of the Court
that Thomas Lyles McGhee one of the heirs of said Alexander
McGhee since the partition of said lands and the report of
the Commissioners, were made had died intestate, leaving Barclay McGhee, Rachel Walker, Jane McGhee, John McGhee Jr. and
Mary Jones McGhee his heirs at law it is therefore ordered,
adjudged & decreed by the Court that the lands alloted to
said Thomas Lyles McGhee, as designated in said report be
vested in said Barclay McGhee, Rachel Walker, Jane McGhee,
John McGhee Jr. and Mary Jones McGhee and their heirs forever.
As tenants in common. It is further ordered that the two surveyors be allowed three dollars per day and the other commissioners two dollars per day each, to be taxed and then
paid one half by John McGhee Sr. in his own right and the
other half by the heirs of Alexander McGhee, deceased, and
the other costs to be divided in the same way.

Pierce B. Anderson   )
        vs   )
John McKinn Jr. & Son.   )

        The death of one of the Defts. John McKinn Jr. is
suggested.

John Rogers   )
 vs   )
F.A. Patton &   )
Jacob Brown   )

   By consent of the parties for the taking of proof,
the order made at last term directing an account to be taken
is continued.

George Schorn   )
  vs   )
Fishers & Rider)

   It appearing to the court that this case is Compromised, at Complts Costs. The Bill is ordered to be dismissed & that Complt pay the Costs for which let execution
issue.   (P-304)

Uriah Kyker   )
 vs   )
John Matlock Exr.   )

   This case coming on for hearing and the affidavit
of Complt. for continuance having been presented; It is ordered that the Clerk and Master report on tomorrow as to the
condition of the legal title to the land in question.

G. Morgan   )
 vs   )
L. Jarnagan &   )
A. Bacum   )

   By consent of Respts Complt is allowed till next
Term for taking testimony.

Gideon Morgan   )
  vs   )
A.H. Henley   )
& Others   )

   By consent of Respondent Complainant is allowed
till next Term for taking testimony.

Thomas J. Caldwell &   )
David Caldwell   )
  vs   )
Jesse Kerr   ) .

   This case coming on to be heard on the Bill Answer
of Respt. and Replication, and it appearing to the Court that
Complts are not entitled to relief; It is ordered that Complainants Bill be dismissed; and that Complainants pay the
Costs, for which let execution issue.

James Vaughn   )
  vs   )
Alexander Hart, adm.   )

This case is by consent Continued as on affidavit of Complt.

Thomas Crutchfield)
vs)
Thomas N. Clark, adm.)

This case is by consent Continued as on special affidavit of Complt, and remanded to the rules.

Robert Campbell)
vs)
Teeners & Others)

This case having been compromised & the costs having been paid, it is ordered to be stricken from the Docket.
(P-305)

Pierce B. Anderson)
vs)
John McKinn Jr. &)
David T. McKinn,)
partners in the)
name of John)
McKinn Jr. & Son.)

This 19th day of September 1842, came on this cause before the Honorable Thomas L. Williams, Chancellor, on a motion to dissolve the injunction on Bill and answer of Defendant David T. McKinn, which were read, heard and understood. It appears to the Chancellor that the equity of the Bill is derived by the answer filed, the Chancellor is therefore pleased to order, adjudge and decree that the injunction heretofore granted in this cause be dissolved, and that defendant David T. McKinn surviving partner of the firm of John McKinn Jr. & Son recover of said Pierce B. Anderson and Onslow G. Murrell his surety in the injunction Bond the sum of Six hundred and sixty dollars, and fifty cents, the Amount of the judgment of the Circuit Court for McMinn County, rendered the December Term thereof 1841, together with the further sum of thirty dollars and twenty seven cents, the interest thereon up to this time, making six hundred and ninety dollars and seventy seven cents, for which an execution may issue, upon said David T. McKinn giving bond with surety to refund if the final decision be against him.

It is ordered by the court that a fine of five dollars be entered against John J. Humphreys, deputy Sheriff of Monroe County, for failing to keep good order during the session of this Court.

(P-306)   By order of the Court James A. Coffin is appointed Clerk and Master of this court for the term of six years from the 20th day of June last, who entered bonds with approved security, which bonds are in the words and figures following, viz - Know all men that we James A. Coffin, Daniel L. Coffin, Guilford Cannon & William Henderson ~~Acknowledge ourselves~~ are held and firmly bound unto James C. Jones Governor in and over the State of Tennessee and his successors in office in

the sum of Ten Thousand dollars, to which payment will and
truly to be made we bind ourselves, and each of our executors
administrators and assign jointly and severally firmly by
these presents. Signed with our names & sealed with our seals
this 19 day September 1842.

The condition of the above obligation is such that
whereas the above bound James A. Coffin hath been appointed
Clerk & Master of the Chancery Court at Madisonville for the
9th Chancery District Composed of the Counties of Monroe &
McMinn in the State of Tennessee and in the Eastern Division
of said State, for the Term of Six Years from the 20th day of
June last; Now if the said James A. Coffin shall truly and
honestly keep the records of said court and discharge the
duties of said office, for the said Term of six years, according to law then the above bond is to be void and of no effect
otherwise to remain in full force and virtue. Given the day
and date above written.

James A. Coffin	(Seal)
Daniel L. Coffin	(Seal)
Guilford Cannon	(Seal)
William Henderson	(Seal)

(P-307)   Know   all men by these present that we James A.
Coffin Daniel L. Coffin, Guilford Cannon & William Henderson
are held and firmly bound unto James C. Jones, Governor in
and over the State of Tennessee and his successors in office,
in the sum of five hundred dollars, to which payment will and
truly to be made we bind ourselves and each of our Executors,
administrators and assigns jointly and severally firmly by
these presents Signed with our names and sealed with our
seals the 19 day of September 1842.

The condition of the above obligation is such that
whereas the said James A. Coffin hath been appointed Clerk &
Master of Chancery for the term of six years from the 20th
day of June last, for the Chancery Court held at Madisonville
in the Eastern Division of Tennessee for the ninth Chancery
District Composed of Monroe & McMinn Counties now if the said
James A. Coffin shall duly collect and pay into the public
treasury all such tax on Causes as shall arise in said Court
of Chancery, at such time and in such manner as is or may be
prescribed by law, then the above obligation to be void, otherwise to be and remain in full force & virtue.

Given the day and date above written.

James A. Coffin	(Seal)
Daniel L. Coffin	(Seal)
Guilford Cannon	(Seal)
William Henderson	(Seal)

(P-308)   Know all men by these presents that we James A.
Coffin, Daniel L. Coffim, Guilford Cannon, & William Henderson
are held and firmly bound unto James C. Jones Governor in &
over the State of Tennessee, and his successors in office, in
the sum of five hundred dollars to which payment will and

truly to be made we bind ourselves and each of Our Executors, Administrators and assigns, jointly and severally firmly by these presents. Signed with our names and sealed with our seals the 19 day of September 1842.

The Condition of the above obligation is such that whereas the said James A. Coffin hath been appointed Clerk & Master of Chancery for the term of six years from the 20 day of June last, for the Chancery Court held at Madisonville in the Eastern Division of Tennessee for the ninth Chancery District Composed of Monroe & McMinn Counties. Now if the said James A. Coffin shall duly collect and pay into the public treasury all such tax on causes as shall arise in said Court of Chancery, at such time and in such manner, as is or may be prescribed by law, then the above obligations to be void, otherwise to be & remain in full force & virtue.

Given the day & date above written.

James A. Coffin	(Seal)
Dan'l L. Coffin	(Seal)
Guilford Cannon	(Seal)
William Henderson	(Seal)

(P-309)

James Stephenson, admr.)
       vs)
Susannah Davis &)
Others, Heirs of J.R.)
Davis, deceased.)

On motion of Susannah Davis one of Defts her Sol. Two months are allowed her for filing her answer.

Court adjourned till tomorrow 8 O'Clock.

Thos. L. Williams

Tuesday Sept. 20, 1842

Court met pursuant to adjournment present the Hon. Thos. L. Williams Chancellor &c.

Robert Frazier and Others)
       vs)
Julius W. Blackburn)
John McKinn Jr. &)
son & Alexander Stowil)

Complts by their Sol filed the bill of reviver to revive this suit so far as the interest of Ann Blackwell was Convenient, in the name of Adeline A. Blackwell who is executrix of said Ann, deceased, and thereupon on agreement of Complainants and defendants by their solicitors it is ordered that said suit so abated by the death of Ann Blackwell be revived, and stand for other proceedings without the necessity of service of process or publication of said bill of revivor, as fully as though process & copies of said bill of revivor were regularly served, or publication thereof made - and by

Consent the death of John McKinn Jr. is suggested, and it is admitted by Complts Sol. that David T. McKinn is the surviving partner of the firm of John McKinn Jr. & Son. (P-310)

James W. Stephenson   (
admr. of John R. Davis   )
Decd.   )
                vs   )
Susanna Davis and   )
Others, heirs at law   )
of John R. Davis, decd.   )
& R.F. Cook & others   )
Creditors of said John   )
R. Davis, decd.   )

      Be it remembered that on this 19th Sept. 1842 this cause came on before the Hon. Thomas L. Williams Chancellor presiding at Madisonville on Bill of Complainant & pro confesso and the matters and things therein contained being seen, The Chancellor is pleased to order and decree and does order and decree that the Clerk & Master of this Court take an account in this cause, that he ascertain the nature and kind & value of the assets of the deceased which have come to the hands of Complainant or that should have come to his hands by due diligence, that he ascertain the amount of the debts owing from said estate & to who, what real Estate descended to the heirs of law of the said John R. Davis and what of said real Estate can be sold with the least injury to the said heirs & that he report to the next court.

William Henderson   )
Adm, of James M.   )
Broyles, decd.   )
                vs   )
Eliza Broyles and   )
heirs at law of   )
said James M.   )
Broyles and   )
Others, Creditors of   )
said intestate   )

      Be it remembered that on the 19th September 1842, this cause coming   (P-311)   on to be heard on the Bill of Complaint & pro- Confesso of respondents before the Hon. Thomas L. Williams, Chancellor presiding at Madisonville and the matters and things therein contained being seen and understood. The Chancellor is pleased to order and decree and does order and decree that the Clerk & Master of this Court take an account in this cause and ascertain the amount and value of the assets belonging to said intestate that have come to the hands of the Complainant or that should have come to his hands by due diligence. What debts are owing by said estate and to whom, what lands if any have descended to any of respondents as heirs at law of the said James M. Broyles, and report to the next term of this Court.

Robert Sneed, Complt.)
   vs   )
Nancy Jane Glass,)
minor heirs of   )
Jesse Glass, decd. &)
her guardian   )
Stephen McCaslin)

   Be it remembered that on this 19th day of Sept 1842
this cause coming on to be finally heard and determined before
the Hon. Thomas L. Williams presiding in Chancery at Madisonville on Bill, answers, Replication & proof, and it appearing
to the Chancellor from the pleadings and proof in the cause
that complainant had purchased of the Father of Nancy Jane
Glass the North West quarter of section seventeen in Township
one, Range two East of the Meredian in the Hiwassee District
for the price of nine (P-312) hundred dollars, which has
been paid, that in Consideration thereof Jesse Glass now deceased had some time previous to June session of the County
Court of Monroe County, 1832, made a deed to the Complainant
for the said quarter section of land, which was at said court
admitted to record and ordered to be registered, that before
registration of said deed the Court House was consumed by
fire and said deed with it, and that the said Jesse Glass had
since departed this life leaving the said Nancy Jane Glass
his only heir at law. It is therefore considered and decreed
by the Court that the title to said Quarter Section of land
be divested out of the said Nancy Jane Glass & her heirs and
vested in the said complainant Robert Sneed & his heirs and
that a copy of this decree be registered in the register's
office of Monroe County, and it is further ordered and decreed
that the Complainant pay the Costs of this cause and that an
execution may issue for the same, as at law and it is further
ordered that Respondent Nancy Jane Glass have six months
after coming of age to except to this decree.

Robert Sneed, Admr &c)
   vs   )
Grimmett & Others   )
heirs at law of   )
 Grimmett, decd.   )
(P-313) and Eli Cleveland)
and Others Creditors)
of said Intestate   )

   Be it remembered that on this 19th Sept. 1842 this
cause Coming on to be heard & determined on the Bill & Pro
Confesso the matters and things therein being seen & understood the Chancellor is pleased to order and decree and does
order and decree that the Clerk & Master of this Court take
an account in this cause, the amount of assets of every kind
& description of the said Grimmett decd. that have come into
the hands of the administrator to be administered, or that
should have come to his hands by due diligence, that he ascertain the amount of indebtedness of said Estate, what lands,
if any, have decended to the defendants as heirs at law of

the decd and that he report to next court his proceedings hereon.

John L. McCarty Exr.   )
of John Walker, decd.   )
        vs   )
Gideon Morgan &   )
R. T. Hanks   )

          The death of Respt. H.T. Hanks is suggested.

McClung, Wallace & Co.)
          vs   )
R.D. Balckstone & Co.)

          Complts by their sol. dismisses their Bill, and
assume the costs for which let execution issue.
(P-314)
Grady and Herbert, Complainants   )
              vs   )
Wm. A. Upton, Thos. L. Upton & David   )
W. McReynolds, Defendants   )

Brach, Power & Bozee, Complts   )
              vs   )
David W. McReynolds, John   )
W. Grady, Wm. A. Upton   )
& Thos. L. Upton, Defendants   )

Hyatt, McBurney & Co. Complts   )
              vs   )
John W. Grady, David W.   )
McReynolds, Wm. A. Upton   )
& Thos. L. Upton, Defendants.   )

H.W. Conner & Co. Complainants   )
              vs   )
John W. Grady, David W.   )
McReynolds, Wm. A. Upton &   )
Thos. L. Upton, Defendants   )

J. & J. McBride & Co. Complainants   )
              vs   )
John W. Grady, David W.   )
McReynolds, Wm. A. Upton &   )
Thos. L. Upton, Defendants   )

R.C. Baldwin & Co. Complainants   )
              vs   )
John W. Grady, David W.   )
McReynolds, Wm. A. Upton &   )
Thos. L. Upton, Defendants   )

William R. Utter, Complainant   )
        vs   )
John W. Grady, David W.   )
McReynolds, Henry Grady   )
Elizabeth Herbert, Wm. A.   )
Upton & Thos. L. Upton, Defts.)

(P#315)   On this 20th day of September 1842, these causes coming on to be heard together by consent of the Complainants, before the Hon. Thomas L. Williams Chancellor &c. on the Bills of the Complainants, judgments pro- confesso against all the defendants, and the inhibits filed in the several causes Because it appears to the satisfaction of the Court that the several Complainants, are entitled to the relief they, pray for; And because it appears further to the Court that the Complainants Henry Grady and Elijah Herbert are the rightful owners of the five negroes, Lewis, Julia Ann and their three Children Caroline, Violet and Herod to indemnify and save harmless the said Complainants as specified in the Mortgage mentioned in the pleadings that the defendants William A. Upton & Thomas L. Upton have the possession of said negroes Wrongfully; and because it appears further to the Court that the said William A. Upton & Thomas L. Upton have the wrongful possession of the other negroes mentioned in Complainants Bill, and that said negroes should be condemned to the satisfaction of the several Claims of the Complainants. It is therefore ordered & decreed by the Court that the said William A. Upton and Thomas L. Upton deliver to the Clerk & Master of this Court the negroes mentioned in the bill of Complainants, to wit, Lewis, Julia Ann, Caroline, Violet, Herod, Jerry, Polly, Almira, Martha, Caswell, Clacy, Angeline and Jim son of Lewis and Julia Ann and (P-316) that the Clerk & Master make sale of said negroes at the Court house door in Madisonville after giving thirty days notice of the time & place of Sale Upon a credit of Six and twelve months taking bond with good & sufficient security for the purchase money -- And because it is not yet known whether the Complainants Henry Grady and Elijah Herbert Will be liable to pay the debt for which the aforesaid slaves, Lewis, Julia Ann, Caroline, Violet & Herod were mortgaged to them . It is ordered by the Court that the proceeds of the Sale of Said Mortgaged Slaves await the further order of this Court and because further it is proper that an account should be taken of the claims of the other Complainants. It is further ordered that the Clerk & Master take & state an account showing the amount due the Complainants respectively and that the Clerk & Master report said accounts and the sales aforesaid to the next Court. It is further ordered that the Defendant D.W. Reynolds surrender to William A. Upton & Thos. L. Upton the note given by them to him as for the purchase money of said negroes.

Caswell Torbett and others)
minor heirs of James   )
Torbett, deceased   )
     vs   )

Robert McReynolds &   )
Maxwell Duncan, admrs   )
of James Torbett, deceased   )
& John Hall and Others   )

   On this 20th day of September 1842 Came on this the
above cause for hearing before the Hon. Thomas L. Williams,
Chancellor &c. (P-317) Upon the Bill of Complainants, the
answers of respondents, the replication and proof and because
it appears to the Court that the negro girl Cynthia had been
given by James Hall to James Torbett & his wife the daughter
of said James and the ancestor of Complts & that it will be
necessary to take an account in the case, it is ordered, adjudged & decreed by the Court that the Clerk and Master of
this court proceed to take and state an account and ascertain
first what is the value of the negro Cynthia in the Bill
mentioned, with her increase together with interest thereon,
and 2nd what is the value of the life estate of Margarett
Hall in said negro with interest thereon and third what is
the value of the hire of said girl Cynthia from the death of
James Torbett, to the death of Margaret Hall, calculating interest thereon from year to year up to the time of taking the
report and further what would be the value of the hire of said
negro from the time she has been in the possession of John
Hall, together with interest thereon, and the Complainants
waive relief as to the taking any further account of the personal estate of James Torbett, deceased, and that he charge
the Respts McReynolds and Duncan as administrators of James
Torbett with the above sums, and that all other points in this
case be reserved until the coming in of said report and that
the question as to the admissibility of the Deed of gift from
David Miller to Margaret Hall and John Hall as evidence and
the effect thereof on the rights of the parties be also reserved.

   And further that the Clerk and Masters ascertain
what advances were made by this (P-318) Administrators of
James Torbett, if any, toward the support and maintenance of
Complts.

Jonathan Thomas   )
  vs   )
Theophilus Smith   )
& Johnson Minton   )

   This cause coming on before the Hon. Thos. L.
Williams, Chancellor, upon the exceptions of Respondent
Minton to the report of Clerk & Master, and because the Court
is not satisfied as to the evidence on which the Clerk &
Master based his report the Court orders that said account
be referred back to the Master to take and state a more perfect account. And because it appears from the evidence in
the cause that said respondent Smith disposed of a note of
hand due the firm of Thomas Smith & Co. for about the Sum of
fifteen hundred dollars, and received for said note a tract
of land in the State of Georgia and took the title in his

own name. And because the Court has been here informed by
the Clerk & Master, that on the taking of the account by
said Clerk & Master in this cause, the said respondent Smith
refused to obey the order of the said Clerk & Master, to answer to interrogatories upon the taking of said account It
is therefore ordered adjudged & decreed by the Court that the
said respondent (P-319)   Theophilus Smith be enjoined from
selling or in any manner disposing of the tract of land aforesaid purchased with the note aforesaid, and that the Clerk &
Master in taking an account examine the parties upon interrogatories upon oath.

Franklin Yoakum admr.   )
of George Yoakum, decd.   )
            vs   )
Mary Yoakum, widow   )
of the said George   )
Yoakum & Henderson   )
Yoakum and Other   )
Heirs at Law of   )
George Yoakum, and   )
Robert Cannon &   )
Others, Creditors of   )
said George Yoakum   )

        Be it remembered that on this 20th day of Sept.
1842, this cause came on to be heard before the Hon. Thomas
L. Williams, Chancellor &c. On the Bill pro Confesso & answers of Mary Yakum when the matters & things being seen and
understood, the Chancellor is pleased to order & decree and
does order & decree that the said Mary Yoakum is entitled to
Dower out of the lands described in Complainants Bill that
the Sheriff of Monroe County summon a jury and go upon the
premises and lay off and allot to the said Mary Yoakum her
said dower of the lands, of which her said husband died seized
and possessed and that the said Sheriff make due return of
his proceedings at the next term of this Court. And it is
further ordered and decreed that the (P-320)   Clerk &
Master take an account in this cause, that in said account he
ascertain the assets which have & should have come to the
hands of the said Complainant and what debts are due from
the estate of said George Yoakum and to whom, what lands have
descended to the said Henderson Yoakum & others heirs at law
of said George Yoakum, and that he report his proceeding to
the next term of this Court.

James W. Lea   )
      vs   )
Robert Wear Adm &c.   )

        Be it remembered that on this 20 day of Sept. 1842
this cause came on to be heard and determined on the bill &
answer before the Hon. Thomas L. Williams Chancellor &c. When
the Chancellor is pleased to order & decree that the Clerk &
Master of this Court take an account of the partnership be-

tween Complainant & respondents, intestate that he ascertain
the amount advanced to the partnership by each of the partners,
the amount paid out by each, and the amount withdrawn from
the firm by each, and that he also ascertain whether there
were any settlement between the said Complainant & his partner E.H. Wear of the matters touching said partnership and if
any what that settlement was ———— and that he   (P-321)
report to the next term of this court.

Hugh E. Martin   )
        vs   )
H. Bacum   )

     Be it remembered that on this 20th day of Sept.
1842 this cause came on to be heard and determined before
the Hon. Thomas L. Williams Chancellor &c. When the Court is
pleased to order & decree that the Clerk & Master take an
account in this cause and ascertain the amount of the debt
due Complainant from respondent and that he report to the
next term of this court &c.

Carter Mayfield, Jesse
Mayfield, Thomas B.
Mayfield, Nancy C.
Mayfield, widow of
William T. Mayfield
David A. Cobb & his
wife, Prissa, Mahalda
Mayfield, James Hill
and his wife Elizabeth
William Mayfield heirs
at law of Jesse Mayfield
decd and Penelope Mayfield
widow of said Jesse deceased.
       vs (Original Bill)
Nancy Mayfield widow
of Pearson Mayfield decd.
Samuel Mayfield, William
Mayfield, Jesse Mayfield,
John Mayfield, James
Mayfield, Standrix Mayfield
Clement Mayfield, Thomas
Mayfield and Pearson
Mayfield, heirs at law
of Pearson Mayfield, deceased
       and
(P-322) Nancy Mayfield & Others
        vs   Cross Bill
Carter Mayfield & Others.

     On this 19th day of September 1842 came on before
the Honorable Thomas L. Williams, Chancellor, the above Causes
for final decree upon interlocutory decree and the report of
the Clerk & Master, and exceptions to said report. After agreement of Counsel, the Chancellor is pleased to order that said

exceptions be disallowed, and that the report be in all things
Confirmed - From said report it appears a fair division of the
Estate, real & personal of Jesse Mayfield deceased had been
made among his heirs and distributes and that defendants to
the Original bill, and Complainants in the Cross Bill, had received their full share in and the Court is further satisfied
that the heirs at law of Jesse Mayfield, deceased, ought to
have conveyed to the Complainants Thomas B. Mayfield & William
Mayfield the title descended to them as heirs, according to
the division made among said heirs, in and to the South West
quarter of Section twenty three, township four, in range
first west of the Meredian the North west quarter of section
twenty six, in same township & range and the North West quarter of section twenty three, in the same township & range
Containing in   (P-323)   all four hundred and eighty acres
lying in McMinn County, Hiwassee District, being the land upon which the said Jesse Mayfield resided at the time of his
death. That these lands, by agreement among the heirs at law
of said Jesse Mayfield and his widow were subject to the en-
tire dower of said Widow and that defendants to the original
Bill were all the heirs of said Jesse Mayfield deceased who
refused to make such Conveyance. The Chancellor is also
satisfied that Complainant in said Cross Bill are not entitled
to any relief prayed by them. Upon the view of these causes
the Chancellor doth order adjudge & decree that said Cross
Bill be dismissed and that the Complainants therein pay the
Costs thereof and that all the right, title and interest in
and to the above described quarter section of land that the
parties in these causes have, be divested out of them, and
be vested in said Thomas B. Mayfield and William Mayfield,
and their heirs forever, subject to the dower of Penelope
Mayfield the widow of said Jesse Mayfield deceased. It is
further ordered and decreed that the defendants in said Original Bill, Nancy Mayfield, Samuel Mayfield, William Mayfield,
Jesse Mayfield and John Mayfield pay the costs of said cause &c.

From which decree the Respondents in the original
Bill & the Complainants in the Cross Bill pray an appeal to
the next term of the Supreme Court to be held in Knoxville on
the first Mon. of July   (P-324)   1843 which to them is
granted upon time giving bond & security according to law and
that they have one month to give said bond.

D.J. Wilson & J. Rowland   )
            vs   )
James Caruthers,   )
W.J. McCatchey and   )
Thos. Caldwell & Others   )

The Demurrer filed by Thomas Caldwell and Wiley J.
McCatchy two of the Respts coming on for argument; And the
Court not being satisfied as to the law in the case, holds
the same under advisement until next Term.

Jesse Kerr   )
    vs   )
Thomas J. Caldwell   )
David Caldwell &   )
Charles Donohoo   )

        The death of Charles Donohoo security for Respts
in the Injunction Bond having been suggested, thereupon came
James Donohoo and Charles Dondohoo into Court by their solicitor G.W. Rowls, and admit that they are the administrators
of said Charles Donohoo, decd. and agree that judgment may
be revived against them without scrie Facias and that Execution may issue, which is done accordingly.

Riley Horn   )
    vs   )
John Copeland.   )

        Be it remembered that at a Chancery Court held at
the Court house in Madisonville on the 20th day of September
1842, this cause came on to be finally heard and determined,
before the   (P-325)   Honorable Thomas L. Williams, Chancellor &c. Upon the Interlocutory Decree, heretofore made in
this cause and upon the Report of the Clerk & Master and it
appearing to the satisfaction of the Court from the report
of the Clerk that Respondent Copeland had advanced to the
Complainant on the 10 of April 1838 the sum of one hundred
and twenty five dollars, the interest on that sum till now
thirty one Dollars eighty seven & one half cents, and that
respondent paid into the entry taker's office of the Ocoee
District for said land mentioned in the Bill the sum of
eighty dollars and seventy five cents and interest on that
sum from 16th November 1838 until now, sixteen dollars and
fifteen cents making in all, the sum of Two hundred and fifty
three dollars seventy seven and one half cents with Interest-
that Complainant has received from Respondent. The Court
therefore pleases to order and Decree, and does order, adjudge
& decree, that the land mentioned in the pleadings viz the
South West quarter of section Twenty seven, in Township and
range two East of the Basis line in the Ocoee District, be
sold to the highest bidder for the satisfaction of the aforesaid sum, by the Clerk & Master of this Court at the Court
house door in the Town of Benton, Polk County, where the said
said land lies, after giving forty days notice of the time
and place of sale in the "Athens Courier" a Newspaper published in Athens, McMinn County. It is ordered that Complainant
have four months in which to deposite with the said Clerk &
Master the said sum Two hundred and fifty three dollars and
seventy seven and a half cents subject to the order of Respt-
And if in said   (P-326)   time he fail to pay the same that
the Clerk & Master proceed to sell as directed.

        It is further ordered that the costs of this cause
be paid out of said sale.

```
Fanny Grimmett        )
    vs                )
Hannah Grimmett       )
& Others heirs at     )
law of Sam.           )
Grimmett, decd.       )
```

Be it remembered that this cause coming on, on this Sept. 20, 1842, to be finally heard & determined before the Hon. Thomas L. Williams on the Bill of Complainant, pro-Confesso and the Report of the Sheriff &c. Which report is in the words and figures following - "The undersigned being unconnected with the parties and entirely disinterested have been summoned and duly sworn to allot and lay off to Fanny Grimmett her dower out of her deceased husbands lands do hereby assign to the said Fanny Grimmett the following described lands, with the improvements thereon, to wit, a tract of land in Monroe County on Sweetwater Creek Containing thirty acres, Commencing at James Taylors Corner on the school land line, thence North with Taylor's line to Martin Low's line, thence thence west with Low's line, thence south to the school land, thence, with the school land to the beginning - being an oblong including the said thirty acres which in our opinion Contains one third of the real estate of which the said Samuel Grimmett died seized & possessed-
(P-327) Signed:

                              B.B. King
                              A. Allen
                              Wm. Lillard
                               Shelly Lee
                              Thomas Laughlin.

Sworn to subscribed   )
the date above   )

It is therefore ordered and adjudged that the Complainant have the land above alloted to her for her dower in the estate of her deceased husband. And the Chancellor is further pleased to order and decree that the Complainant pay the Costs of this suit for which execution may issue as at law.

```
John Henderson adm &c.         )
            vs                 )
Joseph R. Henderson Exr. &c.   )
```

On this 20th day of September 1842 came on the above cause for final hearing upon the Bill of Complainant the answer of Respondent, the Replication and proof and the Report of the Clerk & Master, which is not excepted to, and from which it appears that there is in the hands of Defts the sum of sixty six dollars and eight cents of the assets of the estate of Andrew Henderson, decd. over and beyond what he has disbursed in a due course of administration; and it

farther appearing to the Court that there is also in the
hands of the Respt- two notes executed to him as Executor of
Andrew Henderson, Deceased, by William P.H. McDermott and
Thomas Henderson his security for five hundred and fifty six
dollars and sixty six and two thirds (P-328) Cents, each
being part consideration for the lands sold by Respt. as Executor as aforesaid, belonging to said Estate. It is therefore ordered, adjudged and decreed by the Court that Complt.
recover of the defendant the sum of sixty six dollars and
eight cents as aforesaid; and it is further ordered by the
Court that Respt. on demand by Complt surrender to him the
said two notes on William P.H. McDermott and Thomas Henderson
and that he receive no part of the money due on said notes
and that each party pay half the Costs accrued in this case.

Gideon Morgan   )
    vs   )
James L. Bridges   )

        The 4th exception filed by Complts Sol. to Respt.
answer, the determination of which was postponed until this
Term is sustained; and that Respt is required answer more
fully & explicityly.

Mark M. Hix &   )
Geo. M. Hix   )
    vs   )
The Heirs of C. &   )
C.R. Hix   )

        In this cause the Complts Sol, represents to the
Court that the Decree heretofore rendered in this cause on
the 23rd of March 1842 was erraneously drawn up, and en-
rolled in this, that Eliza E. and Worley J. Hix are named
and described as the heirs of Charles R. Hix when they are
the heirs of Charles Hix mentioned (P-329) in the decree
rendered in this cause as appears from the Bill of Complts-
Therefore it is prayed that the Court orders said Decree to
be amended in this particular and be made to conform to the
Bill and that this amendment & correction be taken as part
of the original decree in this case- It is therefore ordered by the Court that the correction prayed be made in the
former decree.

Richard Swafford &   )
Alfred Swafford Complts   )
    vs   )
Elizabeth Leuter, Guardian   )
Of James B. Leuter &   )
Preston Leuter and   )
Will Bates, Adm. &c.   )

        On this 20th day of Sept. 1842 this cause coming
on to be finally heard and determined upon the Report of the
Clerk & Master and because it appears to the Court that said

report is unexcepted to. It is ordered that said report be in all things confirmed and because it appears from said Report that there is a balance due to the Estate of James L. Leuter deceased, from the said Complainants, of three hundred & sixty two dollars and fifty cents, which sum has been paid into office viz - in Alabama Bank notes $210 - in Tennessee Bank Notes $125 and in Specie $27.50. It is ordered adjudged and decreed by the Court that the Clerk & Master pay the said sum of money over to the administrator of the estate of James L. Leuter decd. (P-330) After first deducting there from the costs of this suit.

The fine of $500 entered against John J. Humphreys D. Sheriff is remitted by the Court.

Gregory F. Hawkins)
    vs)
A.D. Gentry, James)
White, Robt. Daniel)
& John Daniel)

On this 20th day of September 1842 came on the above cause for final hearing before the Honorable Thomas L. Williams Chancellor upon the Bill of Complaint the answers of Allen D. Gentry, James White & John Daniel and the replications thereto the judgment pro confesso as to Robert Daniel: And because it appears to the Chancellor from the proof that Complt. is not entitled to relief and that the land in the pleadings mentioned was subject to redemption, and that Allen D. Gentry the purchaser from John Daniel had a right to redeem and that he tendered to Complainant the sum of forty eight Dollars being the amount of his bid at the Sheriffs sale with ten percent interest thereon, within two years after the sheriff's sale which was refund by Complt - It is therefore ordered adjudged and decreed by the Court that Complainants Bill be dismissed, and that Complt pay his costs and that Respts pay their Costs, for which execution may issue.

And it appearing to the Court that the money tendered being forty eight dollars is (P-331) deposited with the Clerk and Master of this court for Complt - It is ordered by the Court that the Clerk pay the same to Complt or his attorney, together with the amount of one dollar & fifty cents deposited to pay the costs of Complts deed.

George W. Churchwell)
Thomas & George &)
Others)
    vs)
Hiram K. Turk &)
Thos. J. Turk)

The order made at last Term appears to have been made inadvertently. It is therefore ordered by the Court that said order be rescended and this cause reinstated, as it stood at time.

The Clerk & Master having given bond & security, had the several oaths prescribed by law administered to him by the Chancellor, and also the oath against dwelling.

.

www.ingramcontent.com/pod-product-compliance
Lightning Source LLC
Chambersburg PA
CBHW080418270326
41929CB00018B/3080